From Sofia
to Jaffa

From Sofia to Jaffa

The Jews of Bulgaria and Israel

GUY H. HASKELL

Foreword by Raphael Patai

WAYNE STATE UNIVERSITY PRESS·Detroit

Library of Congress Cataloging-in-Publication Data

Haskell, Guy H., 1956–
    From Sofia to Jaffa : the Jews of Bulgaria and Israel / Guy H.
Haskell ; foreword by Raphael Patai.
        p.   cm. — (Jewish folklore and anthropology series)
    Includes bibliographical references and index.
    ISBN 0-8143-2502-5 (alk. paper)
    1. Jews—Bulgaria—History. 2. Jews—Bulgaria—Folklore.
3. Folklore—Bulgaria. 4. Bulgaria—Social life and customs.
5. Bulgaria—Ethnic relations. 6. Jews, Bulgarian—Israel.
7. Israel—Ethnic relations. 8. Israel—Emigration and immigration.
I. Title.   II. Series.
DS135.B8H37   1994
304.8′569404977′089924—dc20   94-12661

Designer: Elizabeth Pilon

To Lili Avrahami,
guardian angel of the Jews of Bulgaria

"There are four types of Jews; Orthodox, religious, secular, and Bulgarian."—*Nora Madjar, Plovdiv*

"I get Bulgarian atmosphere in Jaffa. I do my shopping in Jaffa, they have Bulgarian cheese so I go to Jaffa, hear some gossip, and with that I finish with my Bulgarianness."—*Lili Avrahami, Bat Yam*

"You study sociology. There are such moments in social movements that are not rational."—*Isidor Toliko, Holon*

Contents

Foreword

This book comprises four separate and yet interconnected parts, each of them valuable in its own right. It begins with a survey of how Israeli social scientists—sociologists, anthropologists, folklorists—have responded to the challenge presented by the large-scale immigration of Jews from all over the world, including the total transplantation of entire communities. In discussing this subject, under the title "Israeli Social Science Looks at Immigration and Ethnicity," Dr. Haskell offers a restrained criticism of the limited and one-sided approach that was for long dominant, under the influence of sociologists at the Hebrew University, in the study of the unique cultural diversity offered by the presence of immigrants from several dozen Jewish communities in Europe, Asia, and Africa. I know of no other study that offers anything like his brief diachronic survey of the evolution of Israeli social sciences and its interrelationship with the changing multiethnic scene in the country.

Nevertheless, Haskell found much in the achievements of Israeli social science that was useful for his work on the Bulgarian Jews, and basing himself on them and on approaches he acquired at the famous Indiana University Folklore Institute, he presents in the second part of his book a very specific and valuable survey of the history of the Jews in Bulgaria. It is a history of the community based primarily on what members of the community itself remembered of their past. That is, it is a "folk history," in the sense in which folklorists speak of folk tales, folk poetry, folk music, folk dance, folk art, folk medicine, folk custom, folk belief, and the like. The combination of hard historical data with the remembrance of things past, which have continued to live in the consciousness of the people because of their lasting impact, lends this part a particular significance both historically and psychologically.

Part Three, telling about the the Jews of Bulgaria in Israel, pulls together, and builds upon, the themes of the preceding two parts. It begins with a critical presentation of theoretical approaches by Israeli social scientists, goes on to presenting the author's own understanding of the components of identity as derived from his observation of the Bulgarian Jews in Bulgaria and after their immigration in Israel, and concludes with an examination of the role played by ethnic folkloric expression among the Bulgarian Jews in Israel in four areas of social interaction: language, holidays and celebrations, foodways, and performing arts. While doing this, Haskell manages to provide a rare insight into several crucial aspects of Bulgarian Jewish life in Israel including the following: what they have retained of their old folkways, what they have adopted from the new Israeli Hebrew culture, what kind of new socio-cultural ambience they have created for themselves, what types of new "self" have developed among them, and, last but not least, how they were able to achieve an exceptionally successful adjustment to their new Israeli environment.

The brief Epilogue, which actually constitutes the fourth part of the book, tells the story of what happened to those Jews who had remained in Bulgaria and who, after the fall of the Communist regime, were able to breathe freely for the first time in several decades. It also tells about the most recent developments that took place in Israel in the Bulgarian community. What he found was that in Bulgaria, while there was a resurgence of Jewish life, the number of Jews was so small that the disappearance of the last remnant was but a matter of one or two decades at the utmost. And as for Israel, there too, there seemed to be no question of the fading away of a distinct Bulgarian Jewish cultural element in the amalgam of Israeli society.

This outlook makes Guy Haskell's book a lasting monument to a disappearing Jewish tribe all the more valuable. I wish we had similar studies of each and every one of the Jewish communities who have disappeared, or are about to disppear, in their home countries, and are merging into the new Israeli Hebrew nation.

Raphael Patai

Acknowledgments

I would like to thank my teachers at the Indiana University Folklore Institute for sharing their knowledge and enthusiasm for our field: Linda Degh, Hasan El-Shamy, Henry Fischel, and Roger Janelli. For financial support, I wish to thank the government of Israel for assisting me during a year of fieldwork in Israel, Indiana University for providing me with funds for research in the United States, and Oberlin College for a research and development grant and the H. H. Powers Travel Grant, all of which enabled me to complete the research for this book.

To my wife Cheri, my deepest gratitude, both for the wonderful illustrations which grace this book, and for her patience. To my father, Gordon K. Haskell, whose stories of his childhood in Bulgaria sparked my interest in this fascinating country, and whose assistance, good humor, and keen observations during our research trip to Israel and Bulgaria in the summer of 1992 have enhanced the Epilogue. To my mother, Viola Haskell, who always encouraged my interest in Bulgaria and who took me on my first visit to the country at the age of fourteen.

Finally, to my friends and informants who opened their lives to me in Bulgaria and Israel, thank you.

Introduction

The past twenty-five years have seen intense interest on the part of folklorists in immigration, ethnicity, and ethnic identity. For many researchers in America, immigrant groups have become the folk, replacing European peasantry, the traditional focus of folkloristic inquiry. These scholars have been concerned with the adaptation and transformation of expressive culture in the passage from Old World to New. Individuals change their behavior, and perceptions change in the new environment. Folklorists have been particularly interested in these changes, which manifest themselves in different forms, and can be studied as indicators of ethnic affect and acculturation.

American folklorists have been in the forefront of research on the nature and role of folkloric expression in the lives of immigrants and their progeny.[1] The work produced by these scholars reflects major developments in the field of folkloristics. The 1960s saw the publication of works that addressed the notion of ethnic folklore as consisting of survivals from the old country or revivals in the new.[2] By the end of the decade, works began appearing which saw in ethnicity a phenomenon more complex than a unilinear process of acculturation, and novel and exciting approaches were developed.[3] Just as folklore was being viewed more as process and less as item, so immigrant folklore was being viewed less as survival and more as a dynamic element in cultural adaptation, as well as a symbol of identity and strategic asset.[4]

The contextual, or performance-centered approach to folklore, which was the major new voice on the American folklore scene in the early 1970s, has been incorporated into the study of folklore and ethnicity.[5] This approach emphasizes the study of folklore within its specific performance context.[6] One of the weaknesses of this approach is its tendency to neglect the wider cultural and historical context, as well as the concept of folklore as a function of an individual's particular circumstances and life history. These issues have been addressed in the work of Linda Degh, who has blended elements of the European ethnographic approach with trends in American folkloristics.[7]

The scientific study of folklore in Israel has its roots in America, but has developed along very different lines. Dov Noy, the founder of folkloristics in Israel, studied under Stith Thompson at Indiana University in the early 1950s, but the new directions in folklore research which were developed during the 1960s and 1970s in America did not, until recently, find their way to Israel, and the folklore-as-survival approach continued in Israel long after its demise elsewhere. The study of immigration, ethnicity, and ethnic identity, then, was left in the hands of Israel's sociologists and anthropologists. To date, there has been no comprehensive treatment of the development of sociological, anthropological, and folkloristic approaches to immigration and ethnicity. The first part of this study addresses this lack.

There is a natural tendency among folklorists and anthropologists, both American and Israeli, to choose the exotic, the unusual, or the problematic as the topic of research. In Israel, the least assimilated groups command the greatest attention. For the present study of identity and acculturation in Israel, I have selected a different approach. The subject of this study, the Jews of Bulgaria, is a group well known in Israel for having adjusted swiftly, and for having made a positive contribution to the development of the new nation's institutions.

Between 1948 and 1949, approximately forty-five thousand of Bulgaria's fifty thousand Jews came to Israel. This mass transplantation of an entire community provided a unique opportunity to study cultural and folkloric adaptation from a specific point in time. I conducted a pilot study in 1974–1975 under the auspices of the Urban Studies Project at Tel Aviv University, sponsored by the State University of New York at Stony Brook. The results of this preliminary work inform the structure of the present study.

In 1980 I received an Israel Government Grant to spend a year in Israel collecting data for this study. The main emphasis of the research was on in-depth interviewing and participant observation. In planning a research strategy, special attention was paid to the problems of ethnicity research among a dispersed and assimilated population.

The Jews from Bulgaria in Israel could not be studied with the methods and techniques used in collecting data on geographically coherent, attitudinally homogeneous ethnic communities. It was necessary, then, to interview informants throughout the country: old folks who remained in the small Bulgarian enclave in Jaffa, kibbutzniks and moshavniks, and integrated city dwellers. Informants were sought from the least to the most assimilated to provide as wide a sample of opinions and outlooks as possible.

In-depth interviews were conducted with sixteen informants. The interviews were constructed on the basis of directions suggested in the earlier pilot study. The interviews were structured, but open-ended; informants were permitted to channel discussion to areas they felt were important. Throughout the present study I have excerpted passages from the interview transcripts.

The interview schedule was divided into two parts; life in Bulgaria and life in Israel. Many of the same questions were repeated in both sections. Emphasis was placed on folklore, and groups of questions were designed to elicit types of folklore, context of performance, and attitudes toward preservation and transmission.

Participant observation was directed at all types of events where Jews from Bulgaria would interact: parties, weddings, holidays, immigrant clubs, performances, political rallies. These activities took place largely in the old immigrant neighborhood of Jaffa, and were attended by a small percentage of those immigrants who remained within the ethnic community.

The complexity of the field of ethnicity requires an openminded, eclectic theoretical orientation. In the words of eminent folklorist Richard M. Dorson: "Various processes are operating simultaneously. . . . Generalizations about acculturation must not be applied sweepingly to all immigrant groups."[8] Folklorists in the United States have indeed been at the forefront of multi-discipline research in the field. Israeli researchers have been less open-minded, due in part to the requirements of governmental institutions, and due in part to their mistrust of "soft" data, folklore being perceived as the softest of all. They have, nevertheless, produced an impressive amount of research on immigration, acculturation, and ethnicity, responding to the demographic, political, religious, and ideological factors which are unique to the Israeli ethnic equation. Whereas the development of American folkloristic research on ethnicity has been summarized, Israeli research has not.[9] Part I, Israeli Social Science Looks at Immigration and Ethnicity, addresses this lack, with special emphasis on those works which bear on the subject of this study.

Part II, The Jews in Bulgaria, is a survey of the history of the Jews of Bulgaria. The survey was directed by informant data, i.e., those events, places, persons, movements, and ideologies which were consistently mentioned by informants as having been important in their personal development and worldview, received special attention. These phenomena I have called "components of identity." They are illustrated with excerpts from the interviews.

Part III, The Jews of Bulgaria in Israel, is divided into three chapters. The first expands on the theoretical approaches discussed in Part I, and applies them to the present subject. Three Israeli studies in particular are applied to the present case and are discussed in detail. An original, fourth approach, defining "components of identity," is used to further explain the data. The second chapter of Part III describes these components, and each is discussed and illustrated with interview excepts. The final four components are folkloric, and are treated as part of a general discussion of folklore and identity as they are perceived by the Jews of Bulgaria in Israel.

Until 1990 I had assumed that I had written the final chapter on the Jews of Bulgaria in Israel. Recent events in Eastern Europe proved me wrong. The withering of Communism in Bulgaria led to a renewal of Jewish life there, as well as a new group of immigrants to Israel. I returned to Bulgaria and Israel in the summer of 1992, and the observations made during that trip are contained in the Epilogue.

This study has several objectives: to accurately describe the nature of the concept of identity among the Jews of Bulgaria in Israel based on the perceptions of individual immigrants, with special consideration of the social, political, cultural, and ideological context of their lives in Bulgaria preceeding emigration and in Israel after immigration; to approach this subject using the tools developed by Israeli social science for the unique conditions of Israel, adding the perspective of American folkloristics and an additional theoretical approach; and to describe and analyze the development of these tools.

My attitude toward the question of folklore and ethnicity reflects my training at Indiana University. The work of students and faculty noted above informs my assumptions. It is not my intention here, however, to apply theories and hypotheses developed in America to the present discussion. Rather, I will analyze the field data based on the critical application of Israeli models. In doing so I have surveyed and evaluated applicable Israeli scholarship, discussed its strengths and shortcomings in its application to the present case, and suggest a complementary approach. Thus, even though the historic-ethnographic perspective on ethnicity, which is the basis of the present research, was applied in Europe and America long before it was used in Israel, it is discussed here in the context of developments in Israeli social science, leaving the analysis of its international connections to another study.

In the present work on the Bulgarian Jews in Israel, these trends underlie much of the research. The attitude of this study is eclectic; no single approach is capable of adequately describing and explaining ethnicity. The concepts of survivals, revivals, performance, context, stategy, and identity are all important in gaining a clearer understanding of the present case.

Note: Hebrew and Bulgarian are transliterated according to the style of the *Encyclopedia Judaica*. Words spelled in English in an accepted form are spelled according to convention (e.g. kibbutz, Israel, Massada). A short description of informants mentioned or quoted in the text may be found in Appendix B. Information in parentheses refers to transcriptions of the interviews, and contain informant name and transcript page number. These transcripts may be made available to researchers by contacting the author. Two sample transcripts are reproduced in Appendix C.

The Central Synagogue in Sofia, whose external beauty covers the devastation within. Illustration by Cheri Haskell.

PART I

Israeli Social Science Looks at Immigration and Ethnicity

CHAPTER 1

Confronting Mass Immigration

The study of immigration and ethnicity has been the central problem of Israeli social science since the establishment of the state in 1948.[1] In many ways the manner in which Israeli sociologists and anthropologists have approached this problem parallels the development of Israeli society itself.

Independence, the rise of Arab nationalism, and the displacement of Jews during World War II created the conditions for mass immigrations to Israel. Within three years of independence, the Israeli population had more that tripled, with mostly impoverished refugees arriving from over seventy countries (see Table 1). One of the first works to deal with the social and cultural effects of this immigration on Israeli society was Raphael Patai's *Israel between East and West*.[2]

Patai was born in Budapest in 1910, and came to Jerusalem in 1933 after receiving his doctoral degree at the University of Budapest and rabbinical ordination at the Seminary.[3] There he began his anthropological study of Israeli society and in 1936 received the first doctorate to be awarded by the Hebrew University of Jerusalem. He left Palestine in 1947 to study in the United States on a fellowship from the Viking Fund (now the Wenner-Gren Foundation of Anthropological Research). Patai returned to Israel in 1949 and 1951 to continue his observations, but he was to make his home in the United States, and thus lost much of his influence in shaping the direction of social research in Israel.[4]

A student of Middle Eastern culture, Patai was fascinated by the changes which occurred under conditions of culture contact. Even before the founding of Israel, Patai began publishing work on the cultural upheavals which were taking place in Palestine. His 1947

article, "On Culture Contact and Its Working in Modern Palestine,'
examines the cultural interplay between the Arabs, the British, and
the European and Oriental Jews.

From the early 1940s until his departure in 1947, Patai found it
increasingly difficult to get anthropological research in Israel off the
ground:

> Continued study of the traditional forms and functions among
> the Middle Eastern and Western population groups in Palestine
> as well as the processes of change evinced by them under the
> impact of intensive culture contact convinced me at an early date
> that here was a research field of overwhelming magnitude and
> importance which could be attacked with some promise of suc-
> cess only by a group of scholars working in concert. However,
> after the untimely death of Dr. Brauer, in 1942, I found myself
> the only student of ethnology in the country. When prolonged
> efforts to convince the Hebrew University to introduce the teach-
> ing of the subject (with special emphasis on the Jews of the
> Middle East) proved of no avail, I decided to make an indepen-
> dent effort. With the help of a handful of friends I founded the
> Palestine Institute of Folklore and Ethnology in 1944. In 1945
> we launched a publishing program which was quite considerable
> for local conditions. In the short period of three years the Insti-
> tute published three volumes of the quarterly *Edoth* (in Hebrew
> and English), five volumes of a library called "Studies in Folklore
> and Ethnology," and two volumes of a library called "Social Stud-
> ies." All this was done with very little institutional support.[5]

When Patai left Israel for the United States, he hoped that the
Institute and its publication program would survive in his absence. He
later wrote, "That this was not the case, and that the Institute along with
its publications and other activities became a casualty of the War of
Liberation, will always remain one of the great disappointments of my
life."[6] We can only speculate on the course Israeli social science might
have taken had Patai remained in the country. We can say with certainty, however, that anthropological and folkloristic research would
have played a far more significant role in the description and analysis of
emergent Israeli society and culture than they have to date. Although
the situation has changed significantly within the past twenty years,
Patai described the state of the field in 1953 as follows:

> To this day, five years after the foundation of the State of Israel,
> in a country literally teeming with anthropological problems and

opportunities, there is not a single anthropologist employed by any public or private body, although anthropologists elsewhere have splendidly demonstrated their usefulness in solving practical problems arising out of the contacts between peoples and population groups. The only anthropologists working in Israel today are American students of the field who go there occasionally on a temporary basis and are supported by diverse American funds.[7]

With Patai's departure, the task of studying immigration was taken up with great vigor by sociologists. Leaders in this early work were Shmuel Noah Eisenstadt and Judith Shuval. Utilizing his seminars at the Hebrew University as workshops and his students as fieldworkers, Eisenstadt embarked on a massive project aimed at the development of a framework for a comprehensive examination of immigrant "absorption" in Israel. The use of the term "absorption" by Eisenstadt and most other Israeli social scientists during this period is quite telling. While the term was sometimes used in the social scientific lexicon on immigration, terms such as "assimilation," "acculturation," or "integration" were generally preferred. The term "absorption," and its companion, "modernization," are indicative of the ideological framework which guided Israeli institutions in charge of immigrant settlement, an ideology which Israeli social scientists shared.

The basic ideological tenets underlying the Israeli approach to immigration were *kibbutz galuyot*, the "ingathering of the exiles" from the lands of the Diaspora, and *mizug galuyot*, the "merging of the exiles." The physical and cultural integration of the immigrant communities into a new people and identity was one of the imperatives of Zionist ideology and the leadership of the Yishuv (the pre-state Jewish community in Palestine). This fusion was to create a new Israeli society free of the tainted cultural accretions of the Diaspora. Mizug galuyot did not imply the cosmopolitanization of Israeli culture. Rather, its intention was to distill the common elements from the cultures of the immigrant groups, separating centuries of foreign accretions from the ancient kernels of Hebrew tradition. It was thus assumed that by combining all of these kernels, a new Israeli culture reminiscent of that of biblical Israel would emerge.

The term "absorption," which is used to the present day, implies a high degree of change and adaptation to an existing society and culture. This implication underlies much of the sociological research on immigrants in Israel. Although most Israeli scholars adhered to this view, only Patai presented an actual framework for the realization of this ideology.[8] The fact of the matter was that the leadership, orientation, ideology, and institutional framework of the Yishuv and later the state were primarily East European, and it was into this cultural context that the immigrants were to be "absorbed."

This relationship between the "absorbee" and the "absorber" was mirrored in the relationship between researcher and subject in Israeli social scientific research. Virtually all of those engaged in studying immigration were Jews from Europe and America, while the subjects of their study were mainly immigrants from the Middle East and North Africa. Indeed, very little research has been done to this day on European immigrants to Israel.

This reality is easily understood in the context of the development of Orientalism in Europe, as well as the ethnic composition of the Yishuv and the socio-economic status of the new immigrants. Elements of exoticism, patronage, intellectual curiosity, as well as a sincere desire to help those considered less fortunate played a role in this relationship. It was not until the 1970s that this began to change with the empowering of second-generation Israelis of Middle Eastern and North African origin, the emergence of scholars from their ranks, and increasing criticism of the ethnocentric attitude of the Israeli establishment.

Eisenstadt and his students conducted most of their research during the pivotal years immediately following the War of Independence (November 1947-July 1949). The newborn state had lost one percent of its population (about six thousand men and women) and was economically strained to the breaking point.[9] Yet one of the fundamental ideological concepts underlying Israel's raison d'être was to challenge the institutions and resources of the country with an almost impossible task; the concept of "ingathering of exiles" and the providing of a safe refuge for the world's persecuted Jews led to a policy of unrestricted Jewish immigration which would double Israel's population within the span of three years. Between the establishment of the state in May 1948, and December 1951, 684,000 immigrants poured into Israel from all corners of the globe. Of the total number of immigrants to Israel as of 1964, 49 percent immigrated between 1948 and 1951, 27 percent before 1948, and 24 percent after 1951.[10]

Whereas the majority of immigrants to the Yishuv were from Europe, fully half of the immigrants during the first wave of mass immigration to the state were from the Jewish communities of Asia and Africa. The demographic change, then, from the beginning of the mass immigration in 1948 until 1951 would alter the character of Israeli society and present the Yishuv with a series of problems which would greatly tax its economic and social absorptive capacity. In 1948, 35 percent of Israel's population was native-born, 55 percent was born in Europe and America, and 10 percent in Africa and Asia. By 1952, these figures would change to 27 percent Israeli, 28 percent Afro-Asian, and 45 percent Euro-American-born. By the end of the first decade of Israel's existence, those figures would change even further: 36 percent Israeli, 28 percent Afro-Asian, and 36 percent Euro-American-born. Of the native-born Israelis (*sabras*), an increasing number were of Afro-Asian percentage due to the higher birth rate within this group.

The social and cultural implications of these statistics are staggering. Looking at them objectively one would expect a major dislocation to have taken place in Israeli society, which would have put in question the future viability of the state. Although the effects of the mass immigrations changed Israel greatly, the continuity in Israeli society is truly striking. Perhaps, then, under the unique circumstances of immigration to Israel, the term "absorption" becomes somewhat more meaningful.[11]

Not only the number, but the background and condition of the immigrants who poured into Israel during this period presented difficulties for the government and the existing society. Those who came from Europe were in large part the survivors of the Nazi death camps and refugees from the cataclysm of the war in Europe—the destitute and terrorized remnants of the obliterated Jewish communities of the European continent. Homeless, totally impoverished, physically and psychologically traumatized, most had spent years in displaced persons camps scattered throughout Europe, unable to return to homes that no longer existed, and denied entry to other countries of possible refuge.

Some of these refugees had managed to reach the shores of Palestine through the *Aliyah Bet*, the Yishuv's heroic program of smuggling European Jews to Palestine through the British blockade which had been imposed to enforce the British policy of restricting Jewish immigration to Palestine, as detailed in the British government's White Paper of 1939. Many of those who had attempted to run the blockade on tramp steamers purchased throughout Europe by the Haganah, the Yishuv's underground defense force, were captured by the British and interned in camps, first at Atlit in Israel, and then on Cyprus.[12] One of the first tasks of the Israeli government was to bring these refugees to Israel from the camps as quickly as possible. These shattered and broken survivors of a decade-long nightmare made up a large portion of the 330,000 European immigrants to arrive in Israel between 1948 and 1951.

The second major category of immigrants to Israel during this period also presented very serious problems. Entire Jewish communities from North Africa and the Middle East arrived on Israel's shores with little more than the shirts on their backs. Satisfying their barest economic needs—food and shelter—was the primary concern of the institutions charged with their welfare, but cultural, social, and educational problems would prove even more lasting and difficult to overcome. Sociologist Judith Shuval described the situation as follows:

> The economic and social problems involved in the absorption of such a large population were enormous, especially for a new state which had just come through a war and had not yet had time to establish appropriate institutions to undertake such a task. The most immediate problems were employment and housing; the questions of full social and cultural absorption remained more in the realm of long-term problems. The shortage of investment capital during the first years of the state's existence made the provision of employment opportunities for immigrants extremely difficult, and the result was widespread unemployment. The housing shortage, which had persisted since World War II, was partially alleviated during 1948, when 117,000 immigrants found shelter in abandoned Arab dwellings. However, at the beginning of 1949, it was necessary to establish transit camps on a wide scale. By the end of 1949, there were twenty-four such camps housing close to 60,000 immigrants; by the end of April, 1950, there were 95,000 immigrants living in thirty transit camps in various parts of the country.[13]

The mass airlifts of the Jewish communities of Yemen and Iraq were two dramatic events of this period. "Operation Magic Carpet" succeeded in transporting virtually the entire Jewish community of Yemen from the British protectorate of Aden to Israel. The Jews of Yemen had made their way to Aden across the desert on foot or donkey-back with their few belongings, there to be picked up by a ragtag collection of old airliners and converted air freighters. In all, a total of 47,000 Yemenite Jews were airlifted to Israel "on eagles' wings" (Exodus 19:4). In 1950, the Iraqi government enacted a law allowing the emigration of Iraqi Jews, providing they renounced their citizenship. It permitted each individual to take between six and sixteen dollars out of the country, depending on his or her age. By 1952, 121,512 Iraqi Jews had arrived in Israel as the result of the airlift code-named "Operation Ezra and Nehemiah."[14] No less dramatic, but seldom mentioned, is the fact that within two years (1948–1949) 45,000 of Bulgaria's 50,000 Jews arrived on Israel's shores.

In contrast to many of the immigrants from Europe, especially those who arrived before the establishment of the state, most of the Jews from the communities of Asia and North Africa had little exposure to the Zionist movement or its ideology. The motivations of these people, like those fleeing fascism and death in Europe, were primarily negative: a desire to escape the persecution, or at least the second class (*dhimmi*) status, to which they were relegated in their countries of origin.[15] Although many, in particular the Yemenites, were transfused with a Messianic yearning for the return to Zion with the establishment of a state based on their traditional religious worldview, they were in all respects ill-prepared for the economic, social, and cultural shocks they encountered in the new land.

These, then, were the general conditions under which researchers conducted their investigations during the early years of Israel's existence. To a tiny country which had just lost one percent of its population in a bloody war of independence against extreme odds, reeling from the economic and social impact of the war, and trying desperately to get its footing and set up the basic institutions necessary for the functioning of a modern state, arrived masses of immigrants from either technologically backward and culturally traditional societies, or from miserable camps into which they had been herded after having survived the destruction of their communities and over six million of their brethren. This influx doubled the country's population within three years, and each immigrant expected help from the state in his or her hour of need.

In this context, the greatest problem in conducting social research in Israel was the fact that virtually every variable to be studied was in flux.[16] Equally important, the immigrants themselves were undergoing massive and often debilitating social, cultural, and psychological dislocation and disorientation as a result of their immigration. It was very difficult, then, for the observer to find a stable platform from which to scrutinize changes in any one of these areas. There were very few constants to work with. Under these circumstances, the quality of the work which was carried out, under conditions of extreme stress and with inadequate financial and institutional backing, is all the more impressive.

The results of the research conducted by Eisenstadt and his students appeared in Hebrew in 1951 and two years later in English translation under the title *The Absorption of Immigrants: A Comparative Study Based on the Jewish Community in Palestine and the State of Israel.* This comprehensive work of sociological observation remains to this day a basic text for the student of immigration to Israel.

The Israel Institute for Applied Social Research, founded in 1948 and headed by Louis Guttman, also engaged in the study of immigrants in Israeli society. The government, responding to the public outcry caused by a series of damning articles in the local press on conditions in the transit camps, asked the Institute to undertake an independent study of the adjustment of new immigrants.[17] The researcher chosen to head the project was Judith T. Shuval, a social

psychologist educated at Hunter College, who received her doctorate
in sociology from Radcliffe in 1955.[18] Under Shuval's direction, fieldworkers who were themselves mostly new immigrants collected the
data during 1949–1950.

The fieldworkers used a questionnaire, translated into several languages, and worked under difficult conditions within the transit camps
themselves.[19] By the end of 1949, there was no more abandoned Arab
housing available to provide shelter for the new immigrants. Initially
they were housed in abandoned British army barracks, and when those
were filled to capacity, vast tent cities were erected, usually in isolated
parts of the country. "Conditions were crowded, with large families
occupying a single room. Sanitary facilities were located outside the
living quarters. Families had no private cooking facilities; food was
provided without cost at public dining halls. Few of the transit camps
had any landscaping to break the sordid monotony of row after row of
barracks and tents."[20]

The difficulties the new immigrants experienced in the transit
camps were compounded by widespread unemployment and the appre-
hensions of an uncertain future in a strange land. Shuval's research was
directed toward understanding the ways in which immigrants perceived these difficulties, and how they transformed their perceptions
into actions. "Her basic emphasis had been to distinguish *within* the
immigrants in transit the variables which lead to quicker or slower
acculturation."[21]

Unfortunately, the data generated from this project remained unused for a decade: "The fieldwork was completed at a most unfortunate period in the government's history. The War of Liberation was
finally over. Budgets that had been completely unbalanced had to
become more realistic. The government was in desperate financial
shape and overnight canceled hundreds of activities including this
research project."[22]

During the period 1956–1957, Shuval was the appointed adviser
on social research at the Institute under the United Nations Educational, Social, and Cultural Organization's (UNESCO) program of aid
to member states, and she was able to prepare the data for publication. Although much of the material was published piecemeal in the
form of articles, the complete work did not appear until 1963 under
the title *Immigrants on the Threshold*, which Leonard Weller calls "The
single most comprehensive study of immigrant adjustment."[23]

The study's basic thesis is that cognition, the perception of information and the way information is utilized, is the key to understanding differing rates of immigrant adjustment. The differences in cognition among immigrants were determined to be based on three

elements of the social structure of the immigrants' countries of origin: 1) social and economic conditions, which determine perceptions of relative deprivations in Israel; 2) the religious-secular worldview of the home community; and 3) the degree of social mobility for Jews allowed by the gentile society of the home community.[24] In addition, the degree of adherence to Zionist ideology was determined to play an important role in the adjustment of many of the immigrants.[25] Shuval's main findings of relevance here have been summarized by Weller:

1. Zionist immigrants were more receptive to information about Israel than were non-Zionist.
2. European immigrants were more disappointed with Israel than were Afro-Asian immigrants.
3. European Zionists were less disappointed with Israel that were European non-Zionists. For the non-European immigrant, ideology was not related to acculturation.
4. Immigrants who were Zionists used new information for constructive planning; additional information for immigrants without such commitment was dysfunctional.[26]

For European immigrants, Zionist ideology served to some extent as a buffer against the frustration they encountered in Israel. For the Oriental immigrant, a traditionally religious worldview served a similar purpose initially, though it was not capable of providing them with a framework for interpreting and acting upon new information in the Israeli context.[27]

Although Eisenstadt's and Shuval's works were the most comprehensive of the period, a large cadre of sociologists were engaged in more modest projects during the 1950s.[28] Most significant in the field of immigration was the scholarly work on the education of the immigrants and their children which was published in the journal *Megamot.* Most of these studies leave us with the impression, however, that culture in general, and its expressive manifestations in particular, are insignificant and easily dispensed with trappings of social structure rather than its cognitive base. It is no wonder, then, that intellectual circles of Israeli society today have been shaken by the realization that culturally influenced behavior did not disappear with the shedding of exotic dress nor through some universally compelling process of "absorption" which left behind only rectifiable socioeconomic differences. Rather, fundamental cultural characteristics,

though transformed in the new environment, have persisted and
been passed down to the native-born generations, only to manifest
themselves in ways which are of paramount significance to the stability of Israeli society. This attitude toward culture was most clearly
stated in an oft-quoted statement by sociologist Joseph Ben David in
his 1952 article, "Ethnic Differences or Social Change?":

> It appears that in this country—except for the Arab population
> and perhaps the old Ashkenazic population—there are no eth-
> nic groups possessing definite cultures, but only one society
> characterized by a rather uniform cultural orientation (notwith-
> standing the problematics of this culture), and on the margins
> an ever-increasing number of individuals and groups which
> have not yet become absorbed in it. The important point is that
> even groups hailing from the same country do not see, in their
> common origin or in the cultural tradition therein involved,
> any important or vital societal value. It is therefore doubtful
> whether the discussion should start with the question of ethnic
> differences, and whether anthropological research dealing with
> closed and self-sufficient societies can teach us anything of im-
> portance concerning the situation in this country.[29]

The culture-free, structural approach to the study of immigration in Israel was not challenged until the mid-1960s. The early
1960s saw a continuation of the type of research which had been the
staple of the previous decade. Sociologists were increasingly concerned with "strain," "stress," and "crisis" in Israeli society as it became clear that the majority of immigrants had been neither socially
nor institutionally "absorbed" ten years after their arrival in the country.[30] What Israeli sociology saw as a growing "crisis" in inter-ethnic
relations appears today to have been more the result of its lack of
consideration of cultural issues than the consequence of radical
change in the social realities. According to Harvey Goldberg, an
American-trained cultural anthropologist who immigrated to Israel:
"In general it may be said that we have a good picture of institutional
development and change in Israel over the first two decades of its
existence, with reference to ethnic categories of the population, but
little understanding of the cultural mechanisms which have animated
and expressed these developments."[31]

Moreover, when culturally regulated behavior was discussed, it
was usually in connection with instances where an explanation was
sought for a group's difficulty in adapting to a social norm. As Goldberg argues, "there is a tendency [among Israeli sociologists] to cite
cultural norms derived from the past in cases of maladaption to Israeli

society, [but] less attention is paid to culture when the process of integration appears to run smoothly."[32]

The ethnological study of immigrant folklore passed from the Israeli scene with Raphael Patai's Palestine Institute of Folklore and Ethnology, its journal, and other publications. In 1948, the Hebrew Society for Folklore and Ethnology, which was made up of a diverse group of literary scholars and amateur folklorists interested in recording the Jewish folk traditions of Eastern Europe, began publishing its journal, *Yeda' 'Am*.[33] The systematic and scientific investigation of folklore in Israel did not begin until 1953, when Dov Noy returned to Israel—a new Ph.D. in folklore. Noy had studied for two years at Indiana University under Stith Thompson, and returned to Israel with the tools and drive to begin the scholarly collection of folklore, especially folktales, in Israel.

Noy went right to work. The year of his return he founded the Israeli branch of the Society for Folk Narrative Research and the Israel Folktale Archives at the Haifa Municipal Ethnological Museum, which he directed. This period saw a number of related organizations spring up throughout the country: the Institute for Oriental Jewish Music, the Institute for Religious Music Research, the Institute for Oriental Jewish Dialects, and the Ben-Zvi Institute for Research on Jewish Communities of the Middle East. In order to coordinate the various folklore-related activities of these groups, the Folklore Coordination Board was set up within the Ministry of Culture and Education with Noy as its director.[34]

According to a young scholar and one of Noy's promising students, Dan Ben-Amos: "The primary project of the Israeli folklorist now is to collect the materials available before the traditions brought by the newcomers to Israel are lost in the process of acculturation, and to archive and classify it to provide the foundation of scholarly research."[35]

Another of Noy's students, Elisheva Shoenfeld, wrote the following: "Solange noch Tradition besteht, gibt es unendliche Möglichkeiten, die Kultur einer jeden Volksgruppe zu erforschen und zu studieren, aber wir haben nicht mehr viel Zeit, denn der Tag ist nicht mehr fern, an welchem es eine neue israelische Kultur geben wird, die all das in sich vereint."[36] Noy himself described his hopes as follows:

> The State of Israel is an ideal land for the collecting of tales originating from many diverse parts of the world. Geographic and ethnic groups, rooted in lands thousands of miles away from each other, live in Israel in neighborly villages. A pleasant walk separates Bokhara from Libya, Afghanistan from Lithuania, Tu-

nisia from Romania, etc. Let us hope that Israel folklorists, as well
as international folktale scholars, will take advantage of these
inexhaustive possibilities, before the acculturation processes put
an end or effect a change on the original ethnic 'ego' of both the
story-telling group and the story-telling individual.[37]

It is significant to note that at the same time the Israeli folklorists
were scrambling their forces to rescue as much of the rapidly disappearing folklore as they could before the irreversible advent of "ethnic 'ego' " change, they were aware both of the inevitability of such
change and, as in the case of the sociologists and anthropologists
discussed above, ideologically committed to it. The "Merging of the
Exiles" would require the dissolution of the immigrants' original ethnic egos and culture. Ben-Amos wrote:

> Because of the special circumstances, the Israeli folklorists do
> not conceive of their study as a mere pursuit of intellectual inves-
> tigation in human culture but try to introduce applied folklore in
> the sense that the knowledge of the folklore of other ethnic
> groups may lead to a rationalistic approach in contacts on an
> institutional and hopefully even personal level and will facilitate
> the process of integration of culture.[38]

Essentially, these folklorists perceived of their subject as a perish-
able commodity of value to the academic community and to the nation, which could not withstand the pressures of technology and the
ideological imperative of mizug galuyot. They were saving precious
manuscripts from the fires of modernity, and were doing so with the
most advanced techniques available. Noy was primarily a literary
scholar, and his training, both in Israel and Indiana, taught him to
approach folklore from a literary, humanistic standpoint. It is not
surprising, then, that Israeli folklorists did not apply their folkloristic
expertise to questions of ethnic identity, acculturation, and cultural
transformation.

It is unfortunate that after the demise of the Palestine Institute of
Folklore and Ethnology there were few scholars examining the transformations immigrant folklore was undergoing in the new Israeli setting.[39] In a sense it was a golden opportunity lost. Equally unfortunate
is the fact that there was little interest in the development of the much
talked about new synthetic Israeli " 'folk culture'—songs, dances, and
the like—attempts [at which were] specially numerous in the various
youth movements and agricultural settlements."[40]

CHAPTER 2

The Emergence of Culture

One of the most important areas of settlement for the new immigrants was the *moshavim* (cooperative small holders agricultural settlements). Whether the immigrants were placed in homogeneous communities or not, these new settlements provided an ideal setting for the application of anthropological techniques; they were small, closed communities often consisting of one or more groups of the same lineage or place of origin. One of the earliest of these applications to appear in English was "Reciprocal Change: A Case Study of a Moroccan Immigrant Village in Israel" in 1962, by Alex Weingrod, an anthropologist at the Hebrew University in Jerusalem. Trained in the United States, Professor Weingrod presently teaches at Ben-Gurion University of the Negev.[1] This work would serve as a starting point for later studies, and provides a good example of the "moshav study" genre.

The moshav is a unique type of planned village based on individual ownership of land, combined with communal services, marketing and purchasing, democratic village institutions, and a high degree of cooperation. Unlike the kibbutz, the basic social unit of the moshav is the nuclear family. Between 1920, when the first moshav was established, and 1948, 72 moshavim (pl. of moshav) were founded, and between 1948 and 1958, which includes the period of the mass immigration, 274 moshavim were founded.[2]

During the mass immigration to Israel (1948–1954), many immigrants, especially from the Middle East and North Africa, were transferred from the transit camps to the newly founded moshavim. After 1954, groups of immigrants were often taken directly from the boats which brought them to Israel to the agricultural villages. For most of these immigrants the shock of transplantation to a new country was

compounded by having to contend with a new community structure
and, as few of them were formerly agriculturalists, a new vocation.

From June, 1958 until November, 1959, Alex Weingrod conducted fieldwork in a newly established moshav in the Negev desert
which was inhabited by immigrants from Morocco. He found that
whereas the immigrants had adopted many of the technological and
cultural norms of the new environment, they adapted the imposed
social structure and institutions of the moshav to their own cultural
norms and community structure. Furthermore, he found that the
traditional clan structure, which had experienced a significant breakdown during the years immediately preceding emigration, was reinforced in the new environment to such a degree that the basic social
and economic structure of the moshav was founded on resurrected
forms of communal relationships.

Between 1959 and 1962, Weingrod served as Director of Social
Research in the Jewish Agency Settlement Department, which employed several young sociologists to study developments in new immigrant communities. From among these fieldworkers, Shlomo Deshen
and Moshe Shokeid emerged as key figures in the field. Both were
students of Eisenstadt who served as regional sociologists in southern
Israel in the Land Settlement Department of the Jewish Agency.

Deshen broke from his teacher's methods and emulated Weingrod's example when he found that he could not understand developments in the political structure of the moshav without reference to the
cultural-historical background of the village's inhabitants. Whereas
Eisenstadt implied a relationship between an immigrant's "predisposition to change," his main indicator of assimilation, and cultural background, Deshen made this relationship explicit.

Deshen devoted a significant portion of his research reports to
description of the cultural and political setting in the villagers' region
of origin. With time, he would largely abandon sociological theory
and methodology for those of anthropology, which he found more
applicable to understanding actual cultural processes involving immigrants in the new country.

Deshen's 1964 essay, *Case of Breakdown of Modernization in an Israeli
Immigrant Community*, examined the return to traditional rivalries in a
community which was culturally predisposed to the moshav organizational system, and had for a time functioned productively according
to that model. Changing fortunes and a shifting population led to the
re-emergence of political factions based on pre-immigration regional
rivalries, especially between two communities from the Tunisian Is-
land of Djerba, which had not played a significant role during the
early years of the moshav. This situation is similar to that described in
Weingrod's work. Deshen presents a vivid picture of those aspects of

Djerban culture and politics which would manifest themselves later in Israel. His work provided a model for Israeli anthropologists during the following two decades in describing the process of acculturation and the development of ethnicity in Israel.

The mid-1960s were pivotal years for the development of the role of anthropology in studying immigration to Israel. Finally, Israeli anthropologists would have the institutional backing they had lacked up to this time. Looking back ten years later, Don Handelman and Shlomo Deshen wrote: "The single greatest stimulus for anthropological research in Israel has been the Bernstein Fund for Research in Israel, directed by Professor Max Gluckman of the University of Manchester during the mid- and late 1960s, which has supported ten different extended field studies during the past few years."[3] Indeed, many of today's prominent Israeli anthropologists were given a significant boost as young researchers by this fund, and anthropology as we know it in Israel today was greatly influenced by it.

The main focus of the work carried out under Gluckman's direction was on immigrant acculturation, and the moshav and development town were the preferred sites for conducting research. Of the projects undertaken prior to 1970 under the auspices of the Fund, three were conducted in development towns, four in moshavim, two in kibbutzim, and one in a charitable workshop for old people in an urban setting.[4]

Perhaps the most significant finding of these studies is that cultural continuity was at least as important as social change in the adaptation of new immigrants to their particular social setting in Israel. In their survey, Handelman and Deshen stated: "All moshavim considered . . . have at least one major component in common. They all exhibit strong cultural continuities with their settlers' areas of origin. These cultural continuities should be translated as resources which enabled the immigrants to interpret their new situations and to adapt to them."[5] A statement of this kind is a most significant development when we recall the earlier disregard of culture in the "absorption" studies of Israeli sociology.

One of the shortcomings of both the sociological and anthropological treatments of immigration and ethnicity in Israel was the neglect of the city. Although over two thirds of all Israelis live in cities, which have been the primary sites of immigrant settlement, urban areas have seldom been considered for investigation. The emphasis on agricultural settlements and development towns is, of course, understandable, given both Zionist agrarian romanticism and the ease of studying these more isolated and independent communities.[6] Of the ten Bernstein projects, only one explored an urban setting.

One of the important features of much of the research undertaken by the "Bernsteinites" was their commitment to supplying data to the settlement authorities which could be of value in improving their programs and correcting their mistakes.[7] How and to what extent the data were utilized by these institutions remains a question.[8]

Moshe Shokeid also abandoned the sociological approach for the anthropological. Shokeid conducted research in a moshav settled by immigrants from the Atlas Mountains of Morocco. He examined the settlement authorities' strategy of settling new immigrants in homogeneous communities. Shokeid discussed a case in which this policy had disastrous consequences, when three traditional clan groups battled for power in the new social setting of the moshav.[9]

The Bernsteinites were not alone in conducting anthropological research on immigration and ethnicity in Israel. Trained at Harvard, Harvey Goldberg was an outsider to the Israeli social scientific scene, unlike Deshen and Shokeid who were products of it.[10] Goldberg began publishing studies on various aspects of life in a moshav settled by Tripolitanian immigrants. His concerns lay within the traditional scope of anthropological research and, unlike other Israeli anthropologists working during this period, his sources were drawn primarily from the anthropological rather than sociological literature. His work in the moshav covered such diverse topics as the frequency of father's brother's daughter marriage in the village,[11] the relationship between its autocratic political and egalitarian economic structure,[12] and the organization of domestic wealth within the community.[13] Taken as a whole, Goldberg's work clearly demonstrates the productivity of employing traditional anthropological methodology in the study of Israeli immigrant villages.

Two pioneering books by Weingrod, one dealing with the moshav, appeared in the 1960s.[14] The first few years of the 1970s saw a greater acceptance and institutional backing of anthropological research and a significant increase in publications. The young researchers of the preceding decade came of age during this period and saw their work published in book form. Shlomo Deshen's *Immigrant Voters in Israel*, a study examining the social dynamics of a local election in a development town, was published in 1970 by the University of Manchester, home of Max Gluckman and the Bernstein Fund. In 1971, Manchester published Moshe Shokeid's *The Dual Heritage: Immigrants from the Atlas Mountains in an Israeli Village*. Harvey Goldberg's *Cave Dwellers and Citrus Growers: A Jewish Community in Libya and Israel* saw light the following year. These works offer a concise expression of the historical-ethnographic approach discussed above, and utilized extensive historical material to illuminate the ethnographic present.

The moshav studies have several features in common. First, they argue that social realities in Israel cannot be properly understood without detailed knowledge of the history and culture of the group under consideration and its country of origin. Second, all the studies examine moshavim with Middle Eastern or North African populations, and because of this, extended kinship ties were deemed of special importance in understanding the village's social structure. Third, although all of the studies make reference to a wider theoretical framework, their main concern is ethnographic description. This last point was a departure from the Israeli sociological tendency to fit all data into comprehensive categories and theoretical constructs.

By the end of the 1970s, the anthropological study of immigration had reasserted itself, two decades after the hopeful but short-lived attempt made by Raphael Patai and his colleagues. The young anthropologists working in the field were talented and dedicated researchers, professionally trained in sociology and anthropology. Like the sociologists of the preceding decade, they attempted to make their research of value in the betterment of immigrant life in Israel. Yet these studies left an entire area of cultural expression largely unconsidered. Neither the sociologists nor the anthropologists concerned with Israeli immigrant society addressed the field of folklore, the study of expressive and creative behavior and the aesthetic elements of a culture which inform us of its essence and texture. They had yet to make the leap to considering folklore a valid and significant part of the study of culture, as well as a highly sensitive indicator of the degree, direction, and mechanism of acculturation.

Israeli folklorists, however, were deeply concerned during this decade with those very areas of traditional expression that failed to capture the interest of sociologists and anthropologists. But the main thrust of Israeli folkloristics was not the understanding of an emergent Israeli culture and its expressive manifestations, the attempts of Israeli ethnic communities to accommodate their traditions to the Israeli context, or the alteration of expressive behavior in the new environment. Their main concern was the recording of the rapidly disappearing "pure" folklore, largely consisting of traditional generic forms, of the various immigrant communities. Throughout the 1960s, the approach to folklore which was prevalent in the late 1950s continued with little change. Every major Israeli folklorist expressed similar sentiments regarding the primacy of collecting the vanishing oral remnants of the authentic immigrant culture increasingly eroded by the demands of life in a modern state.

Often, however, the actual activities and research of Israeli folklorists belied their expressed aims. In her report on the First World Conference on Jewish Folklore Research, which was convened in Tel Aviv in September, 1959 under the auspices of the Israeli Folklore and Ethnological Society, Ruth Rubin describes papers which directly

consider the dynamic role of folklore in modern Israeli life. For
example, the folkways of various communities were discussed with
regard to their roles both in the country of origin and contemporary
Israel. One paper dealt with the influence of oriental music on Israeli folk music. Most interestingly, eight different Jewish wedding
ceremonies were presented at the conference: from Hebron, Morocco, Yemen, Salonika, Poland, Bokhara, a kibbutz, and a wedding
in the Israeli army. Despite this apparent recognition of folklore as
an intrinsic and inextinguishable part of contemporary Israeli culture, Rubin stated: "The 'pressure-cooker' atmosphere in Israel and
the rapid integration of the Jewish groups of various origin make the
tasks of folklore and musicology exceedingly urgent. The customs,
traditions, ways of life, songs, tales, dances, proverbs, handicrafts,
folk art, etc. etc.—are becoming quickly effaced and threatened with
complete disappearance. Time is indeed of the essence."[15]

In 1963, a volume of Israeli folktales was added to Richard M.
Dorson's "Folktales of the World" series. The book's editor, Dov Noy,
clearly repeats these sentiments, but adds another goal to the tasks of
Israeli folklore. In addition to advocating their scholarly examination,
Noy hoped that the collecting of folktales in Israel would help Israeli
folklore develop in a specific direction: "Let us hope that the collection and preservation of oral Jewish folktales will lead to a genuine
Hebrew folk literature based on ancient traditions and characteristics
of the entire Jewish people."[16]

The use of folklore collections as aids in the development of a
national literature is not uncommon in developing nations. It is, however, somewhat surprising to read these sentiments from a scholarly
folklorist in the 1960s. The orientation toward Israeli folklore research as the salvaging of the past rather than the study of the present
was repeated in Noy's description of his collectors' attitudes toward
their work: "In the nine years of the existence of the Israel Folktale
Archives a large corpus of collectors has been built up who regard
their work as a sacred mission, salvaging these folk treasures for present and future writers and scholars."[17] Despite this view of folklore
research as more archeological than ethnographic (a view which was
somewhat archaic even in the early 1960s), Noy produced a work of
importance which broke ranks with the kind of collections that had
been published in Israel until that time, and the like of which was not
to be seen again. *Jefet Schwili Erzählt*, published in Berlin in 1963, is a
study of a single narrator from Yemen who immigrated to Israel, and
whose tales were collected by Heda Jason and Noy between 1957 and
1960.[18] Schwili's art was spellbinding and his repertoire enormous
(the collection includes 169 entries). As a modern folklore collection,
the work is impeccable. However, Noy's attempt to place Schwili's

repertoire within his personal and historical context ("folklore and personality") is helpful, but all too brief. We are provided with two paragraphs on Schwili's village, seven pages on his family, three on his life-history, two on his worldview, and four on his narrative style. We learn very little of Schwili's life in and attitudes toward Israel, and the function (or lack of it) of his art in the new environment.

It is clear that Israeli folklorists at this time limited themselves to what they perceived as survivals, allowing them no other option than to view folklore as a static art form incapable of making the transition to modern, technologically-based lifestyles. The theoretical apparatus they utilized was incapable of registering the existence of folklore beyond its range of well-defined generic parameters, and for reasons which are not entirely clear, they seemed unaware that these instruments had been redesigned and recalibrated to the demands of the modern world by young American and European folklorists.

While Israeli anthropologists were disinterested in folklore, and Israeli folklorists were salvaging survivals, there seemed to be little interest in studying the dramatic transformations immigrant, sabra, and ethnic folklore were undergoing during the 1960s. The formation of Israeli behavior models was well under way, and new forms of expressive behavior were being developed in response to the realities of modern Israeli life. Immigrants were turning into ethnics, and ethnics into "veterans," either eschewing or emphasizing their identities, and the abandonment, reinforcement, or transformation of traditional forms of expression were primary vehicles for self-expression. Sabras were growing up and living in a society in which the Diaspora was denigrated, and were developing new forms of entertainment and communication which were based on their own unique range of experiences and satisfied their own particular needs. If any of this was noted by Israeli folklorists, it was with regret.

It is unlikely that Israeli folklorists remained unaware of the dramatic developments in folklore theory taking place in the United States, considering their close ties with American folklorists. What is not clear is why they chose to ignore these developments. The necessity for the interdependence of folkloristic and anthropological research in regard to Jewish materials was made clear by Raphael Patai in a volume which he co-edited with Dov Noy and Francis Lee Utley. He wrote:

> as a student of Jewish culture one knows that Jewish legends and tales can be studied only in the context of Jewish folk custom. If the scholarly consensus is that folk custom is not a legitimate object of study for the folklorist because it belongs to the realm of anthropology, then the Jewish folklorist must be an anthropologist

as well in order to be able to study fully the inseparable oral behavioral components of Jewish tradition.[19]

Although one may argue about the existence and/or legitimacy of such a scholarly consensus, which was strongly advocated by William Bascom,[20] it is difficult to argue for the study of a Jewish folklore isolated from Jewish cultural reality. Nevertheless, it is clear from the works cited above that just such a perspective existed among Israeli folklorists during this period, and that Patai's observation was ignored by both folklorists and anthropologists. The ramifications of this neglect for our present topic are clear. For the scholar interested in the development of ethnicity in Israel, its expression in folklore, and the transformations undergone by the expressive behavior of various ethnic groups in the new country, there was no corpus of theory or data tailored to the Israeli experience to which he or she could refer. For the scholar interested in the development of a native Israeli folklore, there was also little material, as this folklore was considered sui generis tainted.

The period between the Six Day War and the Yom Kippur War (1967–1973) was one of stability and progress in many sectors of Israeli society. The standard of living rose dramatically, Israel felt more secure strategically because of her much-improved territorial position, and more confident militarily after her startling success of June, 1967. As economic conditions improved, Israelis could turn their attention from the problems of basic economic and military survival to improving their quality of life and redressing neglected social problems.

These developments in Israeli society altered the focus of social scientific research. By the 1970s, the immigrants who had come to Israel from the Middle East and North Africa during the mass waves of immigration in the 1950s, and their progeny, began to realize that the promise of swift social and economic advancement and mizug galuyot remained largely unfulfilled. Twenty years after the mass immigrations, the Israeli establishment remained dominated by former Europeans. The prosperity that followed the Six Day War accentuated the lack of opportunities for upward mobility among Jews of Middle Eastern and North African origin, who saw that their attempts at acculturation and accommodation had not eliminated ethnic barriers and prejudices, and that their aspirations, motivated by a largely traditional Jewish worldview, were not identical to those of the establishment. Outward and obvious manifestations of cultural differences, such as speech, dress, and mannerism, became less evident with each generation born in Israel. But, at the same time, Middle Eastern and

North African Jews were increasingly alienated from the socialist, secular Israeli culture. Indeed, there is little to suggest that deeper attitudes and manifestations of Middle Eastern Jewish culture had diminished.

These realizations led to a reassessment of the value of cultural heritages which were more closely linked to Jewish religious tradition than the socialist secularism of the East European establishment. This reassessment would eventually lead to the ascendancy of the Likud Coalition in 1977, supported by a majority of Israelis of Afro-Asian origin, which demonstrated the reawakening and public assertion of a complex of culturally-based attitudes.[21] It is telling that Israeli intellectuals, many social scientists included, were caught off guard by this cultural revival, which manifested itself politically in a support for religious intervention in state affairs, a militant stance toward the Arabs, a religio-nationalistic attitude toward the retention of territory, and the adoration of a political father figure.

The search for meaning within one's own cultural heritage, so popular in the United States during the 1970s, had its impact on the expressions of this dissatisfaction in Israel. Organizations responsible for the fostering, revival, and often re-creation of ethnic folklore increased in number. Ethnic festivals, conferences, and clubs became commonplace.[22] But the resurgence of culture in Israel went far beyond manifestations of ethnic pride and the public display of ethnic folklore. It shook the very foundations of the Israeli establishment and society.

Ethnicity began expressing itself in ways which would finally lay to rest the absorptionist theoretical perspective of the Israeli sociological establishment. In fact, a true mizug galuyot was taking place, but in a direction very different from that envisioned by the old establishment; the majority, not the elite, provided the commanding input. Israel's social scientists now faced the challenge of developing a theoretical framework to study this emerging ethnicity.

Shlomo Deshen, Harvey Goldberg, Moshe Shokeid, and Alex Weingrod were instrumental in awakening interest in the cultural study of ethnicity, culture change, and the reinterpretation of symbols and symbolic behavior. Studies conducted during the early 1970s marked another turning point in the scholarly approach to immigration. For the first time, researchers recognized the significance of expressive and symbolic behavior.[23]

The increase in concern for ethnicity resulted in a symposium on that subject, convened by the Israel Anthropological Association in the Spring of 1975. The papers read at this symposium appeared a year later as a special issue of the new journal *Ethnic Groups*, entitled "Culture and Ethnicity in Israeli Society," and demonstrated a growing sophistication in the treatment of issues related to ethnicity. In his introduction to the volume, Goldberg described the various issues which distinguish ethnicity in Israel from that in other societies. For example, Israelis make a clear distinction between non-Jewish minorities (*mi'utim*) and Jewish "communities" (*'edot*), a system of categorization accepted by Israeli scholars as well. The term "ethnic group" (*kvutsah etnit*) is avoided because of its divisive connotation. Due to the emergent nature of Israeli society itself and the ideology of mizug galuyot, an overtly aggressive expression of ethnic differences is often considered a subversive, anti-national force. The incompatibility of the ideology of mizug galuyot with the increasing recognition of and pride in ethnic differences is bound to produce cognitive as well as behavioral incongruity.

These competing ideologies found symbolic expression in the *mimouna*, a Moroccan Jewish festival which has grown in scope and symbolic significance over the past fifteen years, as well as in other manifestations and cultural expressions. According to Harvey Goldberg,

> the *mimouna* may be seen as part of an overall growth of ethnic consciousness, and attempts to preserve ethnic traditions, both with sponsored and spontaneous manifestations. Among the former we may count lecture series, museum exhibits, radio broadcasts and other programs . . . while among the latter we find the growing popularity of acts of memorialization of revered Rabbis . . . week-end retreats, ethnic journals and so forth. While attention to the culture of the variety of Jewish groups has long been present (though not without ambivalence) within the Yishuv . . . it has exhibited a growing institutionalization in the past decade.[24]

In recent years, the mimouna has become far more than an ethnic event. In fact, it is nearing the status of a national festival. In addition to the display of Moroccan ethnicity, it has become a mandatory stop for Israeli politicians, and other ethnic groups display their dances, songs, wares, and foods as well. On Saint Patrick's Day, all Americans are Irish; on the mimouna, all Israelis are Moroccan. But the mimouna also carries with it the message that all members of the various 'edot are Israeli. In addition to Goldberg's study of the mimouna, new studies of ritual and festival increased in quality and number over the next few years.[25] The inclusion of *The Predicament of Homecoming* by Deshen and Shokeid in the "Symbol, Myth and Ritual" series edited by Victor Turner is also evidence of this shift.

Israel's sociologists also began to question the accuracy of the "absorption" model in understanding emerging social forces in Israel.[26] In a work of impressive scope, Sammy Smooha from Haifa University introduced the concept of "pluralism" in place of "absorption" and injected class and power into the discussion of acculturation.[27] By the middle of the 1970s it was clear that the study of ethnicity was an intellectual force within the Israeli social scientific community.[28] Even Shmuel Eisenstadt, who introduced the absorption model to Israeli social science, tentatively recognized the role of culture in shaping immigrant perceptions and behavior.[29]

The heightened institutionalization of ethnicity encouraged publication and research on the traditions of various communities, particularly those of Middle Eastern and North African origin. The Ben-Zvi Institute for the Study of Middle Eastern Jewish Communities began publishing an attractive and scholarly journal, *Pe'amim*, which is rich in ethnographic materials. Various immigrant societies became active in encouraging scholarly research on their own communities.

Israeli folklorists were also active during the period immediately preceding the Yom Kippur War. The Folklore Research Center of the Institute of Jewish Studies of the Hebrew University of Jerusalem began the most ambitious folklore publishing project since the dissolution of the Palestine Institute for Folklore and Ethnology. The appearance of the first volume of *Folklore Research Center Studies* seemed to indicate a shift in the attitude and approach of Israeli folkloristics.[30] This volume, edited by Dov Noy and Issachar Ben-Ami, contains thirty articles in Hebrew, English, and French, with English summaries of the Hebrew articles. It is an eclectic collection, containing articles written by scholars in a number of disciplines, covering a wide spectrum of folkloristic inquiry. This collection seemed to usher in a period of cooperation between folklorists and social scientists in the study of ethnic folklore in Israel. For example, there is an article by Abraham Stahl, a folklorist, on the changes undergone in the folktales of Oriental Jews following their immigration to Israel, and an article by Harvey Goldberg on the continuity of power relations in an immigrant community before and after immigration. Even more folkloristically oriented is an article by Goldberg which appeared in volume three of the series on the use of patronyms by North African immigrants depending on social context.[31] Unfortunately, the degree of synthesis displayed in the contributions to this series did not result in subsequent institutional or intellectual cooperation between folklorists and anthropologists of significance.

The emerging recognition on the part of Israeli anthropologists of the significance of expressive and symbolic behavior led them into what American folklorists would define as folkloristic territory. The theoretical framework for folkloristic participation in social scientific research had been firmly laid by the beginning of the 1970s.[32] Yet

Israeli folkloristics maintained an emphasis on collection and preservation. Thus, collections of the folktales of the various communities culled from the Israel Folktale Archives continued to be the primary publishing activity in the field, and its analytical focus remains literary and historical to this day.[33] Whereas anthropology and sociology had by this time challenged the founding fathers of their fields, Israeli folklore remained very much constrained by the ideas and methods of its founders.

With the rise of ethnicity and the resurgence of culture in Israel, folklore became an identifying ethnic marker, a source of pride, and subject for display. At the same time, the folk traditions of the many groups in Israel were being continually adapted, resurrected, created, or abandoned to fit new situations and new realities. Finally, each passing year has seen the percentage of sabras grow along with native Israeli culture and folklore. Israel is a highly urbanized, industrialized, and technological society. The power of mass culture is tremendous, yet new folklore has developed in Israel as well.

CHAPTER 3

Introspection and Diversification

The decade of the 1980s solidified the importance of anthropological research in the understanding of Israeli society, especially its immigrant component. It also marked a degree of introspection and self-consciousness within the social sciences previously unknown, as well as an intentional merging of anthropological and sociological approaches in order to develop a closer understanding of the actual social and cultural processes occurring among the second, third, and fourth generations of immigrants. As in previous decades, Israeli sociology continued to produce copious and valuable work in a wide variety of areas relating to immigration and ethnicity:[1] politics,[2] demography,[3] education,[4] as well as comprehensive, general sociological studies.[5] In addition, Israeli folklorists began looking at the role folklore serves in a multi-ethnic, pluralistic society, as well as at the nature of emergent Israeli folklore as a dynamic expression of a developing Israeli culture.

During the 1960s and 1970s, Israeli anthropologists emphasized the importance of a thorough understanding of immigrant cultural background and history to understanding immigrant culture and behavior in Israel. During the 1980s, several of these scholars reached more deeply into the pasts of their subjects, producing social histories of the lives of Jews in their countries of origin. Outstanding among these studies are Shlomo Deshen's *The Mellah Society: Jewish Community Life in Sherifian Morocco*,[6] and Harvey Goldberg's *Jewish Life in Muslim Libya: Rivals and Relatives*,[7] which complements his translation and editing of *The Book of Mordechai*, an early twentieth-century account of Jewish life in Libya written by Mordechai Hakohen, a Libyan Jew.[8]

Goldberg relates that when he began his anthropological research, the first informant he spoke to brought up the subject of anti-Jewish riots which occurred in Tripoli in 1945. He writes: "I remember chiding myself at the time not to get involved with the topic because I was doing anthropology and not political science. Since then, anthropologists' claims regarding the scope of their concerns have been expanded, and my desire to understand the former cultural milieu of Libyan Jews has made the topic of Muslim-Jewish cultural relations central in my research."[9] Indeed, all directions of scholarly inquiry seemed open before Israel's anthropologists as they studied ethnic cultural phenomena in the 1980s. In addition to the stress on history, the importance of the religious component in shaping Israeli society and culture was becoming increasingly evident.

The territories captured by Israel during the Six Day War of 1967 contain areas which were part of the Biblical Land of Israel, considered sacred by many Jews. In addition to the strategic arguments for retaining these territories, a powerful and emotionally charged movement began to develop immediately following the war that advocated the retention of Judea and Samaria as an inviolable Jewish obligation, a sacred trust.

This phenomenon was only one, albeit dramatic, manifestation of the rise of national-religious forces within Israel. More subtle manifestations of the resurgence of religion have arisen during the twenty-five years following that war, but it was only during the past decade that they began to receive the attention they deserve among Israeli social scientists. The implications of considering the religious factor have since been acknowledged as central to the understanding of ethnicity.

The struggle between religious and secular in the Yishuv, and later in Israel, has its roots in the earliest days of the Zionist movement. Although the secular form of Zionism eventually became predominant, religious Zionist groups, and even religious anti-Zionist parties, have always had power disproportionate to their numbers in the political and social institutions of the Jewish state. Nevertheless, the dominant establishment in Israel during the period of large-scale immigration was socialist Zionist, hostile to religion, whereas the majority of immigrants were religiously traditional. The seeds of conflict were thus sown, only to blossom at a later date as the immigrants began to speak up for their own enfranchisement.

Religious categories in Israel differ from those in Western, and especially American, Jewish communities. To say that a person is *dati*, "religious," implies what is termed "orthodox" in the West—adhering to traditional interpretations of *halakhah*, religious law. The Reform, Conservative, and Reconstructionist branches of Judaism have had little influence in Israel. Among the religious, there are two main divisions: black *kippah* (skull cap), and knitted kippah. Wearing the black kippah implies an intentional separation from modernity; knitted implies a greater acceptance. These are, of course, gross categorizations, and there are large variations within these groups as well as important symbolic distinctions. For example, the *haredim*, or "ultra-orthodox," are divided into dozens of groupings depending on affiliation and variety of belief, and form a large variegated sub-category within the black kippah group.

It is fair to say that of all the categories of cultural belief and behavior ignored by the sociologists of the 1950s and 1960s, religion would prove the most powerful, enduring, and glaring omission. This is a clear case of a scholarly community guided by its own priorities and worldview. Anthropologists have always studied the centrality of belief systems in understanding social behavior, so it should come as no suprise that in this area as well anthropological studies were more aware of the enduring power of belief on practice.

One of the pioneers in the social scientific study of religious belief and behavior among immigrants was Shlomo Deshen, who, beginning in the early 1970s, wrote about synagogue life as a central venue for communal activity.[10] Along with the trend toward a more in-depth study of cultural and historical origins, this period showed an awareness of the central role played by religious tradition in the lives of *mizrahi* (Eastern) Jews, a role that was challenged but not negated by their immigration to Israel. The resurgence of ethnic cultural and political awareness and power in the 1970s had strong religious manifestations, as Jewish culture could not ultimately be separated from Jewish religious tradition, despite the best efforts of secular Zionists.

This return to the study of religion as a central component in the study of the anthropology of Jewish life went beyond the study of Israeli society. The interdependence of Jewish studies and anthropology is eloquently stated by Harvey Goldberg in his essay, "Reflections on the Mutual Relevance of Anthropology and Jewish Studies," which serves as the introduction to his 1987 collection of essays by eleven authors, *Judaism Viewed from Within and from Without: Anthropological Studies*.[11] Three of the essays deal specifically with Judaism in Israel, and this collection marks an important turning point, or turning back, to both anthropological and Jewish roots. Here, too, social science reflected, and lagged behind, changes occurring in Israeli society itself, another instance in which it may be said that Israeli social science has been more accurate as an indicator than as a predictor of social and cultural trends.[12]

The term "religion" as a separate sphere of thought and behavior is alien to pre-modern Judaism, if not pre-modern thought in general. The term Judaism itself defines a somewhat unnatural category in Jewish thought before the Enlightenment. To be a Jew was an all-encompassing existence, and the nature of Jewish belief and practice excluded the possibility of a separation between the secular and the

Volunteers help new immigrants at the Bulgarian Immigrants Association.

Bulletin board listing the accomplishments of the Bulgarian Immigrants Association.

...ath and memorial notices for Bulgarian immigrants in Jaffa.

...kiosk in Jaffa appeals to new immigrants from Bulgaria.

A coffee shop in Jaffa frequented by new immigrants from Bulgaria.

Acquaintances meet on the main street of Bulgarian Jaffa.

Mr. Pardo, editor of the Bulgarian language newspaper *Far*, in front of his travel agency in Jaffa. The sign reads "Bulgaria: Hit of the Season."

Old friends, veteran immigrants from Bulgaria, meet at the Davidoff Park in Jaffa for an evening chat.

A typical "skhunah" in Holon, a housing project built for immigrants in the 1950s.

Lili Avrahami, former secretary of the Bulgarian Immigrants Association, with G. Haskell and four new immigrants from Bulgaria in Bat Yam.

Lili Avrahami with the author's father, Gordon Haskell, in Bat Yam.

Yosef Levi, president of the Bulgarian Jewish Religious Council, in the chapel of the Sofia synagogue.

Learning games at the Plovdiv Sunday school.

G. Haskell (center) with two youth leaders at the social club of the "Beit Ha-'Am" in Sofia.

The social club of the "Beit Ha-'Am" in Sofia on a Friday night.

Expressions of a new antisemitism on the main boulevard in Sofia.

religious. Thus, for all but the most westernized Jews living in the Middle East and North Africa, the concept of secular Zionism was, to say the least, baffling, and a secular Jewish state, unfathomable.

If secular or sectarian challenge to faith breeds religious intolerance, then the security of Jewish communal life within these communities bred tolerance within the law, and a more relaxed, open-minded attitude toward practice than that which existed among the Jews of Europe. Confronted with antisemitism from without and apostasy, assimilation, and challenges from secular Jews from within, orthodoxy as a category developed within European Jewry.[13] The more integrated and self-assured religiosity of many mizrahim is referred to in Israel as *masorti*, "traditional."[14]

Judaism pervades the family lives of many mizrahim in Israel, regardless of degree of belief or practice of individual family members. Tolerance of a wide variety of behaviors is the hallmark of this approach, and a more relaxed and secure attitude toward practice is evident. Categories of secular and religious are much less well-defined, and may be of little significance. For example, if an Ashkenazi family lights candles on Sabbath eve, one might safely assume that family members would be dati, or religious, and follow the commandments of orthodox Judaism. The lighting of Sabbath candles in a mizrahi home, however, would give little indication of the degree of practice of the family members. Father might walk to synagogue for prayers the next morning, the children might drive to the beach, and the question of consistency would be unlikely to arise. As Moshe Shokeid states: "This mode of religiosity is characterized by spiritual and emotional involvement and the notion of belonging, rather than by the strict practice of religious observances."[15]

It is in the realm of religion, however, that we can observe an instance of the assimilation of Ashkenazi ideology by mizrahi Jews. Because of the polarization of religious and secular within the Israeli establishment, many mizrahi Jews are becoming more strident, more ideological, and more political in their religious belief and practice. In fact, many of the more orthodox are even adopting Ashkenazi dress. The leaders of the mizrahi religious parties have become physically indistinguishable from their Ashkenazi counterparts, in coiffure, clothing, and decreasing tolerance of others.

A local component of the worldwide return to traditional religion is the repentance (*tshuvah*) movement in Israel. Large numbers of Israelis are becoming, some for the first time, traditionally religious, aided by well-organized recruiting programs run by various orthodox groups. A major contribution to our understanding of this movement is a study by Eli Yassif, folklorist at Ben Gurion University of the Negev, analyzing the folkloric elements within the recruiting speeches given by prominent rabbis in large public gatherings. This study demonstrates the power and viability of traditional narrative motifs in a contemporary setting.[16]

During the initial three decades of Israeli social scientific inquiry, there was relatively little scholarly introspection or theoretical debate. This quiet was shattered rather dramatically by a group of young sociologists, centered at Haifa University in the early 1980s, who challenged many of the assumptions of the Israeli establishment through what Percy Cohen dubs the "radical critique."[17] They criticized both the absorption/modernization model of the sociologists and the cultural/historical model of the anthropologists as being flawed in their understanding of the real mechanisms at work in the adaptation, or maladaptation of immigrants from the East to life in Israel. Rather, they looked to the economic sphere to explain the realities of social and ethnic, or to them, class conflict in Israel, substituting "class" for "ethnicity" as the primary social force.

Indeed, of all approaches used to gain an understanding of ethnic divisions in Israel, the economic had previously been the least emphasized. Because of their predisposition to socialist-Zionist ideals, Israeli social scientists were loathe to point out the possibility of divisions based on emerging economic class. Although Judith Shuval and S. N. Eisenstadt touched on the subject in the 1950s, they believed that economic differences would disappear with the success of immigrant "absorption."[18]

In a series of articles published in the first half of the 1980s, Deborah Bernstein and Shlomo Swirski discussed the creation and persistence of ethnic and class differences on what may generally be called a Marxist model.[19] According to these studies, there is an emerging ethnic class division in Israel which is structural and not created by chance. This division exists in employment, income, education, and social status, and is becoming greater rather than diminishing with time. This class distinction is presented as having been intentionally developed by the dominant European establishment, which imported Jews from North Africa and the Middle East to form an Israeli proletariat.

The ideas of this "radical critique" were essential in forcing Israeli social scientists to look at their own theoretical assumptions, in causing them to become more introspective. It reintroduced economics and social class into the discussion of the development of ethnicity. It revealed many of the gross shortcomings of the absorption/modernization model, as well as the sometimes too-narrow focus of the cultural/historical model in understanding the complex components that make up identity.

As in all radical critiques, Bernstein and Swirsky went too far by impugning a malevolent master plan to the Israeli establishment. In fact, there is no evidence of such a plan, and I think it fair to grant the planning and immigration authorities nothing but the highest motives in their attempts to deal with the mass immigration of impoverished Jews from over seventy countries within a very short period of time. Even with the best of intentions, even with historical hindsight, it is not entirely clear that with the limited financial and manpower resources of the day the authorities would have had it in their power to implement even the most enlightened of plans.

Bernstein also makes the same error committed by the absorption/modernization studies which she criticizes when she underestimates the power and persistence of immigrant culture. She writes: "the negation of Oriental culture has led to its almost complete disappearance, leaving behind it little creative experience or expression."[20] In one sense, then, Bernstein arrives at the very same conclusion as did Ben-David, advocate of absorption and modernization, almost three decades before.[21]

In their 1985 article, "Variations in Ethnic Identification among Israeli Jews," Hannah Ayalon, Eliezer Ben-Raphael, and Stephen Sharot attempt to reconcile the sociological and anthropological perspectives of ethnicity, by pointing out its multivalent, polymorphic nature:

> Recent studies have provided divergent accounts of the meanings, strength, and relative importance of identification with the *eda* and *edot ha-Mizrah* among Middle Eastern Israelis. Those who have focused on the *eda* rather than the 'Oriental' or *Mizrahi* . . . identification have tended to be anthropologists who approach the subject from a perspective that emphasized the cultural, primordial, expressive, non-rational components of ethnicity. Those who have focused on the 'Oriental' identification have been sociologists who have emphasized the socio-economic, political, instrumental, rational components of ethnicity.[22]

This balanced and well written study examines various definitions and manifestations of ethnicity in interviews with 826 male residents of Be'er Sheva of Iraqi, Moroccan, Polish, and Rumanian origin. The results indicate that the nature of ethnicity is fluid, dynamic, and strategic, rather than static and paradigmatic. The authors point out the need to balance our understanding of ethnic identification with the broader identifications of citizenship and nationality. Group identity and integration are also not mutually exclusive: "A high level of ethnic identification may have little effect on integration-mindedness if it is not accompanied by either cultural or political separatism.[23]

This 'symbolic ethnicity' has long been recognized by folklorists and anthropologists as being of central importance to groups that continue to value identification with the culture of origin at the same time fully identifying with the dominant culture. As Israel seems to be moving in a similar pluralist direction, Israeli social science may find much of value in this literature.

In 1986, Sammy Smooha of Haifa University published a comprehensive study entitled *Social Research on Jewish Ethnicity in Israel 1948–1986: Review and Selected Bibliography with Abstracts*.[24] The bulk of the work consists of a bibliography of 614 works on the subject, mostly in the fields of sociology, anthropology, social psychology, education, and geography (had Smooha paid more heed to the reemergence of religion as a central factor in Israeli society he might have limited his bibliography to 613 entries, the number of *mizvot*, "commandments", orthodox Jews find in the Bible). It is a remarkable compilation, of great interest and utility to researchers and students in the field. The book also contains a core list of one hundred selected works ordered by subject, and a list of active researchers in the field with affiliation and address.

Smooha begins this impressive work with an essay titled "Three Approaches to the Sociology of Ethnic Relations in Israel," essentially a revision of the central premise of his 1978 work, *Israel: Pluralism and Conflict*.[25] He divides sociological research in Israel into three approaches: the cultural, the class, and the pluralistic. The first refers to what I, and Smooha in his previous work, call the absorption/modernization approach, into which he casts the cultural/historical approach of the anthropologists. The second refers to what Percy Cohen calls the "radical critique" of Israeli sociology, the Marxist and neo-Marxist school emerging from Haifa University. The third is Smooha's approach, which attempts to bridge the gap between the two. In fact, Smooha's pluralism refers both to a pluralistic society and to a pluralistic, or eclectic use of scholarly approaches depending on the context of the group being studied.

Smooha's essay is an admirable attempt to provide a comprehensive framework for examining the very issues discussed in this essay. From the vantage point of cultural anthropology, however, his inclusion of works in his first category does not make sense. It is clear from the foregoing discussion of the development of the anthropological study of immigration and ethnicity in Israel, that the consideration of the centrality of culture in understanding the emergence of ethnicity was a radical departure from the absorption/modernization model of the sociologists, both in theory and in methodology. In effect, the anthropologists advocated much of what Smooha calls the "pluralist" approach, in which the "underlying premise is that the ethnic phenomenon differs from place to place and from one period to another; hence, a uniform set of concepts, be they based on assimilation or on class inequality, will not succeed in explaining the vast disparities that mark ethnic situations."[26]

This very point is made by Alex Weingrod in his introduction to *Studies in Israeli Ethnicity: After the Ingathering*.[27] Most of the seventeen articles included in the collection grew out of a conference held at Ben Gurion University in Be'er Sheva in June, 1980. Weingrod divides the studies in his collection between "culture" and "social change" perspectives, the first broadly referring to the anthropological, the second to the sociological approach. He further divides the studies along an "inequality" theory/"symbolic" or "mobilization" theory axis. The former posits that ethnicity becomes an important social fact when ethnic groups are clustered in lower social and economic niches which reinforce their group identity and solidarity. The latter recognizes the changing nature of ethnic identity according to changing context, and views ethnicity as a resource which can be put to economic, political, and symbolic uses.[28]

Perhaps the best summation of the cultural/historical approach of Israeli anthropologists can be found in Harvey Goldberg's contribution to the collection, "Historical and Cultural Dimensions of Ethnic Phenomena in Israel."[29] Here Goldberg discusses the study of a wide variety of ethnic phenomena, including demography, ethnic boundaries, ethnic definitions, and religion:

> Our theoretical stance sees culture as a system of meanings, embodied in symbols, which are analytically separate from social structure, though they constantly interact with it . . . the way that cultural conceptions of institutional spheres (politics, stratification, religion) are linked together in a given society is a historical and, hence, variable matter, so that ethnicity, in any given instance, must be viewed in the context of these broader configurations, and cannot be fully understood in isolation. . . . This is not to say that ethnicity can be understood only as a particular phenomenon in each society, with no contribution from cross-cultural comparisons. What it does claim is that such comparisons which ignore the historical and cultural dimensions of these questions are likely to be superficial and misleading.[30]

It would seem that Goldberg's categorization of the cultural/historical approach would fit more appropriately into Smooha's "pluralist" than "cultural" category. It is just such misunderstandings of the nature of culture and culture theory on the part of many of Israel's sociologists that predisposes them to repeat the mistakes of earlier scholars.

The 1980s saw the largest new immigration to the country since the massive waves of the 1950s. Emigration of Jews from the Soviet Union, which began with *detente* between the United States and the Soviet Union during the 1970s, became a flood with the policy of *glasnost* during the early 1980s, and finally a deluge with the end of Communist hegemony by the end of that decade. The closing of many Western countries to large numbers of Soviet immigrants channeled more and more Jews to Israel, amounting to hundreds of thousands by the end of the decade.

The other large group of immigrants of the 1980s came from Ethiopia. In a dramatic operation reminiscent of the airlifts of Jews from Iraq and Yemen in the 1950s, over fourteen thousand Ethiopian Jews were evacuated within the span of a few days in May, 1991. Once again, the Ministry of Absorption was confronted with tremendous challenges in dealing with the massive influx. Although the Jews of both Ethiopia and the Soviet Union required housing, food, health care, and jobs, the cultural differences between them created quite different problems in the long term.

Despite the much greater size of the Soviet *aliya* (immigration), the Ethiopians have received more ethnographic attention. This may be the result of a number of different factors. The "exoticism" of the Ethiopians may hold more interest for social scientists, just as the Yemenites did forty years earlier. The smaller size of the group and its greater concentration within the general population may make it easier to study. Finally, the confluence of academic and settlement activity proved fortuitous for these studies.

During the 1980s, Ben-Gurion University of the Negev became one of the key centers for innovative research on immigration, as well as other areas of social concern, in Israel. A new journal, *Israel Social Science Research*, was introduced by the University, and a number of talented scholars were attracted to the institution, leaving their mark on the study of this new aliyah. A special issue of the journal appeared in 1985, edited by Michael Ashkenazi and Alex Weingrod, containing ten articles on a wide variety of issues.[31] This work follows a comprehensive study by Ashkenazi and Weingrod on the absorption process in Be'er Sheva, which is the most comprehensive description of the actual mechanisms of the absorption process provided in the literature. The study has an applied focus, was sponsored by the Ministry of Absorption, and ends with ten specific recommendations. According to the authors, "the Israeli officials responsible for the absorption programs are dedicated, experienced, and intelligent persons. Moreover, they are consciously concerned not to repeat the mistakes and failures that were made during the mass immigration of the 1950s."[32] The question as to whether the government agencies in charge of immigration had in fact learned lessons from earlier experiences is explored both in this work and in a study by Jeff Halper, "The Absorption of Ethiopian Immigrants: A Return to the Fifties."[33]

The 1980s marked an increase in innovation among young Israeli folklorists, as the first generation of native scholars began to come into its own. Work of this period demonstrates a growing independence of thought, as well as increased contact and cooperation betweeen students of Israeli culture both in Israel and abroad. An intellectual openness combined with the universal acceptance of the miraculous web created by electronic mail, fax machines, and computers has created an ever smaller academic world, and this is especially true in the already cozy field of Jewish studies.

Aliza Shenhar,[34] Haya Bar-Itzhak,[35] Yoram Bilu,[36] and Issachar Ben-Ami[37] have all contributed to our understanding of the function of folklore in contemporary Israeli immigrant society. A signal of the maturation of the discipline can be found in a marvelous survey of the history of folkloristics in Israel by Galit Hasan-Rokem of the Hebrew University and Eli Yassif, which appeared in 1989 as a special issue of the *Jewish Folklore and Ethnology Review* on the "Folklore and Ethnology of Israeli Society," edited by Yael Zerubavel of the University of Pennsylvania. The article provides a comprehensive framework for examining the development of the discipline in Israel, as well as references to many obscure sources. The present study examines folklore only in its relation to the social scientific study of immigration and ethnicity. Hasan-Rokem and Yassif's essay is essential to an understanding of the contributions of folklorists to the study of Israeli and Jewish culture as a whole.

The special issue of the *Jewish Folklore and Ethnology Review* provides an invaluable contemporary snapshot of scholarship in the field. It includes articles on the latest scholarship on Ethiopian, Yemenite, Kurdish, and North African immigrants, as well as several important directories and bibliographies. It should serve as a companion to this study in providing the widest possible coverage of the field.

The present study both builds on and departs from previous studies of ethnicity in Israel. It owes its greatest debt to the first generation of Israeli anthropologists, who dedicated their professional lives to understanding the place of immigrant culture and nascent ethnicity in the changing dynamic of Israeli society. Shlomo Deshen, Harvey Goldberg, Moshe Shokeid and Alex Weingrod have provided rich and detailed descriptions of the communities they studied over the span of thirty years, always open to new ideas and new ways of understanding the fascinating process of human adaptation to the miraculous circumstances of Jewish return and rebirth. Each has demonstrated untiring curiosity and willingness to try new methods and ideas, providing insights into the widest variety of cultural adaptations. Most recently, Shokeid has followed a different kind of migration, studying the wrenching emotional and cultural crises of identity experienced by Israeli immigrants in New York.[38] Alex Weingrod adapted the tools of the folklorist in his study of the *hillula*, or pilgrimage to the grave of a saint, by Israelis of North African descent.[39]

In this summary, I have concentrated on the effects general developments within Israeli society have had on the ways in which Israeli social scientists have looked at immigration and ethnicity. At the same time, scholars living in other countries, especially the United States and Britain, have been engaged in the study of these questions and have made major contributions to the field. Because they were not responding as directly to developments in Israel in conducting their research, and because their work does not appear to have had as great an impact on the directions in which Israeli social science developed, their work has not been included here. With the development of new, instantaneous communications technology and the increasing mobility of scholars, especially between the United States and Israel, geographical distinctions have become less and less a distinguishing factor among scholars, and for future comparisons I would not continue such a distinction. Among these scholars, to name a few, are Jay Abarbanel, Herbert Lewis, Milford Spiro, Walter Zenner, Walter Weiker, and Dorothy Willner. I hope to document the contributions of such scholars in a future study.

The present study is both historical and cultural. It is based on the premise that it is impossible to understand the present divorced from the past. In the case of immigrants, the researcher must first gain a comprehensive picture of the lives of the community and the individual in the country of origin in order to understand the process of individual and cultural adaptation in the new home. Second, generalizations about immigrant groups not based on intensive fieldwork, including participant observation and in-depth interviews over time, tend to be superficial if not inaccurate. Third, human beings are dynamic, adaptable and adaptive creatures who create their own realities depending on individual and community needs. These realities include individual and group identities, and these identities are expressed symbolically. Therefore, it is important to contemplate symbolic expression and interaction, which in modern, pluralistic societies have been the primary domain of the folklorist, in order to grasp the ever-changing nature of ethnicity.

Israeli social scientists have studied, almost exclusively, immigrants from the Middle East and North Africa. In fact, it is largely these groups which are considered "ethnic" in Israel (much as Blacks and Hispanics are sometimes referred to colloquially as "ethnics" in the United States). This is another example of Israeli social science uncritically following trends in Israeli society. In the present study, the group under consideration was European and westernized before immigration. Not only were they not considered a "problematic" group, they served as an example of successful integration, a model to be followed. Popular stereotypes concerning Bulgarian Jews abound: modest and generous, uncomplaining and industrious, pulling themselves up by their own bootstraps. Perhaps by studying such a group, we may be able to obtain some insight into what constitutes, and what factors led to, the perception of the successful adaptation of an immigrant group to life in the Jewish state.

This study focuses on the nature of symbolic expression, of folklore, as a primary indicator of immigrant attitude and affect. It attempts to find common ground between anthropological and folkoristic theory and approach, and demonstrate the efficacy of folkloristic inquiry in gaining a deeper understanding of the forces which drive the creation of cultural identity.

The unused synagogue in Plovdiv, the second largest city in Bulgaria. Illustration by Cheri Haskell.

PART II

The Jews in Bulgaria

CHAPTER 4

From the First Century to the Ottoman Conquest

An individual's identity, the way one sees one's self in relation to others and to the world, is created from elements so various and complex that they are difficult to isolate. Yet there are always events, people, places, and ideas which can be identified as being of exceptional importance to one's present self-image. There are almost certainly other elements of which one is not consciously aware. Occasionally some of these elements can be isolated and reconstructed by the trained observer.

Ethnicity is both an individual and a group phenomenon. Within a group of immigrants from the same place, no two will perceive of their relationship to the old home, the new home, and to other immigrants in quite the same way. Yet the very term "ethnicity" connotes a collectivity of common experience and sentiment: language, food, faith, folklore, worldview, memory. Reliance on memory alone in reconstructing this common experience is a tricky affair.

When two navigators standing on the bridge of a ship check solar declination at a given point in time, and add and subtract for various standard deviations, they should end up with the same position, assuming they use correctly calibrated sextants. The sextant of human memory, however, is never calibrated in precisely the same way as any other, and each shows the distortions, additions, and subtractions which have occurred as the result of individual experience. Nevertheless, those memories may tell us a great deal about the individual's sentiments and attachments at the present time. For a clearer picture of the past they must be triangulated with observations from other vantage points.

Although it is clear that each Bulgarian Jew in Israel will perceive of himself or herself through the prism of his or her own experience, it is also true that there have been pivotal collective experiences which have influenced the identity of the group as a whole. This fact emerged from the interview data and has guided the historical research for this study. This section will begin with a survey of the history of Bulgarian Jewry from the arrival of the first Jews within the borders of what is today Bulgaria, until its departure for Israel, a period of about two millennia, paying careful attention to those events, ideas, and cultural transformations that influence ethnic identity in Israel today.

In light of current practice in anthropological and folkloristic research, the examination of the past in order to illuminate the present would seem self-evident. As the student of the development of either of these disciplines knows, however, this was not always the case. In Part I, I surveyed the development of this approach in Israeli social scientific methodology, especially the early pioneering research of Shlomo Deshen, Alex Weingrod, and Moshe Shokeid. These scholars, and many others who followed, have shown us the shortcomings of examining any Israeli immigrant group in synchronic isolation, and the present study hopes to follow their example.

Interview data guided the development of components of identity, discussed below. Most of these components have their roots in Bulgaria, and it is the purpose of this section to help illuminate those relevant historical components. As the historical research was retroactively directed by informant sentiments, representative excerpts from the interviews have been included in the discussion to illuminate key points and help reveal the coherence of what may appear to be disparate elements.

After Albania, Bulgaria is probably the least studied and documented country in Europe. This holds true for historical study, and even more so for ethnographic.[1] The Jews of Bulgaria, always a small minority within the country, have been awarded even less attention. Only in the present century do the sources provide us with a clearer picture of Jewish communal life in Bulgaria.

Bulgarian Jewry is usually treated as a sub-division of the larger Balkan Sephardi community. Although Bulgarian Jewry shares many historical and cultural features with other Balkan Sephardim, its singular demographic make-up and historical experience created a people whose attitudes, culture, and relationship to gentile society were unique, and resulted in the dramatic cultural and social transformations and events during the last century which have no parallel in Jewish social and political history. This uniqueness is a key factor in understanding Bulgarian Jewish attitudes and identity both in Bulgaria and in Israel.

There is significant evidence of Jewish habitation in the area since at least the destruction of the Second Temple in Jerusalem in 70 C.E.[2] It was not until the second half of the first century, however, that Jews settled in larger numbers along the Danube and in Macedonia. The first organized Jewish communities were founded by Romaniots, the term used for the original Jewish population of what was to later become the Byzantine Empire. Although Hebrew was probably used among the Jews themselves, Greek and Latin were the linguae francae, and the Romaniots maintained an abiding identification with Greek language and culture even after the Iberian influx of the late fifteenth century. The Romaniot communities were organized around the *Kahal Kadosh Romaniyah* (the Holy Romaniyot Community), and a synagogue of the so-called "Gregos" existed in Sofia until 1819, and one that was active in Adrianople until it burned down in 1905. Greek-Romaniot names are still common among Jews of Bulgarian origin.[3] The Romaniots were among the first of many communities in what would become the amalgam of Bulgarian Jewry.

The sixth century saw the influx of Slavic tribes into the region and their subjugation of the local populations. Primarily agricultural, these tribes were organized in unique, loosely-knit communal groupings called *zadrugas*.[4] They had little contact with the urban centers where Jews were concentrated, and largely resisted Greek cultural influences.[5] In 681, the Turko-Uigir (Volga) Bulgars crossed the Russian Steppes and entered Bulgaria, easily subduing the local Slavic population. The Bulgars themselves were soon assimilated culturally by the Slavic majority, adopting its language. There is strong evidence that these Bulgar tribes were closely related to the Khazars, whose leaders would convert to Judaism within a century. The extent of the influence of Jewish thought on the Bulgars is unclear, but there is evidence of a degree of affinity between the Jews and the Bulgar tribes which appears to have persisted after their Slavicization, and even after the nation's acceptance of Christianity in 864–865. Vicki Tamir, historian of Bulgarian Jewry, wrote:

> For centuries Bulgaria was free of anti-Semitism despite persistent efforts of neighboring Byzantium to contaminate the Slavic populace and clergy with theological Judeophobia. A curious affinity for Judaism, exhibited by the proto-Bulgars, survived in Bulgaria long after the nation's Christianization. There are no records of anti-Jewish manifestations before the fourteenth century, when King Ivan Aleksandur, married to the Jewess Sarah/Teodora, convoked a synod against Christian heretics and Jews.[6]

Allegations of unsuccessful Jewish attempts to convert the heathen Bulgarians to Judaism during the reign of King Boris I (852–889) are

without historical verification. Early Bulgarian Christianity remained a
syncretism of pagan, Christian, and Jewish beliefs and practices long
after Bulgaria became nominally Christian. According to Nissan Oren,
scholar of Bulgarian history:

> A curious insight of the contemporary religious situation is af-
> forded by the 106 questions submitted by Bulgarian representa-
> tives to Pope Nicholas I (858–867). Among the questions on
> which guidance was requested were the proper regulations for
> offering first fruits; the law concerning amulets; which day is the
> day of rest—Saturday or Sunday; which animals and poultry
> may be eaten; whether it is wrong to eat the flesh of an animal
> that has not been slaughtered; should burial rituals be per-
> formed for suicides; how many days must a husband abstain
> from intercourse with his wife after she has given birth; should a
> fast be observed during a drought; should women cover their
> heads in houses of prayer; and so on. The names of the Bulgar-
> ian princes at the time—David, Moses, Samuel—may also show
> Jewish influence.[7]

Vicki Tamir goes so far as to relate several contemporary Bulgarian
folk beliefs to Jewish origins.[8] There is little doubt that Saint Cyril and
Saint Methodius, who devised the Cyrillic script soon after Bulgaria's
conversion to Christianity, were influenced by Jewish thought and
teachings. By the ninth century, communities of the Kahal Kadosh
Romaniyah had been organized in Sofia, Pleven, Nikopol, and Vidin,
and were treated with tolerance by the non-Jewish majority.[9]

The centuries-long seesaw battle between Bulgaria and Byzan-
tium resulted in the conquest of Bulgaria by the Byzantine Emperor
Basil II in 1018, followed by nearly two centuries of Greek rule. Although this period could hardly be termed a peaceful one for the Jews
of the region, with constant invasions and general lawlessness being
the rule of the land, in many ways it was characterized by a trans-
Balkan Jewish cohesion which would be an important feature of the
Ottoman period. Byzantine domination broke down national boundaries to trade, and Jews throughout the Empire were united by the
language of Byzantine commerce and public affairs. The Jews in sub-
jugated Bulgaria were in a particularly good position as the virulent
antisemitism prominent in the surrounding lands of the Empire was
not shared by the Bulgarians, who continued to regard them largely
without malice.

The Second Bulgarian Kingdom, which reached the height of its
power under King Ivan Asen II, proved to be a haven for the Jews of
Europe, just as it would prove to be a haven for the Jews of Iberia

more than two centuries later. As the Latin Church was increasingly undermined by various heresies, including native Bulgarian Bogomilism, the Jews, the archetypical scapegoats, suffered increasingly from Christian violence. The association of Jews with heresy, combined with the upheavals and religious fervor of the Sixth Crusade, caused a major dislocation in European Jewish life, terror, and a continual search for refuge. Bulgaria provided a safe haven, and Jews from other parts of Europe settled within the kingdom. They were permitted to join the already existing Jewish communities, and engage in free trade. As a result of this "tolerance" toward the Jews on the part of Bulgaria, Pope Gregory IX called for a "holy war" against the kingdom. These immigrants created a new community within Bulgarian Jewry, and were among the first large populations of Ashkenazim to take up residence in the country. With King Ivan Asen's death in 1241, the deterioration of Bulgarian greatness began, which would eventually result in the loss of sovereignty itself, first to Serbian, and then, finally, to Ottoman domination.

The ascendancy of Ivan Aleksandur to the Bulgarian throne in 1331 heralded two paradoxical events in the history of Jewish life in Bulgaria. Four years later he divorced his wife in order to marry the Jewess Sarah, who converted to Christianity and took the name Teodora. Although Queen Teodora continued her contacts with Jews and often interceded on their behalf with the King, she was unable to prevent the convocation of a holy synod in Veliko Turnovo in 1360, which condemned the Bogomils, Adamites, Hesychastes, and Jews. This marked the first official antisemitic action undertaken by a Bulgarian government.

Vicki Tamir, whose *Bulgaria and Her Jews* is the first comprehensive history on the subject to appear in English, argues that the Holy Synod's antisemitic accusations of Jewish proselytizing and arrogance were the result of both Jewish refusal to accept Christian proselytizing, and Jewish power in the capital and court. She concludes that "had the Jews not presented a real threat, albeit unintentionally, they would not have been declared enemies, and their 'heresy' would not have been lumped with that of the Bogomils."[10] It seems Tamir does not accept what I believe to be one of the fundamental axia of Jewish history; that antisemitism is rarely the result of any action on the part of its object.

Despite the events in Turnovo, Jewish life in the rest of Bulgaria continued largely undisturbed, and the realm would continue to provide a haven for the increasingly terrorized Jews of Central and Western Europe. In 1376, the Jews of Hungary were expelled, and sent down the Danube on barges. Many settled in Vidin and Nikopol, and Rabbi Shalom Ashkenazi founded the first rabbinical school in Bulgaria in Vidin.

The Hungarian Jews were quickly integrated into the larger Ashkenazi population, and their numbers would be augmented following the invasion of Buda by Suleiman I in 1526.[11] Due to widespread terror and genocide in France and the Provence, many Jews arrived in Bulgaria in 1394.

With the fall of Adrianople to Sultan Murad I began the conquest of Bulgaria by the Ottoman Empire, which ended with the subjugation of Nikopol and Vidin in 1396. Under Ottoman rule, the Jews of Bulgaria would be free from the evil of Christian antisemitism which had periodically threatened them during the preceding centuries. It should be clear from the foregoing summary, however, that when compared to Jewish life in much of Central and Western Europe, Jewish life in Bulgaria during the period preceding Ottoman rule was relatively secure and free of terror and persecution. This relative tolerance has characterized Bulgaria throughout her history, and one can only speculate as to its causes. One thing seems clear, however; if the peculiar form of antisemitism which developed in Europe is partially a result of theologically-fostered paranoia and hatred, then the relative apathy displayed by the population of Bulgaria toward matters spiritual may serve as at least a partial explanation for the largely symbiotic relationship between Jews and gentiles in the country. Bulgarians appear to have been equally suspicious of Christianity, Judaism, and Islam, and this indifference to Revealed Truth may in part explain their distaste for bombastic ideology, Nazism included. Whatever the reasons, the fact remains that the relationship between Jews and gentiles in Bulgaria during this period stands in stark contrast to the intolerance which was the hallmark of that relationship in most of Europe.

CHAPTER 5

The Ottoman Period: 1389–1878

The consolidation of Turkish sovereignty over Bulgaria provided its Jewish population with a measure of security and protection unmatched anywhere in Christian Europe. From a Jewish perspective, one might say that the conquest of Bulgaria came in the nick of time, for the convocation of the Holy Synod in Turnovo in 1360 was an unprecedented incident of state-sanctioned antisemitism, and one might conjecture that Bulgarians would have found it difficult to resist a European climate which was increasingly antisemitic.

Antisemitism as practiced in Europe was not a universal phenomenon, and the attitude of the Ottoman Empire toward its minority populations was quite different from medieval Christianity's attitude toward Jews and Moslems. In fact, the tables were turned: the Christians in Bulgaria were treated miserably, whereas the Jews were generally respected and valued, and were granted relative autonomy in the running of their own affairs. Unlike the Christians, who were largely illiterate peasants, the Jews could not only govern themselves efficiently, but their acumen in trade and diplomacy and their linguistic competence was of great benefit in linking the Empire in a comprehensive, cosmopolitan network.

Whereas the Jews of Christian Europe were a despised religious minority, the Jews of the Ottoman Empire were, for the most part, a protected national minority. The *millet* system allowed them to exercise control over their own law, religion, language, and education. In exchange they were expected to respect Ottoman authority and pay special taxes.[1] The Turks showed little interest in converting the subject populations to Islam, although many Bulgarians did so, due to the relative weakness of Christian tradition in the country and the benefits which were granted to Moslems.[2] The Turks were content to bleed the peasants dry through taxation, and allowed the Jews to conduct their commerce for them.[3]

It is important to understand that the conquest of the Balkans by the Ottoman Empire was not seen by the Jews, whether in Greece, Bulgaria, or Serbia, as a national catastrophe. They did not share the sense of national loss experienced by the Christians, for their own nationality and identity were not threatened by the Turkish conquest. In fact, they have never had a dual identity, even when they gave their loyalty and even lives to the Bulgarian state. Asked whether she felt more Jewish or more Bulgarian in Israel, Zhanti Zohar replied: "Jewish, of course we felt we were Jews, how could it be otherwise? If you're a Jew, can you be a Bulgarian? No, you can't go and make something like this [makes sign of the cross]" (Zohar, p. 8). On the contrary, the Empire could grant Jews the continuity and security lacking so long on the Peninsula, and the institutionalized tolerance of the new regime must have been greeted with a collective sigh of relief.

At the time of the consolidation of the Turkish conquest, there were Jewish communities in Vidin, Nikopol, Silistra, Pleven, Sofia, Yambol, Philippopolis (Plovdiv), and Stara Zagora.[4] Bulgarian Jewry as a distinct entity would cease to exist, and Bulgaria itself would have no autonomy for five centuries. Until the resurgence of national identity in the nineteenth century, Balkan Jewry under Ottoman rule can be regarded in general terms as a single social and cultural unit. There existed, however, certain regional differences. The Bulgarian communities, dominated by Romaniots, would be enlarged and diversified by a series of immigrations created by antisemitic activity in Europe reaching fever-pitch. As a result of the destruction of over two hundred Jewish communities within the Holy Roman Empire, inspired or rationalized by accusations that the Jews had caused the Black Plague (1348–1349), and increasing incidents of blood-libel accusations and anti-Jewish terror, a large group of refugees was created which was looking for a safe haven. A letter was sent to Bavaria, Moravia, and Hungary by three Jews who had previously fled persecution in France and Germany inviting these refugees to find shelter under the Sultan.[5] After their gradual banishment from Bavaria in the fifteenth and sixteenth centuries, many Jews came to Bulgaria, founded a synagogue in Sofia, and Judeo-German was heard for a long time in the streets.[6] An independent Ashkenazi synagogue existed in Sofia until the exodus of 1948, although most of the congregation was Sephardi.

The subsequent influx of Jews seeking sanctuary from Christian genocide would radically change the character of Balkan Jewry and would absorb both the Romaniots and Ashkenazim in its culture and language. In March of 1492, after a two-century long nightmare of persecution, degradation, forced conversion, and autos-da-fe, Ferdinand II of Aragon and Isabella I of Castille issued edicts expelling all Jews from Spain. Three months later, between one hundred and one hundred fifty thousand still-professing Jews left the country. This was perhaps the most traumatic event in Jewish history between the destruction of the Second Temple in Jerusalem by the Romans in 70 C.E., and the Holocaust in our time.[7]

It was not an event which occurred in isolation, however, but the most severe and catastrophic of a series of expulsions which began early in the thirteenth century. In 1290, England expelled its Jews; in 1306, the Jews were exiled from the Royal Territories of France; during the fifteenth century, Jews were banned from all the major cities of Germany, with the exception of Frankfurt am Main; in 1498, the Jews of Portugal, including those who had fled from the Spanish expulsion six years earlier, were cast out; in 1501 this scenario was repeated in Provence, and in 1507 in the Kingdom of Naples. By the sixteenth century, the Jewish population had been forcibly shifted from west to east, and the two largest Jewries in the world resided in Poland and the Ottoman Empire.[8]

In contrast, this was a period of relative quiet in the Ottoman Empire, and skilled tradesmen and artisans were needed by the government. Sultan Bayazid is reported to have said, in regard to the expulsions from Spain: "They say that Ferdinand of Spain is a wise king, yet he has impoverished his own land in order to enrich mine."[9] According to Tamir:

> Four separate waves of exiles reached the Bulgarian lands, entering—presumably after 1497—via Salonika, Constantinople, Adrianople, and Ragusa. The first and second contingents settled in Nikopol, while a third chose Sofia. The fourth allegedly arrived later, sometime between 1499 and 1540, establishing the 'Holy Aragon Congregation' in Plovdiv. To the existing Romaniot and Ashkenazi synagogues, a third type, the Sephardi, was now added, enriching with its own customs and ritual the already variegated milieu. In time a uniform, well-organized, cohesive community would arise, which would communicate in the Hispanic language of the Iberian Jews while utilizing the creative forces of all its component parts.[10]

The main cities of Sephardi settlement were Constantinople and Salonika, the latter of which would become the center of Jewish life and scholarship in Europe and would eventually boast a Jewish majority.[11]

There were divisions even within the Sephardi community of Bulgaria, and synagogues were established by communities of common origin from regions or even cities in Iberia. But the size and strength of the Sephardi community very soon absorbed the indigenous Romaniots and Ashkenazim, and Ladino became the language of the Jews of the Balkans. Despite the periodic influx of Jewish refugees fleeing persecution in other parts of Europe (especially Italy and Hungary), Judeo-Spanish culture dominated the Jewish communities of the Balkan Peninsula until the advent of nationalism in the area in the nineteenth century. It would also serve to differentiate them from the Ashkenazim dominant in the rest of Europe.

The vast majority of Jews lived in the cities, and made their livings as merchants and artisans. They had little contact with the Bulgarians, who were mostly peasant vassals of the Turkish feudal lords and their Bulgarian lackeys. Turkish, Greek, and Ladino were the languages of trade, and Hebrew the language of scholarship and religion. Few Jews, therefore, had any use for the Bulgarian language, which degenerated during five centuries of intellectual neglect.

During this period the Jews of Bulgaria began a tradition of communal cohesion and cooperation which would develop and endure until the mass immigration to Israel beginning in 1949. In 1640 a single rabbi was appointed for all of the communities; Sephardi, Ashkenazi, and Romaniot.[12] The Jews governed themselves according to Halakhah, and were largely independent of the surrounding gentile communities.

Bulgarian cities, in which almost all of the Jews lived, were multiethnic, and many had a Turkish majority. This fact is of great importance, not only for the development of Bulgarian Jewry, but for the development of Bulgarian society as well. This result of Ottoman sovereignty would play a role in shaping Bulgarian attitudes, and would continue to have an impact on shaping Bulgarian-Jewish relations even after independence. As Nikolai Todorov, Bulgarian historian, states: "we cannot but draw attention to the fact that for centuries the Bulgarians lived in towns with mixed populations. This has been an important element in the formation of the Bulgarian national consciousness and it is perhaps one explanation for the absence of an awareness of exclusiveness and national egoism in the formation of the Bulgarian national consciousness."[13]

The sixteenth century saw the flowering of Jewish culture and community in the Balkans, and has even been termed the "Golden Age of Balkan Sephardim."[14] It was also the century in which the Ottoman Empire reached the height of its power, and saw the beginning of its long and agonizing decline. This correspondence and interdependence of fortunes further demonstrates the confluence of Ottoman and Jewish interests in the area: "the Sephardic Jews were most productive in the sixteenth century because they came from a country burgeoning with creative sap and entered a region under the dominance of a power at the zenith of its conquests."[15] Yet, as we shall see, the final expulsion of the Turks from Bulgaria would allow startlingly progressive developments in which the Jews united their fortunes with the Bulgarians until they themselves could realize national independence.

Of all the subject peoples of the Empire, the Jews have left the most complete account of their communal life. Records of the communal organizations, *haskamot* (ordinances), and Responsa are our chief sources of information, as well as the records of the religious courts, *Batei Din*, which regulated relations among Jews. According to Tamir, the pictures of Jewish life obtained from these documents during this period "do not even remotely resemble the martyrologies reflected in Jewish documents of the same period from Central and Western Europe, where Jews were nearly always heartily disliked. . . . The general picture of Jewish life and legislation painted by these documents is one of continuity, relative stability, and prosperity by the standards of the age."[16]

Bulgaria during the Ottoman period is often described by writers and historians as in hibernation, and in many ways this characterization is correct. The overwhelmingly peasant population was subject to oppressive taxation and a feudal system which led to almost total intellectual, political, and economic stagnation.[17] Even those Bulgarians in the region's mixed cities did not assert themselves creatively, and Bulgarian Jewry was affected by this national apathy, although it always maintained a vigorous communal and economic life. During the "Golden Age," Bulgarian Jewry participated only marginally in the creative activity of the Balkan Jews. The rising frequency of military conflict along the Empire's Danubian border would have an increasingly disruptive effect on Jewish life. Yet as the Jewish communities in Bulgaria were self-governing, wealthier than the peasant population, and had the means of making a livelihood which was not rooted directly in the soil, they often suffered less from the destructive force of incursions from the North than did the Bulgarian peasantry. On the other hand, their Jewishness could enrage the invaders and call down upon them antisemitic wrath, in addition to the usual pillage and plunder.

The most important seats of Jewish learning and rabbinical productivity in Bulgaria were Nikopol, until the seventeenth century, and Vidin, until the nineteenth. As Danube ports, these cities were important economic centers and, as a result, boasted proportionally large Jewish communities. For this reason also, they became primary targets for the sultan's European foes, and suffered repeated destruction. We may speculate that with the increasingly tenuous nature of life on the northern border, Jews began to establish themselves in greater numbers in the cities of the interior. Isidor Toliko, born to one of the few Jewish families remaining in Nikopol at the beginning of this century, was not unaware of his city's history. He proudly related that:

> Nikopol was a very ancient city, with very ancient roots in Judaism.[18] Two hundred years before the period when I lived there, it was a blossoming city for Jewry. Don't forget, it's a port on the Danube. A very important cross-roads. It had connections with the Western World, for trade and culture was quite developed. After the development of technology, the trains and everything, it lost its importance, became economically depressed, and of course the Jews emigrated to different places. (Toliko, p.1)

By the end of the sixteenth century, Bulgarian Jewry was threatened both from within the Empire and without. With the decline of Ottoman power came a decline in Ottoman tolerance, and several discriminatory decrees were issued restricting Jewish rights. In 1592 and 1598, Prince Michael of Wallachia crossed the Danube and laid waste Vidin, Pleven, and Nikopol. Nikopol was burned to the ground, in Vidin two synagogues were destroyed, and both communities were decimated.[19] These communities recovered their losses only later, with the large influx of Jews fleeing the Chmielnicki massacres in Poland (1648–1649), which also added to the Ashkenazi population of the country. These immigrants too would quickly assimilate with their Sephardi brethren.

By the second half of the seventeenth century, the rule of law within the Empire had become so corrupt, and the local governments so contemptible, that a general malaise set in among the Jews of the Balkans that we might characterize as a national depression. In order to check the increasing military pressure on his borders, the sultan raised taxes to fund his militia, and this, combined with corruption, inefficiency, and apathy made life increasingly difficult. To the external military threat and the internal strife and oppression was added a danger from within, as Jews turned to the false messiah, Shabbatai Zevi, for redemption. The spiritual devastation which resulted for the Jews of the Balkans marks a turning point in their history. Tamir writes:

> It is generally viewed as the chief cause of the precipitous deterioration of Jewish morale and the decline of Sephardi scholarship. Goaded with the promise of instant redemption, large numbers of Jews embraced Shabbetai Tsevi as the Messiah, but when he chose apostasy over death, abysmal depression (rather than a wholesome return to nationalism) ensued. The erstwhile cohe-

sion of the communities, already challenged by Messianic agitation, completely cracked, and community life came to a standstill.
With the level of education steeply dropping, knowledge of Hebrew became the esoteric distinction of a small rabbinical class,
and religious observance lost its meaning. . . . Grimly pessimistic
over Turkish obscurantism, on the one hand, and Christian devastation, on the other, the Jews turned to mysticism for solace. The
trend was markedly stronger in Solonica and Constantinople than
in Bulgaria proper.[20]

There appear to be two possible explanations for the relative lack
of Messianic fervor among the Jews of Bulgaria. As noted earlier,
Bulgaria was a backwater of the Ottoman Empire, and all intellectual
and spiritual innovations seem to have reached Bulgaria in diluted
form. This held true for Bulgarian Jewry as well, so that we may
conjecture that the Messianism which rocked Salonika and Constantinople would follow this pattern and affect the Jewish communities in
Bulgaria with lesser force. Secondly, it was noted at the beginning of
this chapter that the Bulgarians themselves seldom showed much enthusiasm for abstract spiritual matters, and took up the cause of both
Christianity and Islam with less than wild abandon. This was pointed
out as being one of the reasons for the relative lack of religiously
inspired Judeophobia, and we might conjecture that this attitude affected Bulgaria's Jews as well. Thus, one can attribute the comparative
lack of enthusiasm for Shabbatianism to a religious moderation which
seems to have been one of the characteristics of Bulgaria's inhabitants,
both Jewish and gentile.

The confluence of neo-Messianism and the beginning of Ottoman
decline affected Jewish intellectual and communal life to such an extent that it never fully recovered, and the bright star of the Balkan
Sephardim gradually faded into obscurity. The two centuries between
the appearance Shabbatai Zevi and the liberation of Bulgaria from
Turkish rule saw the atrophy of Jewish life in the Balkans, especially in
matters cultural and spiritual. The lively intellectual atmosphere
which had thrived for centuries in Salonika and Constantinople became dull and mechanistic, and Bulgarian Jewry, always on the
fringes, sank further into anonymity. By the end of the Ottoman
period, Jewish education, which is the very core of Jewish national life,
was described as follows:

The Jews of the Ottoman Empire were permitted to do business
throughout the Empire, and dealt more with matters of substance than of spirit. That influenced the education of boys. The
Rabbi would enter a few youths into his seminary and teach

reading and writing: I never heard from the elders of the community that they had studied Talmud. Most would be satisfied with learning prayers and the portion of the week with Ladino translation. Girls were prohibited from all study. Ignorance reigned supreme.[21]

This spiritual and educational decline created a vacuum in Jewish life which threatened the very existence of Balkan Jewry. The ways in which this vacuum was filled differed substantially among the various communities of the Empire, depending on differences in environment and historical, economic, political, and social circumstance. But Bulgarian Jewry filled this vacuum differently than the other Balkan Jewish communities, setting it on a unique course toward a surprising destiny. Whereas other communities continued to decay in the rubble of the Ottoman Empire, the Jews of Bulgaria chose to transform the very definition and course of Jewish existence, and infuse it with a new meaning and purpose. At the precise moment in history when Bulgarian Jewish life could no longer draw sustenance and the strength vital to its continuation from traditional sources, it found new wellsprings of inspiration—it reinterpreted and adapted itself to the realities of a new and rapidly changing world. Traditional Judaism was replaced by Jewish cultural, social, and political nationalism embodied in the Zionist movement, which became the creed of the Jews of Bulgaria who emerged from five centuries of Ottoman rule completely changed, strengthened, and revitalized.

CHAPTER 6

From Liberation to
World War II: 1878–1940

Both political independence and the ideological basis of nationalism that supported it were in many ways foreign imports to Bulgaria. The country had been shielded by Ottoman domination from the ideas and changes created by the Reformation, Renaissance, and Enlightenment. With the defeat of Turkey by the Russian army and the liberation of Bulgaria in 1878, an independent country re-emerged in Europe which had not existed for five hundred years. The challenge to the Bulgarian leadership was extreme, and the story of how it developed the most enlightened of constitutions out of the ashes of oppression is fascinating.[1]

In a sense, Bulgaria had been left out of a series of developmental phases in European history, and this fact produced a nation, for a time at least, in many ways unique on the continent. The same may be said for Bulgaria's Jews. Although winds of change had been blowing from the West and Russia for decades, they were unable to effect a substantive reawakening of Jewish creative potential until after liberation. More than a century of conflict and cleavage produced by radical modern thought in Jewish communities throughout Europe left Bulgarian Jewry largely untouched and unmoved. The Jewish community of Bulgaria remained homogeneous and unremarkable. It could not boast the cacophony of irreconcilable beliefs and philosophies that both enlivened and threatened European Jewry as a whole. With few exceptions, Bulgaria had no Hasidim and Mitnagdim, nor socialists and communists and Bundists and Zionists of a dozen persuasions. Bulgarian Jewry in the nineteenth century could boast no great thinkers, scientists, philosophers, or rabbis. It could, however, boast of a united and well-organized community in control of its destiny and certain of its identity.

Russia served Bulgaria her independence. That fact, along with a sense of pan-Slavic brotherhood, affects Bulgarian policy to the present day. Several months after independence, pressure from the West forced the convening of the Berlin Congress of July, 1878. Fearing the rise of a large, powerful, pro-Russian Bulgaria, the Congress divided the country into Bulgaria and Eastern Rumelia, and sliced off parts of Thrace and Macedonia. This act embittered Bulgarians toward the West, and would result in devastating irredentist adventures. Because of it Bulgaria instigated the Balkan Wars, joined the Central Powers in the First World War, and the Axis in the Second. One can only speculate as to what Bulgaria might have achieved had she not devoted so much of her economic and spiritual energies to desperate attempts at regaining territory over the next sixty years.

In 1879, an assembly of notables met at Turnovo to draw up a constitution that established Bulgaria as a constitutional monarchy with full protection and autonomy for its minorities.[2] This constitutional security provided the social basis for the dramatic changes which occurred within Bulgarian Jewry during the fifty years following independence, transforming it in fundamental ways. Language, culture, politics, religion, worldview, and basic community structure were all involved in this metamorphosis, and change in each of these areas influenced change in the others. Examining these changes in historical isolation might lead the researcher to conclude that a basic alteration of Jewish character had taken place during the late nineteenth and early twentieth centuries. In a sense, this observation is accurate, for the observer in 1930 met a people very different from that which existed in 1880. But this conclusion is only partially correct. The revolutionary changes that occurred within Bulgarian Jewry were not without roots, nor were they the result of foreign influence alone. They were an outgrowth of a Bulgarian-Jewish experience which was unique, and they represent the continuity of this experience to accommodate a new reality, and not its rejection.

Structure of the Community: From Plutocratic to Democratic Rule

Independence found Bulgaria's Jewish communities organized along plutocratic lines, headed by the most "prominent" (i.e., wealthy) families and governed by the "notables" (*chorbadzhis*). This system had been fostered by the Ottoman authorities, which dealt with subject minorities through a system of institutionalized graft and influence-peddling. Nevertheless, as long as the Empire received its due, the Jewish communities were permitted to conduct their affairs according to their own wishes. The responsibility for the continuation of this form of internal governance lies within the communities themselves.[3]

Whether or not there was resentment and opposition to the rule of the notables before independence is difficult to determine. That there had been at least some opposition is clear, for within a decade of the liberation of Bulgaria there began a fateful power struggle between the old leadership and democratic reformers. Had there not been deep-seated resentment within the community, it is unlikely that reform measures would have achieved such swift success.

The Ottoman Empire recognized the Jews as a religious minority under the millet system, which granted the various communities within the Empire a degree of autonomy in conducting their internal affairs. It is essential to the understanding of Bulgarian Jewish identity to recognize the difference between the Christian and Moslem concepts of religious minority, especially as put into practice by the Turks. Islamic law grants *ahl al-kitab*, the "People of the Book," a special protected (*ahl adh-dhimma*) status. Whereas pagans were converted or killed, Jews and Christians were permitted to live under Moslem protection. However, because of the meta-conflict between the Ottoman Empire and Christian Europe, the Christian minorities under Ottoman rule were often subject to ruthless oppression, as was often the case for Bulgaria's Christian majority. The stateless and militarily defenseless Jews were treated with greater tolerance.

Although Bulgaria showed a tolerance toward her Jews in the centuries preceding Ottoman domination which was unique in Europe, this tolerance did not preclude antisemitic occurrences. The interpretation of these manifestations of antisemitism is the basis for a fundamental difference between the conclusions drawn by Tamir in her work, and by myself in the present study.

Tamir interprets the existence of antisemitic incidents in Bulgaria, even though less frequent and violent than elsewhere in Europe, as indicating the existence of deep-seated antisemitic attitudes among the Bulgarian people. Simply put, Tamir feels that if antisemitic acts took place in Bulgaria, Bulgaria was, therefore, fundamentally antisemitic. The present study takes a different approach, one based on both an interpretation of the historical record and, more importantly, the evidence contained in interviews with Bulgarian Jews in Israel. The positive sentiments expressed by informants regarding the Bulgarian people directly contradict Tamir's interpretation. The nature of oral history does not allow for the direct extrapolation of contemporary views to general principles. However, twentieth-century attitudes of Jews toward Bulgarians and of Bulgarians toward Jews may help illuminate what has heretofore been a baffling anomaly in the history of European antisemitism.

The interview data are absolutely consistent. All informants agreed that, although there were antisemitic circles in Bulgaria, the vast majority of Bulgarians were not antisemitic and relations between Jews and gentiles were excellent. Haim Molkho, a kibbutznik, Yosef Eldzham, a retired bank clerk, and Avi Cordova, a professor of sociology, agreed on this point: "Relations were excellent. There was almost no difference between Jews and gentiles" (Molkho, p. 10). "Our neighborly relations were with no differences, we used to live as if we weren't Jews and Bulgarians. We had very good neighborly relations. Both the young people and the adults" (Eldzham, p. 2). "It was completely clear to me that I was a Jew, and that as a Jew I was a minority within another people. But there was no animosity toward that people, there was no feeling of the 'goy' " (Cordova, p. 9).

For Tamir, antisemitism does not exist in degrees; it either is or is not present in an individual or population. The fact that antisemitic incidents pepper the history of Bulgaria provides her with ample proof of endemic and widespread antisemitism harbored in the hearts of the Bulgarian Christians. Yet, in a Europe in which antisemitism was indeed endemic and pervasive, the pivotal fact in the history of the Jews of Bulgaria is the startlingly small number of antisemitic acts committed there, despite pressures from outside. Religious tolerance existed in Bulgaria before the Ottoman conquest, and it was reinforced by five hundred years of Ottoman rule. In effect, the absence of antisemitism in Bulgaria was protected and reinforced. The decades following liberation would see this attitude put to the severest of tests.

As Bulgaria struggled toward democracy, starting brilliantly on that path but then faltering, Bulgarian Jewry was engaged in a revolutionary enterprise unique in the Jewish world. Within forty years of liberation, the Bulgarian Jewish community had democratized and secularized itself, and emerged from this process inspired and strengthened by the Zionist dream.

After independence from Ottoman rule, the Turnovo Constitution set down the principles for the governance of religious communities in the country.[4] Bulgarian Jewry was to be led by a democratically elected committee, headed by a chief rabbi who was, in effect, an employee of the state. The first chief rabbi, Gabriel Almosnino, was appointed in 1897. Born in Nikopol and educated in Jerusalem, he was to play an important role in the turmoil within the Jewish community during the following years.[5]

According to Bulgarian law, the Jewish community was a voluntary organization of citizens of the Mosaic faith. Failure to pay tax to the organization, however, would result in the denial of various services: marriage, burial, circumcision, a place in the synagogue, and various certificates and permissions. Thus, although the Jewish community organization was never officially recognized by the government, it was in reality the representative power, and was not interfered with until the promulgation of anti-Jewish legislation during the Second World War.

The story of the democratization and consolidation of Bulgarian Jewry is the story of the development and eventual dominance of Zionism in Bulgaria. The total Zionization of the Jews of Bulgaria was the result of the development of an original, native philosophy which predated the emergence of Zionist ideology in the rest of Europe. In fact, organized Zionist activity appeared in Ruse as early as 1864.

On his way to Constantinople in 1896, Theodor Herzl was surprised by the multitude of Bulgarian Jews who greeted him enthusiastically in Sofia. "Even before Herzl's appearance, there were Zionist societies like Ezrat Ahim in Sofia, Carmel in Plovdiv (Philoppopolis), and Dorshei Zion in Khaskovo. Bulgarian Jews founded the settlement of Hartuv in Erez Israel as early as 1896."[6]

One of the fascinating developments in the Zionization of the Bulgarian Jewish communities was the support it received from the religious authorities. In contrast to the development of Zionism elsewhere in Europe, where it was often considered foreign and antithetical to Judaism and where there were bitter struggles between religious and Zionist Jews, Bulgarian Jewry perceived no contradiction between Zionism and Judaism. In fact, the two were viewed as complementary and integrated bases for Jewish existence. Marcus Ehrenpreis, who succeeded Almosnino as chief rabbi, played an active role in preparing the Bulgarian delegation to the first Zionist Congress in Basel in 1897, which he also attended.[7] The rabbis strongly supported the Zionist movement, and, in effect, voluntarily subordinated themselves to the democratically elected committees despite their superior legal status in the eyes of the Bulgarian government.

One year after the Basel Congress, the first Bulgarian Zionist Congress was held in Plovdiv, which preceded Sofia as the center of Bulgarian Zionist activity.[8] The Congress was headed by Yosef Marko Baruh, a charismatic speaker, adventurer, and eccentric.[9] Ya'akov Nitsani, chronicler of Plovdiv Jewry, sets the stage thus:

> From the spiritual point of view everything was ready: a thirst for knowledge, difficulties in solving the Jewish question, disagreements with the methods of the Alliance [Israelite Universelle], the leaders of the community halted the march to

redemption—just like the Bulgarian Kulaks. With the example
of the liberation of the Bulgarian people, stories of the heroism
and adventure of the national heroes, they were waiting for a
man who could strike the spark and light the lamp. And he
came. He was the wonderful Yosef Marko Baruh.[10]

The First National Congress of Bulgarian Jewry was held in 1900.
Its most significant contribution was the transformation of synagogue
congregations into organized communities. The twenty years between
this First Congress and the Second in 1920 would see the total reformation of organized Jewish life in Bulgaria, and the end of the struggle for its soul. The Second Congress, with its Zionist majority, "pro-
claimed the religious and national solidarity of all Jewish inhabitants
of the country, regardless of origin, language or citizenship."[11] This
proclamation arose from a unified ideology and purpose that per-
vaded Bulgarian Jewish society, giving it the strength to weather the
trials of the coming two decades, and the unity and determination to
make the exodus to Israel. There is perhaps no arena in which this
conflict and transformation was more significant and symbolic than in
the struggle for the destiny and soul of the children.

Education: From Meldar to Hebrew School

The liberation of Bulgaria from Turkish rule found education in the
country in a dismal state. Thirty years after the liberation, 53 percent
of Bulgarian men and 83 percent of Bulgarian women were illiterate,[12] and over 80 percent of the population was peasantry.[13] The
Jewish population, involved in trade, concentrated in the cities, and
following its education-oriented tradition, fared somewhat better, having the highest literacy rate of any group in the country.[14] Nevertheless, by Jewish standards its educational system was totally inadequate,
both in religious and secular fields. The traditional form of Sephardic
school, the *meldar*, was incapable of adapting to the new conditions,
and could not satisfy the needs of a community thirsting for education. The rapid secularization of Bulgarian Jewry would require a
completely new approach to Jewish education. Ya'akov Nitsani describes the decline of religion and religious education as follows:

> [The teachers of the *meldar*] taught Ladino writing and told the
> pupils many legends from the commentaries and the Book of
> Yosippon and other books and folk legends. They knew how to
> tell these stories with great conviction in flowing Ladino. . . . The
> synagogues and study houses were empty. Only with difficulty

could they scrape together a few quorums. Even on the Sabbath the number of worshipers wasn't large. Only those celebrating a wedding, a birth or, God forbid, a funeral would bring their families to the synagogue. The synagogues only saw a crowd on the High Holidays. . . . the tower of strength of the Jews was destroyed.[15]

If the tower of religious strength of Bulgarian Jewry had been destroyed, there were soon attempts to rebuild it in a new mold. The first, ultimately unsuccessful, attempt was made by the Alliance Israelite Universelle, which sought to replace traditional piety with Francophile humanism sprinkled with a minimum of Judaica. The second, more successful, attempt was based on the awakening of Jewish nationalism animated by Zionism, with its bedrock of Hebrew schools and youth movements.

The light of day which shone on Bulgaria after liberation glaringly exposed the backwardness and inadequacy of Jewish education. The enlightened leadership of the community urgently sought ways to improve the education of Jewish children and expose them to the benefits of modern Western learning and science. At the same time, the elimination of Ottoman "obscurantism" revealed to the Jews of the West the inadequate level of education prevailing among the Jews of the East. This led to the birth of the Alliance Israelite Universelle in 1860:

> The French Jews, contemplating the deplorable conditions among their Oriental brethren, were aroused to a feeling of solidarity. These beneficiaries of Emancipation desired to propagate the doctrines and principles of modern tolerance. They were filled with missionary zeal because they were convinced of their being torch bearers of a higher type of civilization. Consciously or unconsciously, the founders of the Alliance were agents of cultural imperialism of France.[16]

The initial popularity of the Alliance schools led to an interesting development. Most Jews at the time of liberation had only a cursory knowledge of the Bulgarian language. Ladino was their first language, followed by Turkish and Greek, the languages of trade. With the founding of the Alliance schools, however, many Jews learned French before Bulgarian. By the turn of the century, nonetheless, Bulgarian had become the first language of the Jewish youth and, as pointed out by both Jewish and Bulgarian informants, the Jews were known for their fine, if accented, Bulgarian. Nevertheless, the multilingual and cosmopolitan education of the Jewish children would continue to differentiate them from the largely unilingual Bulgarians.

This linguistic shift was certainly not unique. Similar shifts had occurred within various Jewish communities in Central, Eastern, and Southeastern Europe, with the rise in linguistic nationalism and the enfranchisement of minority groups.

The first Alliance school opened in 1870, and by 1878 there were schools in Shumen, Ruse, and Samokov. By the turn of the century, the Alliance had fifteen schools and employed 98 teachers for 3,890 pupils.[17] The Alliance system included four years of elementary instruction, three years of progymnasium, and the option of high school. The curriculum conformed to that of the state schools, with the exception that all topics were taught in French, exclusive of Bulgarian language, grammar, history, and geography. In addition, rudimentary Jewish religious topics were taught, often by former teachers from the meldar.[18] According to Tamir, who gives Sha'ul Mezan as her source, the Jewish illiteracy rate was slightly over 1 percent in 1910, whereas among Bulgarians it was 11 percent. These figures are contradicted in an article written in 1929 by Stoyan Omarchevsky, former Bulgarian Minister of Education. He gives the Jewish figures for literacy in Bulgarian for 1910 as 60.69 percent, and for Bulgarians as 33.7 percent.[19] This was also a period of large-scale publishing activity in the Jewish community, and numerous journals appeared in Ladino. An example of the evolution of linguistic competence can be seen in the development of the daily *Ha-Shofar*, which was originally published in Ladino. The newspaper ceased publication during the First World War, and when it resumed in 1919 it was published half in Ladino and half in Bulgarian. By 1924 it was published entirely in Bulgarian. In addition, there were a number of Hebrew periodicals in print at this time.[20]

The impact of the Alliance, and French language and education, on Bulgarian Jewry should not be underestimated. The disparagement of Ladino as the crude dialect of the uneducated and the refusal of the Alliance to teach Ladino in its schools were important factors in the demise of the language as the mother tongue of Bulgaria's Jews. French opened the doors to better jobs and the liberal professions, and allowed Jews to enter the worlds of international commerce and diplomacy.[21] In many countries of the former Ottoman Empire, however, knowledge of the French language increased the alienation of the Jews from the majority population. In addition to being Jewish, they were now considered francophile and part of the foreign elite. For many Jews this double alienation, both from traditional Jewish culture and from the indigenous society, led to a greater sense of anomie and a further breakdown of Jewish communal cohesion. The Jews of Bulgaria, however, consciously and forcefully halted this process in midstream.

The rejection and eventual expulsion of the Alliance Israelite Universelle from Bulgaria by the united Jewish communities was a most significant event in post-liberation Bulgarian-Jewish social history. The decision to oust the Alliance was the result of two seemingly contradictory trends: one toward independent Jewish nationalism, the other towards greater identification with Bulgaria and Bulgarians. Although the influence of Alliance education would be significant and lasting, it was the expression of these two trends which would prove paramount in understanding the nature of Bulgarian Jewish identity in Israel following the mass emigration.

Aron Rodrigue, chronicler of the Alliance in Turkey, concludes that its westernizing influence actively facilitated the embracing of Zionist ideology which, in turn, led to the demise of the Alliance:

> The flocking to the Zionist movement of many of the graduates of [Alliance] schools after 1908 was part of the larger revolt against the society by the very groups that it had itself brought into being. By the twentieth century, the new Jewish middle class was chafing under the rule of the notables and had begun to abandon the Alliance with which the latter were associated. The excessive centralization, paternalism, and authoritarianism of the organization did not sit well with the new dynamic elements that wanted a greater say in the education of the youth. The instruction received in the Alliance establishments had provided a kaleidoscope of possibilities for social action to increasing numbers.[22]

The generation raised in the Alliance schools soon became their adversary, accusing them of fostering one of the greatest sins against Zionist ideology—assimilation. Preceding the Hebraization of Jewish schools came the formation of numerous and powerful Zionist youth movements, such as the sport-oriented Maccabi,[23] leftist Ha-Shomer Ha-Za'ir[24] and Po'alei Ziyon,[25] and Revisionist Betar. These movements were perhaps the most influential institutions in Jewish education, and provided a social outlet and a center of activity for most Jewish children. Outside of school, the youth movement was the social center of Jewish youth until emigration. Avraham Ofek, a sculptor living in Jerusalem who left Bulgaria at age fourteen in 1949, described his childhood in the movement: "I didn't have a life outside of it. You understand, from morning until night only that. And in actuality, really in the end, when we had already packed our things and immigrated, there couldn't have been a more settled decision, more complete or more desired" (Ofek, p. 11). Mikha Kalev of Kibbutz Yad Mordekhai was a leader of Ha-Shomer Ha-Za'ir. He stated: "Bulgarian culture was very important, but you have to understand, during the period of our youth, we had a beautiful youth, especially in the youth movements, that was the center of life" (Kalev, p. 13).

By the turn of the century, agitation for the replacement of French by Hebrew in the schools was intense. In 1906, Pazardzhik was the first community to elect a Zionist-controlled school board. Sofia followed suit in 1910, and by 1912 the Alliance was no longer a factor in Jewish education and Hebrew education had taken its place.

The universality of Hebrew instruction in Jewish schools in Bulgaria by the early twentieth century was a unique development outside Erez Israel. At the same time, the first language of the home had become Bulgarian, and Bulgarian Jewry, as many other contemporary Jewries as well as other minority groups, was thus linguistically divided by generations. The generation that was educated under the meldar system spoke Ladino as its first language; the generation of the Alliance was gradually turning to Bulgarian, but also knew French; and the generations of the Hebrew schools spoke Bulgarian first, knew Hebrew, and were acquainted with Ladino in varying degrees of competence. Of course, knowledge of these languages varied from town to town and from family to family, often depending on economic and educational level (Ladino being the language of the old and the poor), as well as the availability of Jewish schools. Interview data consistently demonstrates this basic generational differentiation. Lili Avrahami, former secretary of the office of the Bulgarian old age home in Rishon Le-Ziyon and the Ihud Olei Bulgariyah, remembered her childhood in Pazardzhik: "In our house two languages were spoken, both Ladino and Bulgarian, because we had a grandmother at home" (Avrahami, p. 4).

The Zionization of Bulgarian Jewry went hand in hand with its democratization:

> By World War I there was a Zionist majority in every Jewish institution, and in 1920 the Second National Convention of Bulgarian Jewry, held twenty years after the first one, gave formal sanction to the Zionists' de facto control by voting new Zionist statutes binding upon all Bulgarian Jews. From now on, all the institutions—consistory, schools, synagogues, etc.—would be officially in Zionist hands, and the Zionist element would remain predominant all through World War II, though formally condemned to inaction between 1939 and 1944.[26]

Zionism in Bulgaria became far more than an ideology to which a sector of the Jewish population adhered, as was the case in other European countries. Zionism became indistinguishable from Judaism, it became part of the way of life, tradition, worldview, culture, and even folklore of the Jews of Bulgaria. This was a synthesis of outstanding significance in the development of Bulgarian Jewish identity. Isidor Toliko, a retired postal clerk, stated this feeling clearly: "The Zionist idea was identified with our nationalism, that is, a Jew had to be a Zionist and if one wasn't a Zionist then one was a traitor, one who is assimilated" (Toliko, p. 6).

The worldview of the young adult generation of the mass immigration was centrally affected by life in the youth movements. At a developmental stage rife with rebellious tendencies, the youth movements offered children a complete social life, a purpose, and an adventurous vision of the future away from school and parents. Lili Avrahami described her involvement in the movement during her childhood in Pazardzhik:

> all the activity, all the folklore . . . one cannot say that it was something big and huge; it began in the movement and ended in the movement. That's it. The Zionist movement, the concentration was in the school and the synagogue . . . and in those yards our entire lives were concentrated . . . our lives began and ended in one place—quite small, quite compact, and I think confining to a certain extent. It confined us from general development I think. It began and ended there. (Avrahami, p. 18)

Although the growth of Zionism in Bulgaria was an organic phenomenon, it was not the result of developments within a Jewish community in isolation. The Jews of Bulgaria benefited from Ottoman rule while the Christians suffered under its yoke. Yet despite Russian provocations during the period of liberation, the Bulgarians did not seek wholesale vengeance against the Jews for their superior position during the Ottoman period. There were sporadic instances of anti-Jewish violence, but soon the Jews and Bulgarians had reestablished their former relationship of mutual tolerance and respect.

The Jews were caught up in the atmosphere of liberation, yet channeled their enthusiasm mostly inward, rather than abandoning their national autonomy and joining with the Bulgarian national awakening. Herein lies another difference that sets Bulgarian Jewry apart from the Jews of the rest of Europe: whereas in most European countries Jews were prominent in the various national parties and movements, as well as in the cultural life of the nation, and Zionists were in the minority, in Bulgaria there were very few Jews involved in national politics and public life, and the Zionists made up the large majority. According to Nissan Oren:

> Lacking meaningful identification with the national and nationalistic aspirations of the Bulgarian majority, the Jews of Bulgaria

identified more closely with the ideals of modern Jewish nationalism, of which political Zionism became the dominant expression.
Prior to the First World War, as well as during the interwar years,
active affiliation by Jews with any one of the various political
parties in the country was generally the exception. The only party
which succeeded in making substantial inroads into the Jewish
community was the Communist party. The proportional representation of Jews within the Communist-led wartime resistance movement far exceeded their proportional representation within the
general population. This situation was a natural reaction to the
rise of authoritarianism, with its cryptofascist admixtures. Politically, the overwhelming majority of the Jewish population operated only within the framework of the Jewish community. Jewish
political energies were largely exhausted by infighting—first, between Zionists and anti-Zionists, and, in later years, with the emergence of the Zionists as the preponderant majority, among the
various Jewish factions.[27]

In Bulgaria, Jewish nationalism drew inspiration and strength
from Bulgarian nationalism, but remained true to itself; two parallel
national movements with many similarities which, by their very na-
tures, would diverge in their ultimate fulfillment. The youth movements provide an illuminating example of this development.

The most widespread and popular of the Zionist youth movements was Maccabi, which was primarily a confederation of Jewish
athletic clubs without affiliation to a particular Zionist party or ideology. Founding members of Maccabi walked on foot to attend the First
Zionist Congress in Basel in 1897, and the first Maccabi club was
founded the same year in Plovdiv.[28] Maccabi was formed after the
model provided by Yunak, the Bulgarian athletic youth movement
similar to the Sokol organizations in other Slavic countries. It followed
the Zionist ideologue Max Nordau's teachings of "Muscle Judaism"
(*Yahadut Ha-Shririm*): "National feeling was turned into symbols,
armbands, movement uniforms, etc. . . . [Maccabi's uniform] was in
the colors of the Zionist flag: white shirt, blue pants, decorated with a
ribbon in the Bulgarian colors. The hat was also blue and white. Two
flags fluttered over all festivities and marches: the Zionist flag and the
Bulgarian national flag."[29]

Isidor Toliko of Holon expanded on this phenomenon: "There
was a Jewish organization, the Maccabis, and the Jews would lift the
blue and white flag and march in the main cities, and the Bulgarians
accepted that as normal. Something like that couldn't happen in Vi-
enna, or Berlin, or Paris, not in St. Petersburg, not in Moscow . . .
those are the roots of Zionism in Bulgaria" (Toliko, p. 21).

Ha-Shomer Ha-Za'ir (The Young Guard) was founded in Bulgaria in 1923 for a different, if related purpose. By that time, Hebrew education was firmly established, but it was then felt that in order for the language to become truly revitalized a framework would have to be developed for fostering it outside of the classroom. Ha-Shomer Ha-Za'ir was intended to provide a vehicle for continuing Hebrew education, and its first motto was "Hebrew: at Home, in the Street, in the Schools."[30]

In 1929, former Bulgarian Minister of Education Stoyan Omarchevsky wrote: "It is very doubtful whether there is so great a tolerance regarding education for minorities in any other country in the world."[31] The development of an independent Jewish educational system could not have occurred without the tolerance and support of the national government. By 1927 there were 9 Jewish schools for children 5 to 7 years of age, with 16 teachers serving 525 pupils; 22 schools for children 7 to 10 years with 71 teachers serving 2,139; and 7 seven schools for children 10 to 14 with 47 teachers serving 674 pupils.[32] As one can see by the numbers, there was a severe shortage of teachers, especially for the younger grades. Dozens of teachers were brought in from Palestine to fill this need, and the ties between the Jewish communities in Bulgaria and Palestine were thereby strengthened. In addition, attempts were made to match the curriculum in the Bulgarian Jewish schools to that of the Yishuv.[33] Hours were lengthened, and the entire government curriculum was taught in Bulgarian. In addition to Hebrew studies and Hebrew language and grammar, Bible and Jewish history were taught eight to ten hours a week.[34] Almost 80 percent of all Jewish children attended Jewish schools, for which most of the funding was collected from the community. The national and municipal governments did contribute to their upkeep, covering 13.3 percent of the costs.[35] Of all my informants, not one had attended a state school if there was a Jewish school available.

The combination of an extensive system of Jewish schools supplemented by youth organizations, all supported by a united and powerful Jewish community oriented toward Zionism and Palestine, produced a new generation unlike the Jewish youth anywhere else in the world. Shlomo Dagan, leader in several youth organizations in Bulgaria and activist in his home kibbutz Yad Mordekhai, stated that:

> What is important to note is that the community, is that in every city in Bulgaria you could find a community organization, even in small communities, and I'm not talking about Sofia. In Sofia there was a very large community. There was a Jewish hospital, a large synagogue, along with smaller neighborhood synagogues, a

burial society, incredible mutual aid, an old age home. Not a rich community, in which there were millionaires, and for one reason or another the government wouldn't help. But in any case a framework developed which was very important in the communal life of the Jews, daily life. Until the war. And that was true also of the smaller communities. Even if you went to a community of fifty or sixty families, like in Samokov, or other holes in the wall. There were forty, fifty, sixty Jewish families. Despite that you found a community which was organized with a community office, though a small one. With a small room for a synagogue, and an elementary school, a Jewish school. In Sofia the two schools which existed were full of students. There were very few Jewish children that didn't go to the Jewish schools. Very few. And that's important. . . . In some way, I wasn't aware of it when I went to school. It was my growing up, and the war. I think that the community, the community organization, had incredible influence. From a national standpoint it was very important. (Dagan, p. 17)

Nothing shows evidence of this unique development more vividly than the album prepared in Hebrew in Israel by Bulgarian immigrants entitled *Maccabi Bulgariyah*. In all the towns and cities of the country with a significant Jewish population, there was a Maccabi youth group. On page after page are pictures of Jews of all ages marching down main streets of big cities and small towns in the uniform of the movement, carrying the Bulgarian and Zionist flags; of Jewish youth in Bulgarian national costume preparing for a folk dance performance; of young men and women in athletic garb competing in local, national, and international contests; of the Maccabi contingent being greeted by King Boris III on Bulgaria's independence day, and of thousands of uniformed Maccabeans placing wreaths on the monument to Bulgaria's national hero Vasil Levski during the Maccabi national convention.[36] It would be impossible to find these images in any other country in Europe; the latest were taken in 1940, and then, after a four year hiatus, from 1944 until the mass migration beginning in 1948. Jews from other nations of Europe look at these pictures and find it difficult to believe that they were taken on the same continent as their own Poland, Czechoslovakia, or Germany. Yet in the Bulgarian setting they appear natural.

Cultural and Social Transformation

The society and culture of the Jews of Bulgaria during the period between liberation and emigration were possessed of the usually in-

compatible qualities of stability and dynamism. Drastic changes occurred in the life of Bulgarian Jewry during that seventy year span,
the most concrete of which was the doubling of the Jewish population during the period. Following independence there were approximately eighteen to twenty thousand Jews in Bulgaria. By 1888, that
number had risen to twenty-four thousand; by 1900, thirty-three
thousand; by 1910, forty-one thousand, and by the 1930s, about
fifty-five thousand Jews lived in the country.[37] Yet the core of group
identity and purpose remained intact and, in fact, was substantially
strengthened and focused by the increase in the Jewish population.
This reinforcement took place both in the realms of social organization and cultural development.

This was a period of transition and of metamorphosis, and the
confluence of internally instigated change and external developments
ultimately led to the voluntary dissolution of Jewish society in Bulgaria. These developments also had an impact on social and cultural
change and the creation of group identity.

The Jewish community in Bulgaria in 1878 was similar in many
respects to the Sephardic communities that existed throughout the
lands of the former Ottoman Empire, excluding the large centers of
Salonika and Constantinople. Just as Bulgaria was a backwater of the
cultural life of Europe, so Bulgarian Jewry was shielded from developments in the rest of the Jewish world. Even ritual religious life had
declined to the extent that services were held in the homes of several
of the notables, complete with Ark and Torah scrolls, rather than in
the synagogues, until eventually, "when religion and tradition began
to weaken, these quorums ceased to function and the religious objects
passed into the hands of the community."[38]

Both to Jews and Bulgarians, however, national identity was not a
function of degree of religious belief or practice. Just as a Turk who
failed to practice the rites of Islam was no less a Turk, or a non-
practicing Christian no less a Bulgarian, so a non-practicing Jew was
no less a Jew. Thus, for the Jews of Bulgaria, the decline of faith did
not automatically result in the assimilation so widespread in Western
Europe. Nevertheless, a gap was created by the atrophy of religion
which needed to be filled in order to ensure the vitality of the community. As discussed in previous chapters, that gap was filled by the
awakening of Jewish nationalism. As we shall see, this new ideology
became as much a part of Jewish culture in Bulgaria as religion had
been previously. Lili Avrahami remarked that: "The root of my Jewish
existence was because I was a Zionist and not because I was religious"
(Avrahami, p. 9). Isidor Toliko said: "in the Jewish tradition I was
completely ignorant, everything that I knew was from what the Zionist
movement translated and published in Bulgarian" (Toliko, p. 8).

For almost three centuries, Ladino had been the voice of Bulgarian Jewry. That its demise could come about so swiftly without fundamentally damaging Jewish identity is evidence of the Bulgarian Jews' flexibility. Changes which began with the liberation of the country and the resurgence of Bulgarian national identity were strengthened with the coming of the Alliance Israelite Universelle. The renaissance of the Bulgarian language and the introduction of French as the language of the elite led to a loss of prestige for Ladino in the eyes of the young, and the relaxation of religious observance, associated with tradition-oriented Ladino, furthered this process.[39] To the young generation, "Spanish was the language of the grandfathers and grandmothers, and seldom the parents."[40] The rise of Balkan nationalism hastened the process of the weakening of traditional Sephardic culture and language, and Ladino moved out of the public realm and remained only as the language of the home.[41] With the rise of the Bulgarian urban population and the increasing involvement of Jews in Bulgarian national life, the Bulgarian language quickly replaced Ladino as the first language of the Jews. Despite all efforts to the contrary, Hebrew would never flow easily from the mouths of Bulgarian youth, but its psychological significance and appeal was of great importance in the shaping of their identity.[42]

The dramatically swift eclipse of Ladino language and culture was, naturally, most difficult for the older generation, the "grandmothers and grandfathers," to accept. In his novel, *Farewell Salonika*, Leon Sciaky captures this anguish in his description of the feelings of an old Jewish woman viewing the changes taking place:

> Life had changed enough about her. Had not the Jewish woman discarded the veil? Had not Western fashions come into the city to change the appearance of the younger generation? New schools had been opened and were now teaching in foreign tongues. The young people were forgetting the traditions of their fathers and made little of age-old customs. God preserve us. She did not want to live the day when Spanish, the language of our ancestors, would be forgotten.[43]

The rapid-fire advent of Westernization, Bulgarianization and Zionization weakened the major institutions of traditional Sephardic culture. Emigration would deliver the final blow. The following chapter will investigate exactly which aspects of Sephardic culture survived this devastating onslaught. Ladino as the primary mode of communication would not be one of them.

The cultural and religious changes that led to the demise of Ladino did not occur in Bulgaria in isolation. They were influenced, at least in part, by the changing political and economic circumstances which affected Bulgaria as a whole, and drastically altered the unity of the Balkan Sephardim. The independence of the Balkan states from Ottoman rule marked their end as a cohesive entity. Tracy Harris, researcher of Ladino, remarked:

> Because of new international trade agreements as well as new customs restrictions, relations with the Sephardic communities of Salonika, Constantinople, Sofia, and Bucharest, which were active during the epoch of the Ottoman Empire, became increasingly difficult to maintain. The Jews were put into contact with non-Sephardic merchants and buyers. As a result, the ties which had unified the diverse Sephardic communities were broken, and Judeo-Spanish lost its role as the international cohesive language of the Balkan Sephardim.[44]

There were also general economic trends which affected the Jews. The artisan class, which included many Jews, became increasingly proletarianized as the result of trade agreements with Western Europe that flooded Bulgarian markets with its goods.[45] In addition, the removal of the Ottoman support network could not but cause major economic dislocation. Artisans and peasants, their livelihoods destroyed by the disruption, formed a vast labor reserve. An example of this change can be seen in the fact that in 1878, Sofia could boast fifty to sixty shoemakers, while in 1896, the number would drop to four or five.[46]

Many Jews had fled Bulgaria following the Russo-Turkish War (1877–1878), but most returned at the first opportunity. Upon their return, however, many suffered from anti-Jewish attacks instigated by the Russian troops, and from their association with the vanquished Turks. This, combined with economic factors, led to a steady increase in the Jewish population of Sofia as Jews fled the violence of the countryside for the relative security of the capital city. In 1881, there were 4,272 Jews living in the Sofia. By 1910, there were 12,862. Before the expulsions from Sofia during the Second World War, the city would host roughly half of Bulgaria's approximately 50,000 Jews. An indication of severe economic conditions, as well as the Jews' adoption of both Bulgarian and Jewish nationalism, was their participation in the armed forces:

> Bulgarian Jews fought in the Turkish army when Bulgaria was under Turkish rule, and after independence they joined the Bulgarian army in their thousands. Many Jewish soldiers distinguished themselves during the Serbo-Bulgarian war of 1885 and

were described by Prince Alexander of Bulgaria as "true descendants of the Maccabeans." Despite growing anti-Semitism no restrictions were placed on Jews entering the army or even the officers' training schools. Five thousand Jews fought in the Bulgarian army in the Balkan Wars (1912–1913) and several thousand of them were killed. In World War I a number of Jews reached senior army ranks, among them three Jewish colonels, Graziani, Tajer, and Mushanov. Over 7,000 Jews were killed in the war, among them 28 officers. Between the wars, Jewish soldiers continued to enjoy equal rights in the Bulgarian army until 1940 when Bulgaria allied herself with Nazi Germany. All Jews were removed from the Bulgarian army and organized into labor units to perform manual work.[47]

The impoverishment experienced by the Jews during the time of the Russo-Turkish was followed by general economic recovery. Many cooperative ventures were established, including enterprises and banks. A large middle class of merchants and professionals developed with this economic recovery, and up until the Second World War, the commercial district in Sofia would shut down on Yom Kippur, due to the preponderance of Jews among the businessmen and shopkeepers. With the gradual political and economic stabilization of the country, the Jewish community began to prosper. Although legally permitted to enter all areas of public life, Jews nevertheless seldom reached the higher echelons of Bulgarian society.

Several of my informants were fond of saying that, in Israel, a Bulgarian would often be appointed assistant manager, but rarely manager. It appears that the same was true in Bulgaria. It is hard to determine now whether this was due to culturally or socially inculcated aspirations, anti-Jewish "gentlemen's agreements," or the legendary Bulgarian Jewish honesty and hard work ethic much touted in Israel. N. M. Gelber wrote in 1946:

> They were pre-eminently engaged in trade but, industrious and persistent as they were, did not dominate commerce or banking. In a few enterprises leading positions were occupied by Jews, but not in the country's infant industry. They were typical tradespeople and only in a few cases merchants of higher rank. The economic structure of Bulgarian Jewry was, in fact, not particularly diversified. The Jews had clung to certain occupations for decades, if not centuries. Jewish business leaders, such as appeared in Germany, Austria or Czechoslovakia, simply did not emerge from the small Bulgarian-Jewish group. Even where a particular branch was exclusively

controlled by Jews, they did not dominate the field in question as a whole. This circumstance is to be attributed to the activity of the Greeks and the Armenians as well as of the Bulgarians in commerce, industry, and later in banking which surpassed that of the Jews. The weakness of the Jews' social and political position in Bulgaria . . . made them no match for their Christian competitors. Emancipation had indeed opened for them careers in the medical, legal and engineering professions, but even there Jews were not well represented.[48]

There were virtually no Jewish professors or teachers outside of the Jewish school system, and few writers or artists. It appears that this was the result of both external exclusion and self-limitation. Another occupational trend was the rapid proletarianization of the Jewish community, as more and more Jews became wage earners and fewer were self-employed.[49]

The 1934 census shows a Jewish population of 48,565, or .8 percent of the total, living in thirty-two communities.[50] Of the total population 84.5 percent was Orthodox Christian (5,120,890), 13.5 percent Moslem (821,298), .7 percent Catholic (15,704), .4 percent Armenian (23,476), .1 percent Protestant (8,371), and 1,802 persons listed as "others." Today, following significant emigration and assimilation, minority groups constitute only about 10 percent of the Bulgarian population. In 1880, 30 percent of the population was made up of various minorities, chiefly Turks and Greeks.[51]

Although the Jewish population was on the whole better off than the Christian (of which 80 percent lived in the villages and were largely illiterate), it had a significant sector which lived in poverty. The best known Jewish neighborhood, Yuch Bunar in Sofia, housed mostly lower-class Jewish families struggling to get by. Much of Jewish poverty was ameliorated, however, by Jewish self-help organizations, cooperatives, and banks. In addition, a unique form of grass-roots social-economic cooperative was developed. Shlomo Dagan, who immigrated from Sofia in 1947, described one type of cooperative association:

> In Bulgaria there were all kinds of unions, social unions. Twenty or thirty families would join together and create a community life. They would get together every Sunday, go out together on trips, pray together in the same synagogue, get together in a home. They contracted a doctor . . . and if someone had paid his membership the union would pay the doctor and all of the members of that group would go to the same doctor—a kind of sick fund. It was a fund for mutual assistance. If a son was being married off, everyone came to the wedding. If there was a death

in the family, so everyone would come. There were several associations like that which were on an entirely voluntary basis, not for profit. So that was quite developed. It didn't include the whole community, but in the community there were several associations like that. So that of course had its influence at home to a certain extent. Now and then, several times a year, you would get together with several Jewish families, friends would come, we would come, friends from the same association. That was when I was a kid. (Dagan, p. 11)

With a Zionist majority in power, these associations took on a Zionist flavor, and the ideals of Jewish unity and social justice were strongly in evidence in their activities. One such organization was the Ge'ulah Bank, which provided cheap capital to Jewish merchants and businessmen, and another was the Aliyah Bank, which moved to Israel with the emigration and is still in operation today.[52]

In addition to the taxes levied by the community, virtually every Jewish home donated regularly to the various funds for the building of the Yishuv. Every home had its blue and white collection box from the Keren Kayemet Le-Yisra'el (Jewish National Fund). Jews also gave generously to Keren Ha-Ge'ulah, Keren Ha-Yesod, and Keren Ha-Hagirah (the Immigration Fund), which supported the 'Atid agricultural training farm near Pazardzhik, preparing young Jews for the rigorous life on the Jewish agricultural settlements in Palestine, several of which were founded by Jews from Bulgaria.[53]

The Zionist revolution in Bulgaria went beyond the politics of the community, beyond cooperative economic activities, and even beyond the education of the children. The ultimate goal of Zionist ideology is aliyah and the rebuilding of the Land of Israel. But preparations for that ultimate fulfillment required the metamorphosis of the Jewish community and its members. This metamorphosis was to change the "diaspora mentality" and fundamentally alter the nature of Jewish society and culture. Of all the countries of Europe, only in Bulgaria did reality come to resemble ideology.

The language, symbols, holidays, dances, songs, images, longings, and goals of the Zionist movement suffused the community, supplanted many of the Sephardic traditions withering from exposure to modernity, and filled some of the spiritual emptiness left by the fading of traditional religious observance and belief. Lili Avrahami described her perception of tradition and nationalism: "Our concept of Judaism is only national, even though I know that my grandfather . . . sat in the synagogue every day and read books. I didn't even know what it was, what he was doing there. He studied. We knew that he studied, that he believed, but we didn't pay attention to it, we weren't interested in what he was studying and what he was doing. With us Judaism doesn't have any relationship to religion" (Avrahami, p. 7).

In addition, the Zionist movement provided the Jews, especially the Jewish youth, with a meaningful alternative to the wholesale adoption of Bulgarian culture and values (a process which was, of course, most pronounced among the young). Yet because of their secular education, knowledge of Bulgarian, and familiarity with Western values and technology, the youth led the way for the rest of the community. They also took as models the symbols of Bulgarian nationalism and independence, if not their substance.

All the major Jewish holidays were celebrated in the home, with the exception of Rosh Ha-Shanah and Yom Kippur, which were for many Jews the only days on which they would enter the synagogue.[54] Yet the most important Bulgarian Jewish holiday had little to do with Judaism. Yom Ha-Shekel (Shekel Day) was celebrated on Lag Ba-Omer, a religious holiday. Although Yom Ha-Shekel has its roots in Jewish tradition and philanthropy, in Bulgaria it was a celebration originally intended to help raise money for the Jewish National Fund.[55]

The holiday took place around the 11th of May, Saints Cyril and Methodius Day, which was the national celebration of the Bulgarian cultural renaissance, and was influenced significantly by it. Although originally intended merely as a way to help encourage donations to buy land for the Yishuv, Yom Ha-Shekel had become a celebration of Jewish solidarity and independence, as well as an occasion to demonstrate solidarity with the Bulgarian state. Marches were held in every town with a Jewish community large enough to support a parade. The day was packed with assemblies, sporting events, picnics, speeches, ceremonies, and memorials.[56] The marches, uniforms, symbols, and significance of the day became such a central part of Jewish consciousness that its origins seemed almost irrelevant. It served as a handy vehicle for a community greatly in need of an occasion to congratulate itself and show off its accomplishments. In addition, the task of contributing to the building up of the Yishuv was for the Jews of Bulgaria more of a *mizvah* (sacred obligation) than keeping *kashrut* (dietary laws) or attending synagogue. Lili Avrahami related this story from the period she worked for the Department of Corrections in Lod:

> There was always an argument. The Poles [Jews from Poland in Israel] always told the Bulgarians: "You're gentiles. What do you have to do with Judaism, you don't know anything! You're gentiles!" So one [Bulgarian] Jew, a man who worked there as a prison guard, one day almost got into a fight. And I saw it. He said: "What are you talking about!? What? We aren't Jews? Do you have any idea what kind of holidays we had? We had Yom

Ha-Shekel!" And they laughed: "What is Yom Ha-Shekel? It's a day for the Jewish National Fund. So that's your big holiday!" So afterwards, and until today, they get together sometimes and say: "Oh, what great Jews you are, you have Yom Ha-Shekel!" But that's our holiday. Yom Ha-Shekel, that's our holiday! (Avrahami, p. 19)

The task of determining the relative significance of the various cultural influences that shaped Jewish society in Bulgaria during this period is not an easy one. Sephardic, Bulgarian, European, and Zionist influences all converged to create something new and composite. Nevertheless, both the historical and the interview data point consistently to the fact that Zionist influence, as an ideology, political power, cultural force, and prime shaper of worldview, was the most compelling of all.

By the 1930s the Jews comprised perhaps the most urbanized and cosmopolitan sector of Bulgarian society. Yet at the same time that Zionism was supplanting Judaism in the spiritual realm, it was developing its own symbols, traditional behavior, and expressive culture in the folkloric. Originally, this study intended to examine the ways in which Bulgarian culture was altered by Israeli culture among the immigrants from Bulgaria in Israel. It soon became evident that the real question was how Sephardic culture became altered and replaced by Zionist culture in Bulgaria. In essence, a significant portion of the acculturation process had taken place before the Jews of Bulgaria boarded the boats that took them to Israel. The Sephardic roots of Bulgaria's Jews are still much in evidence, but they are confined to specific areas of Bulgarian-Jewish life. The Zionists provided a mythology, customs, songs, holidays, dances, a meaningful social context, and even the dreams of the youth. The area in which Sephardic culture remained unchallenged was in the kitchen.

The dark clouds of Fascism which were rolling across Europe in the 1930s found a Jewish community in Bulgaria unlike any other. Introverted and self-assured, yet involved in the life of the nation, Bulgarian Jewry had both unity and direction. Although antisemitism was relatively mild in the country, the Jews nevertheless embraced an ideology that viewed it as endemic, the only solution to which was Jewish territorial and national independence. In the 1930s, Bulgarian Jewry held its fate firmly in its own hands, but not for long. Zionist predictions would soon come true in unimaginably hideous form.

CHAPTER 7

The War Years: 1940–1944

Of all the countries of Europe, only in Denmark and Bulgaria did the majority of Jews escape the clutches of the Nazi murderers and their indigenous lackeys. This dramatic and astonishing fact has produced a large body of literature, much of it partisan and polemical. In the case of Bulgaria, the literature has centered around the question, "Who saved the Jews of Bulgaria?" As Nissan Oren, historian of Bulgarian politics, has pointed out, the proper question should be, "How is it that Bulgaria's Jews were not exterminated?"[1]

Credit for saving the Jews of Bulgaria has been attributed to the Bulgarian masses, the Communist Party, King Boris, and even Bulgarian incompetence.[2] In contrast to these partisan accounts stand the works of Oren and Frederick B. Chary. Chary's dissertation, which was later published in book form, is a masterpiece of historical writing founded on painstaking examination of documents and interviews from libraries, archives, and informants around the world.[3] What is revealed by this research is that the salvation of Bulgarian Jewry was the result of a complex set of factors involving ideology, politics, the course of the war, self-interest, and personal sacrifice. The most crucial factor was the timing of events.[4]

This is not the place to present a detailed discussion of the anguish which was Bulgarian Jewry's portion between 1940 and 1944. It is necessary, however, to examine those events and persons which had a profound impact on the attitude of Bulgarian Jews toward Bulgaria and their own national identity. There is no period of history that influenced Bulgarian identity in Israel more directly than this. Although historiographically unproductive, the question, "Who saved the Jews of Bulgaria," would become a central theme in the Bulgarian-Israeli consciousness.

The interpretation of the events of 1940–1944 that follows is based largely on perceptions of the nature and extent of antisemitism in Bulgaria. We noted earlier that Tamir views antisemitism as both endemic and widespread, and that this conclusion is consistantly contradicted by the interview data collected for this study. It is not the purpose here to evaluate these opposing views. It is important, however, that the sources of Jewish perceptions of the past, and thus perceptions of the present, are understood.

Anti-Jewish actions took place in several cities in Bulgaria around the turn of the century: Vratsa in 1890, Pazardzhik in 1895, Lom in 1903, and Kyustendil in 1904. In comparison to similar actions elsewhere in Europe, these were relatively minor, isolated incidents. According to Peter Meyer, historian of eastern European Jewry: "The most favorable conditions for the development of the Jewish communities prevailed in the first third of the twentieth century, roughly in the years 1900–1930. In this period there were no anti-Jewish excesses, relatively little open discrimination, and considerable opportunities to develop Jewish cultural life."[5]

The comparative lack of antisemitic sentiment in Bulgaria during earlier periods was discussed previously. With liberation and rapid social and economic development, however, new opportunities for conflict arose which had violent consequences in other European countries. The fact that these developments did not lead to Bulgarian-Jewish conflict is explained in part by Oren:

> Being few in number, they [the Jews] never constituted an acute problem for Bulgaria. While in most other East European countries the urban preponderance of the Jewish population constituted a threat to the rising middle class, in Bulgaria the conflict of interest did not arise. Although moderately influential in the economic life of the country, the Bulgarian Jews played no political role of any significance. They were an unassimilated and largely introverted national group. Historically, the Jews had been barred entry into state bureaucracy and the professional army. They were left in peace, however, to develop their own ethnic cultural life.[6]

This picture of constructive isolation was repeated by Chepo Pasi, the electrician at Kibbutz Yad Mordekhai:

> I think that the Jews had a good life, because they lived, in actuality, in a ghetto. A spiritual ghetto. In general they lived within Jewish neighborhoods, there was a Jewish school, and

there were Jewish youth movements which were very active. So that I think that Jewish life, which was very active, gave the Jews fulfillment, and it was concentrated around the synagogue, school and Jewish community. (Pasi, p. 12)

In addition, the recurrent pattern in Eastern European countries of a rising Christian urban middle class clashing with an entrenched Jewish middle class was not repeated in Bulgaria, due to the small number of Jews and the large number of available opportunities to conduct business in the cities. Also, since five centuries of Ottoman domination had eliminated all traces of an indigenous Bulgarian nobility, the resentment produced by a system of Jewish agents and middlemen for royalty did not exist in Bulgaria. "In the final analysis, the small number of Jews made antisemitism largely irrelevant as a political or economic agent."[7]

Lack of enthusiasm for, and even opposition to, antisemitic activities cannot be attributed solely to the small number of Jews in the country. Examples can be cited of countries and regions with a minimal Jewish presence in which antisemitic attitudes are strongly in evidence. Bulgarian tolerance toward ethnic minorities and the reinforcement of that tolerance during the Ottoman period was previously noted. This characteristic, abhorrent to Nazi ideology, was decried in a letter from Adolf-Heinz Beckerle, German ambassador to Sofia, to the Reich Chancellory on June 7, 1943:

> I beg you to believe me that my service is doing everything possible to reach a final solution to the Jewish question in conformity with decisions taken. I am deeply convinced that the Prime Minister and the Bulgarian government also desire a final settlement of the Jewish problem and are trying to reach it. But they are forced to take into account the mentality of the Bulgarian people, who lack the ideological conceptions that we have. Having grown up among Turks, Jews, Armenians, the Bulgarian people have not observed in the Jews faults which would warrant these special measures against them.[8]

The consistency of response by informants regarding antisemitism in Bulgaria is astonishing. All of them strongly resisted the notion that antisemitism was present in more than a small proportion of the population. The historical record indicates that this conception may be somewhat idealized. Nevertheless, it is a central factor in the development of Bulgarian-Jewish identity and attitudes toward Bulgaria and her people. Haim Molkho of Kibbutz Urim

echoed the sentiments of most informants when he stated: "In my
opinion it was a wonderful place, one could live in peace, there were
no pogroms, here and there there were some incidents, but it was
nothing" (Molkho, p. 1).

This idealization is particularly evident in the minimizing of restrictions on Jewish participation in public life. Many rationalized this
fact by stating that the Jewish community looked inward, and that few
were interested in careers in the professional army, the state bureaucracy, or political life. The fact remains, however, that very few Jews
were able to attain positions in these areas; the historical record on
this is clear. Yet these restrictions did not appear to be of significance
to my informants. Throughout the fieldwork, the question arose, why
were the Jews so forgiving of the antisemitism that did exist in Bulgaria and was a part of daily life? The answer, although difficult to
accept, is simple; everything is relative. Lidia Barukh, who came to
Israel from Vidin in 1952, felt that "the conditions weren't very good,
but the conditions weren't as of those who suffered in other countries"
(Barukh, p. 3).

The Jews of Bulgaria were not deported to the death camps, and
though most experienced severe hardship, they found this hardship
bearable. They found it so because the Jews of Bulgaria were tena-
cious, optimistic, modest, and united. They also found it bearable
because they were aware of the fate befalling the rest of European
Jewry. Each informant was asked the following question: "What happened to you and your family during the war?" The inevitable answer was "Nothing." When pressed further they would tell stories of
suffering and deprivation which they made sound more like inconve-
niences then tragedies, and sometimes even described as positive
experiences. Avi Cordova, who came to Israel with his family at age
ten and teaches sociology at Tel Aviv University, analyzed this phenomenon as follows:

> There are perhaps two or three reasons, one of which is that it
> was relative. After all, they knew what happened in Europe. And
> I think it's natural that they say 'nothing happened.' But if the
> Red Army had been held up another six or seven months, it
> [deportations] might have started in Bulgaria. The other reason
> is that those Jews love the Bulgarians as a people. They don't
> have the feeling of jealousy or spite toward the Bulgarians. On
> the contrary, they lived with them very well. There was no feel-
> ing of strangeness between the Jews and gentiles in Bulgaria, at
> least not in the generation that I knew. They were very inte-
> grated within the Bulgarian culture such as in the songs and way
> of life. In spite of the fact that they preserved their Jewishness

> don't forget that they spoke Bulgarian and weren't some kind of
> sect. (Cordova, p. 20)

Somehow, at least in retrospect, Bulgarian Jews took expropriation,
forced labor, expulsion, indignity, and impoverishment during the
war in stride.

Bulgaria never forgave England the Treaty of Berlin, and never
relinquished her irredentist claims. She fought and lost the Balkan
Wars over them, and she joined the Central Powers in the First World
War in order to win back territories she felt were rightfully hers.
Britain was disliked for her policy in the Balkans which helped deny
those claims, and America, although better liked, was largely unknown.[9] In Nazi Germany, Bulgaria saw another opportunity to press
her claims against Yugoslavia, Greece, Romania and Turkey, and Hitler was happy to promise her anything in order to convince her to join
the Axis. In addition, King Boris III was preoccupied with preserving
the monarchy, which he would be unable to do if Germany conquered
Bulgaria.

The atmosphere in the country began to change after 1933, partly
as a result of the increase in German economic and political influence
and the influx of students returning from their courses of study in
German universities. The number of antisemitic right-wing groups
increased. They included White Russian emigres, Macedonian nationalist revolutionaries, the Bulgarian National Socialist Party, the National Society for Political Renaissance, the Homeland Defense, the
Ratnitsi, the Association of Bulgarian National Legions, and the youth
organization Brannik. Peter Meyer relates that "according to all Bulgarian and most German sources, the influence of these groups on
public opinion was small."[10]

In 1940 there were approximately 55,000 Jews in Bulgaria of a
total population of 6,100,000 (0.9 percent): 45,000 were Bulgarian
citizens, 5,000 were aliens (Turkish subjects and refugees from Germany, Austria, Poland, Romania, and Hungary), and 5,000 were from
Dobrudja, annexed from Romania in 1940. In addition, the new territories of Thrace and Macedonia contained 12,000 Jews.[11] The fates of
these groups during the war would differ radically.

The pro-German government was willing to accept Germany's
terms of alliance, including its demands that it take measures to "solve
the Jewish problem." Because of strong Slavophile sentiments and
gratitude toward Russia for her role in Bulgaria's liberation, Bulgaria
refused to declare war on the Soviet Union. Even the opposition,
made up of Agrarians, Democrats, and Social Democrats, supported
the government's irredentist claims, and so at first did not oppose the
anti-Jewish measures.

In December of 1940, the first anti-Jewish law went into effect in Bulgaria. This was the infamous *Zakon za zashtitata na natsiyata*, the Law for the Defense of the Nation, based on the Nuremberg laws, with some modifications[12]:

> It barred Jews from citizenship, public office, army service, the ownership of property, the publication of newspapers, film production, intermarriage, and the employment of non-Jewish domestic servants. Jewish participation in commerce, industry, the professions and educational opportunities were limited to the population ratio. Forced labor for Bulgarian Jews was introduced. . . . Registration of property owned by Jews was ordered.[13]

In addition, the Law set up a Commissariat for the Jewish Problem, whose task it was to oversee the disenfranchisement and impoverishment of Bulgarian Jews, as well as to install the apparatus for eventual "resettlement in the East."[14]

Open opposition to the Law came from several quarters, and belies the notion that all Bulgarians accepted the government's anti-Jewish measures passively. Chary points out that as antisemitism became more powerful in Europe, Bulgaria's intellectuals began to value increasingly the relatively good relations between Jews and non-Jews in the country:

> They emphasized the favorable relations, and the myth of the absence of anti-Semitism grew up. Although this was not strictly true, the myth became as important as the fact, for a large section of the Bulgarian intelligentsia became committed to fighting the growth (or, as they preferred to think of it, the appearance) of anti-Semitism in their country. In 1937, a Jewish journalist, Buko Piti, published a book of statements of some one hundred and fifty leaders of Bulgarian society denouncing anti-Semitism and the reasons for its absence in Bulgaria.[15]

This "myth" of the total absence of antisemitic sentiment in Bulgaria before the war seems to have been adopted by the Jews as well, as evidenced in the interview data. Nevertheless, it served an important role in activating intellectuals from many areas of Bulgarian society to take bold action:

> The Union of Bulgarian Writers sent a letter to the government and parliament not to pass a law which would "enslave part of the Bulgarian people and would blemish modern history." The Executive Council of the Union of Bulgarian Lawyers in a de-

tailed exposé to the government emphasized that the proposed
new law would be a blow undermining the Constitution, which
explicitly prohibits any "division of the Bulgarian people into
higher or lower categories." In a letter to the Minister of the
Interior the Executive Council of Bulgarian Doctors expressed
its dissatisfaction with the measures being planned against the
Jews.[16]

Despite these protests, the Law went into effect, and government
oppression increased. In addition to the ideological support of these
measures on the part of many members of the government, Germany's demands that Bulgaria take more drastic steps against her
Jews increased as Bulgaria pressed her demands regarding territory,
and King Boris struggled with Hitler to keep his country and his
troops out of the actual fighting. Numerous laws were promulgated;
in August, 1942, all Jews were required to wear the yellow star. Cur-
fews were put into effect and Jews were allowed to shop only at specific times, usually when most products had already been sold out.
Viska Uziel, who spent the war years in Pleven, described the effects
of the restrictions on the Jews:

> We in Pleven remained there the whole time, but we were like in
> a ghetto. We had been spread throughout the city, not only our
> family, all the Jews. But then, when the fascists came, when the
> influence of fascism came to Pleven, it was forbidden for us to be
> on certain main streets. We were forbidden to go to the cinema,
> to any public place on the main street. We could stay outside
> until nine o'clock. There was one hour when we were allowed to
> go shopping. For example, in the morning they bring the fresh
> vegetables. First the non-Jews finished their shopping, what was
> left was left. After eleven we could go out. Still there was great
> help from the Bulgarian people. There were gentiles who had
> very close relations with the Jews, they would keep for them the
> (vegetables) either for money, or for the good feeling they got
> from helping them. (Uziel, p. 8)

Jewish organizations, except the official Consistory, were banned,
and the Jewish school system collapsed.[17] More property was confiscated. All Jewish males were pressed into the forced labor battalions.[18]
Isidor Toliko, who spent many months in forced labor, described the
hardships which were inflicted:

> I'll tell you what happened to all the Jews in Bulgaria. First of all,
> they prevented them from being able to work and make a living.

That is, if someone had a business he had to dissolve it, if he was a clerk, they had to throw him out according to the law. In addition to that, they did as the Germans, took people to forced labor. . . . I can tell you, all of the men, invalids, with physical handicaps. Without exception, it was enough that he was called a male from age eighteen to forty-five. Later in the last years, even to age fifty . . . I worked like that like a slave . . . in the Balkan mountains. We built them roads, but not with the tools they have now, everything was done with a shovel and that's all. . . . Eight months every year. In the winter they weren't interested, because it's a cold country, everything was covered with snow, we couldn't work. . . . That's how I worked for four straight years. (Toliko, p. 3)

Several concentration camps were set up. The camp at Samovit housed at one time 520 persons, including most of the leadership of the Jewish community.[19]

The beginning of 1943 saw intense pressure on Bulgaria to deport her Jews to the concentration camps of Eastern Europe. On February 22, 1943, the Commissar for Jewish Problems, Alexander Belev, and Nazi extermination "troubleshooter" SS Hauptsturmführer Theodor Dennecker, signed an "Agreement for the deportation of the first batch of 20,000 Jews to the East German territories."[20] Bulgaria allowed her Jewish nationals in Thrace and Macedonia, and other areas under Reich control, to be deported. Twelve thousand Jews from Macedonia and Thrace were deported and killed.[21] Hypocritically, as these Jews were not "Bulgarian," there was little protest within the country over their murder. The death of twelve thousand Jews was apparently a small price to pay to regain the coveted territories.

Although the Belev-Dannecker agreement was approved by the government, part of it was not made public knowledge; the remainder of the twenty thousand Jew death-quota was to be filled by the deportation of Jews from Bulgaria proper, who were to be rounded up on the nights of March 10 and 11 in greatest secrecy.[22] On March 5, the authorities in charge of the operation attempted to requisition supplies for the deportation from the local government in Kyustendil. When it refused to cooperate, the authorities requisitioned the supplies from the Jewish communities. When word of the impending deportation leaked out, an unprecedented drama unfolded which would stymie the implementation of the Final Solution in Bulgaria.

The leaders of the Jewish community in Kyustendil met with local government leaders, including several members of the Sobranie. That same night a Bulgarian delegation headed by vice-president of the Sobranie, Dimiter Peshev, set out for Sofia. Suprisingly, the delegation

included Macedonian revolutionary representatives, not well known
for their liberal attitudes or aversion to violence. The delegation demanded an audience with Minister of the Interior Gabrovsky, and
insisted on an immediate countermanding of the deportation orders.
They could do this on the legal grounds that the Belev-Dannecker
agreement, approved by the government, included no provisions for
the deportation of Jews from Bulgaria proper. Gabrovski complied
and the orders were cancelled.[23] This heroic action, which cost Peshev
his seat, set into motion an unprecedented series of protests:

> a storm of protest against the planned deportation arose even in
> the government camp. Protests were sent to Parliament, the cabi-
> net, and the King by unions of Bulgarian writers, lawyers, physi-
> cians, by town meetings, by noted men, and even by some officers
> of the army. Protesting deputations arrived from Plovdiv, Kus-
> tendil [sic], Iambol, and other cities. Especially strong protests
> were made by the Bulgarian Orthodox church and its Exilarch,
> the Metropolitan Stephen of Sofia [who was a personal friend of
> the chief rabbi, Dan Ziyon]. Even in the Sobranie, a group of pro-
> government deputies, headed by the vice-president of the Cham-
> ber, Peshev, protested the deportations.[24]

These events did not occur in a political vacuum, however, and
although many of the protesters were sincere in their feeling that
Jewish persecution had gone too far, many others were responding to
developments in the international arena. Germany was being turned
back on several battle fronts, and Bulgarians began thinking of the
consequences of their actions in the event of an Allied victory:

> By this time, the realization that Germany was losing the war had
> become widespread. Influential elements within the left, the cen-
> ter, and even the reactionary right, had come to realize the futil-
> ity and possible adverse consequences of Bulgaria's allowing the
> Jews to be exterminated. This interplay of political forces consti-
> tuted striking proof of the existence within the Bulgarian body
> politic of political pluralism, which had survived even at the
> height of the crypto-Nazi regime.[25]

This wave of protest did not halt the government's increasing
persecution of the Jews. Many in the government viewed the events
of March–May 1943 as a delay in the inevitable deportation of the
Jews. In June, all Jews were ordered to leave Sofia; 19,339 Jews left
for towns in the provinces, most moving in with relatives, friends,
and even strangers in the Jewish communites of cities and towns

throughout the country. Several families often crowded into small homes and apartments. The refugees' homes in the capital were appropriated by the government. Even this action was not completed without open opposition.

On May 23, a march was organized in the Jewish quarter of Yuch Bunar, and thousands rallied at the city center to protest the expulsion orders. The march was broken up by the police, and many were arrested. Historian Reuben Ainsztein relates:

> And when on the following day the Bulgarian police entered the Jewish district, it met with the resistance of organized Jewish groups and was forced to retreat. Similar demonstrations all over the country made the Bulgarian police chief report that "the native Bulgarian population expresses its complete solidarity with the Jews and is taking part in their actions. Every attempt to deport the Jews has met with not only the peoples' indignation, but also with their resistance. We are forced to give up our plan to resettle the Jews in Poland."[26]

The question of the role of King Boris in the anti-Jewish measures in Bulgaria remains unclear. However, it is known that Boris was in control of the government, and little transpired without his approval. There are those, including some of my informants, who hold that he delayed implementation of anti-Jewish measures as long as possible, and even that he was killed by Hitler because of his refusal to deport the Jews.[27] The existing evidence does not support this hypothesis, and it appears that he had no great love for the Jews, but could use them as a bargaining chip with his Nazi masters.[28]

With each battle Germany lost, the government became more aware of the possible consequences of its anti-Jewish measures. In November, 1943, a new cabinet was formed, headed by Dobri Bozhilov, which began to make concessions on matters affecting the Jews, at the same time it was secretly sounding out the Allies on possible agreements. Bulgaria, mostly through the cunning of the King, had managed to make all its political gains without committing men to the field in significant numbers, and the Bulgarian population had weathered the war largely unscathed. In January 1944, mass bombings of Sofia and other cities created panic in the populace. The plan to deport the Jews from Bulgaria was withdrawn. Belev, Commissar for Jewish Affairs, was brought up on criminal charges of graft. In August, with the Soviet army poised on its borders, the government abolished all anti-Jewish laws.[29] On September 9, 1944, the Red Army entered Bulgaria.

The historical record of the fate which befell the Jews of Bulgaria between 1940 and 1944 is complicated, and the reports and their interpretation are often contradictory. Although not deported to the death camps, the Jews were severely persecuted, and their lives and society were totally disrupted. They were threatened with imminent extermination and forced into banishment, forced labor, and poverty. One would expect these events to have a traumatic and debilitating effect which would cause demoralization and desperation. In fact, the opposite occurred. The Zionist predictions had been confirmed, and the social framework created by the movement served to sustain the community through the worst of times.

CHAPTER 8

From Liberation to Emigration: 1944–1949

September 9, 1944 is the date of the liberation of the Jews of Bulgaria from the oppression of a crypto-fascist regime and the threat of annihilation. To call it the date of Bulgarian liberation is fatuous. Bulgaria and her people had wholeheartedly and democratically chosen to enter the alliance with Nazi Germany, and once again suffered the infamy of a self-destructive choice. For the Jews of Bulgaria, the years 1944–1949 would prove as momentous as the preceding four. They were years filled with struggle, confrontation, renewal, hope, and ultimately, true and final liberation.

Political Struggle: Zionists versus Communists

Bulgaria's Jews participated only minimally in the national political arena, and most of their energies were expended within the community. Although Jewish membership in the Bulgarian Communist Party (B.K.P.) was small, it was disproportionately large for their number in the total population. During the war years, 260 Jews joined partisan units to fight the fascists, and 125 fell in the struggle.[1] But after the war, with the increasingly virulent anti-Zionist stance of the B.K.P., most Jews cleaved to the Jewish-Zionist cause. Nissan Oren writes: "In Bulgaria, unlike most other East European countries, Jewish influence within the Communist party was moderate, if not meager. While a few Jewish Communist intellectuals did play a role, particularly in the educational and propaganda fields, the popular sentiments of the Jewish community were directed at Zionism more so than in previous years."[2]

A special section was set up in the B.K.P. whose task it was to gain Jewish support and oppose the now re-established Zionist organizations.[3] The struggle between this small minority, which enjoyed governmental support, and the vast majority of Zionists was long and bitter.

Even barring international political considerations, the Communist attitude toward an independent Jewish community was inevitable since it was dictated by ideology. In a socialist state, all sectors of the population have a duty to eschew their individual cultural and political identities in order to join the common struggle. Thus, the Communist effort to dismantle the Jewish community was the result of a comprehensive ideological imperative. This viewpoint was expressed by Prime Minister Georgi Dimitrov:

> In the gloomy and detestable Fascist days, our people did not allow the genocide of the Jews. Bulgaria was the only country under Fascist rule in which the life of the Jewish people was saved from the animal's claws of the Nazi murderers and cannibals. This fact binds our Jewish brothers in eternal gratitude to the democratic and aristocratic [sic] Bulgarian people and to the "Fatherland Front." Now that we build a new Bulgaria,— democratic, independent, strong and rich, the greatest duty of the Jewish people in Bulgaria is not to be different, but to participate in the most active and loyal way with all their might and ability in the construction of our homeland.[4]

The Jews, however, having maintained a vigorous and independent life on Bulgarian soil for over a millenium-and-a-half, and having just emerged from the clutches of oppression and threatened extinction, had a different agenda.

As the new regime was settling accounts with the previous one through special war tribunals, from which the sentences issued were among the harshest in Europe, the Jewish Communists were wresting the reins of power from the Zionist leadership by force, and a protracted campaign of coercion and intimidation ensued. Yet the Jewish community fought tenaciously against every attempt to usurp its independence.

In 1946, Vitali Haimov, president of the Zionist Organization, claimed thirteen thousand active members. "Zionist organizations continued to function in the face of continuous harassment. Independent weeklies were published until 1948 by the General Zionists and Po'alei Zion. The majority of Jewish youth were organized by He-Halutz Ha-Za'ir and Ha-Shomer Ha-Za'ir."[5]

Great diversity continued to be the rule in the Bulgarian Zionist camp. Nevertheless, the various groups were firmly united against the Communist takeover. The Federation of Zionist Parties included, in order of numerical importance, Po'alei Ziyon, He-Haluts/Ahdut Ha-'Avodah, General Zionists, Ha-Shomer Ha-Za'ir, and Revisionists/ Betar. According to Tamir: "the preponderant share had a leftist-socialist orientation, and a politico-administrative affiliation with Israel's (Palestine's then) MAPAI and what would later be MAPAM [Labour Party]. Whether the process of impoverishment had produced a larger Jewish working class, which identified more easily with Labor Zionism, or the new Marxist climate in Bulgaria had affected the ranks of Zionism too, is essentially unimportant."[6]

Unimportant or not, the fact that most Jews had leftist leanings did not imply sympathy for the Communist attempts at cultural destruction. Until 1947, two parallel power structures existed within the Jewish community; one supported by the government, the other by the people:

> On the one hand functioned the officially-sponsored organizational network of the Jewish People's Committees, connected with the Central Consistory and, through it, to the Jewish Committee and the Minorities Committee of the Fatherland Front. On the other hand, a parallel pro-Zionist organizational network was created, headed by the pre-war Zionist leaders and linked with international Zionist organizations, as well as certain institutions in Palestine. . . . [although subject to constant violent attacks by the Jewish Communists,] the Zionist Organization developed broad activities, which were neither directed nor even supervised by the authorities. Youth clubs, women's organizations, . . . Jewish schools, social activities, and publications all flourished. Furthermore, almost to a man, Bulgarian Jews participated in activities organized by the Zionists.[7]

As a result of Jewish tenacity in the face of Communist strong-arm tactics, the government was forced to take action in order to defuse the threat of Jewish independence, pluralism not being one of the hallmarks of the Communist system. It had two options: outright repression of Jewish autonomy, or cooptation of the Zionist leadership. It chose the latter.

In May of 1946, the Zionists were invited to join the Communists in an equal-representation agreement in the Consistory, which was the Central Jewish Committee of the Fatherland Front. However, a pro-Communist majority was assured by representation on the Committee of a small group of Jewish Social Democrats.[8] This agreement marked the end of Zionist independence.

In October, 1947, the Zionists were accused of maintaining a dual allegiance by the Communists. On November 23, the official Jewish Communist organ, *Evreiski Vesti* [Jewish News] demanded the merger of all Jewish organizations with the Fatherland Front; in January, 1948, they complied. In March of that year, Chief Rabbi Hananel was accused of making political reference to the ruins of the Temple in Jerusalem, and religious autonomy was suppressed. By March of 1949, all Jewish activity in Bulgaria had ceased. "On April 2 . . . the Central Committee of the United Zionist Organization sent its last circular letter (no. 28), calling on all branches to discontinue their activities. This was the final act of organized Zionism in Bulgaria."[9] The circular was sent out to a community which no longer existed. By 1949, there remained in Bulgaria only five thousand Jews. Between 1948 and 1949, forty-five thousand of Bulgaria's fifty-thousand Jews had left Bulgaria forever.

Economic Dislocation and the End of Jewish Education

The war had left Bulgaria in dire economic straits. The economy was in disarray and the population was impoverished. The Soviet Union prepared no Marshall Plan for its sphere of influence. On the contrary, it appropriated much of what was left of the economic infrastructures of its new satellites for its own use, even relocating entire industries within its own borders. Disinherited and disenfranchised, the Jewish community, which had escaped the clutches of death, was now left in abject poverty. Newspaper reports from the period illustrate the terrible reality:

> The economic level of the Jews of Bulgaria has sunk to nothing. Poor Jews, who make up ninety-five percent of the total Jewish population in Bulgaria, have no roofs over their heads, and there is no possibility of their normalizing their lives soon.[10]

> We continue to exist by selling our belongings as before.[11]

> We knew very well that in poor Jewish neighborhoods life was not good. But what we saw in Yuch Bunar was shocking: there it is very bad; they are dying of starvation.[12]

Because of this desperate poverty, it is not surprising that the Jews were anxious to have at least part of their expropriated property returned. On March 2, 1945, the government passed the Law of Restitution. This law provided for the return of all Jewish property and the restoration of all Jewish rights. But the Fatherland Front had its own reasons for not actively fulfilling the provisions of the Law. The ultimate goal of the regime was the elimination of private property. More important, however, was the fact that government coffers were sorely strained and, all rhetoric aside, the needs of the nation were put before justice for the Jews. In fact, only a small percentage of Jewish property stolen during the war would ever be returned, and this paltry amount was further reduced by the high inflation of the time.[13] In fact, of the approximately 4.5 billion leva appropriated by the fascists, only 126 million was returned.[14] The pattern of grandiose rhetoric and promises followed by minimal action would become standard for Bulgaria's treatment of her Jews.

Fortunately, international Jewish relief organizations were active in helping the Jews of Bulgaria through this difficult time, and this aid allowed most to survive until their departure from the country.[15] The government was satisfied to allow the Jews to fend for themselves, particularly in view of the fact that the Jews had shown ingratitude to their "saviors," the Fatherland Front, by insisting on maintaining their cultural autonomy and refusing to self-destruct.

The cornerstone of cultural as well as political autonomy was the independent Jewish school system. As soon as the war ended, one of the first tasks the Jewish community set itself was the reconstruction of the comprehensive network of schools which had existed before the war. The Bulgarian regime recognized the threat of independent education, and immediately moved in to control it.

The Jewish Communists who had forced their way into control of the Jewish institutions made drastic changes in the school system, which hitherto had been based on "Zionist education, an Israeli atmosphere, and the Hebrew language." They replaced Hebrew with Bulgarian, removed the pictures of Herzl and Trumpeldor, threw out the blue collection boxes of the Jewish National Fund, took down the maps of the Land of Israel, forbade the singing of Hatikvah, and banned the Zionist flag. These radical measures only inspired intense activity and rebellion in the Jewish community, and served to strengthen its resolve.[16]

The desperate economic condition of the Jews following the war and the government's refusal to make just restitution could not but strengthen the resolve of the Jews to leave Bulgaria. A people employed mainly as merchants and traders, the uniformity of the Communist system offered them few opportunities for economic growth. But the main impetus for immigration was not economic. Avi Cordova described the situation as follows: "In comparison to the Jewries of Central Europe, it's difficult for me to define Bulgarian emigration as an emigration of refugees from Fascism. I think that even if there weren't Fascists, the Zionist consciousness in Bulgaria was very deep and I can't explain it" (Cordova, p. 5). Very soon after September 9, 1944, it became clear that the new regime saw little room for an independent national minority within its borders. The destruction of Jewish education simply confirmed this suspicion.

Brihah and Aliyah

In December of 1944, David Ben Gurion, leader of the Yishuv, visited Bulgaria.[17] His visit exemplified the close links between the Jewish communities in Bulgaria and Palestine, which were soon to merge forever. As the Communist authorities curtailed the activities of the Zionists in Bulgaria, the Jews began looking toward Palestine with increasing commitment. With the cooptation and domination of the Zionist leadership by the Communists, the Jews concentrated more and more on Aliyah Bet, the "illegal" immigration to Palestine in defiance of British restrictions. On December 2, 1946, a Zionist delegation to Prime Minister Georgi Dimitrov received confirmation that all Jews were free to emigrate. This promise would not be put into practice before the partition of Palestine was sanctioned by the United Nations.[18]

The government's attitude toward Jewish emigration was changeable and confusing, and, when it was finally allowed, the government found itself in direct conflict with the Jewish Communists, who consistently opposed it. Despite Bulgarian and British restrictions, many managed to get to Palestine illegally. Between September 1944 and October 1948, seven thousand Bulgarian Jews arrived in Palestine in defiance of both the Bulgarian and British border police.

Most of the immigrants of the Aliyah Bet were young and committed to the cause of Jewish redemption. Many joined kibbutzim, and most were immediately recruited to the Haganah. In this regard, the Bulgarian authorities displayed an ironic paradox: as the struggle against Zionism within Bulgaria intensified, the government increasingly supported the Haganah and Israel's War of Independence.[19]

The Bulgarian government archives have been closed for this period until very recently, and we do not yet know for certain the reasons the regime allowed the Jews to emigrate. We do know that by the late 1940s, Bulgaria attempted to homogenize its population by encouraging the emigration of other minorities, including Greeks, Turks, and Armenians.[20] Thus, the authorities probably saw the establishment of the State of Israel as a way of further reducing ethnic pluralism in a manner which would appear ethical to the outside world, and at the same time absolving itself of responsibility for making full monetary restitution.

Two pivotal events can be identified in the arrival at this decision: Soviet Minister Gromyko's speech at the United Nations advocating the partition of Palestine, and the vote in favor of this position. "Only after the United Nations Partition Plan was voted upon did the regime permit the emigration of able-bodied young men and women, who were to join in the 'fight against imperialism.' "[21]

During the period of Aliyah Bet, and later, when the government allowed young people to leave, most of Bulgarian Jewish youth left their homes and families to make the journey. Haim Molkho, a founding member of Kibbutz Urim, described his experience:

> I came to Israel with the Youth Aliyah. In my group there were one thousand children. We came via Turkey by train, Syria, Lebanon, and to Israel. . . . My parents, my brother and sister remained in Bulgaria. My brother came two years after me, and my parents came four years after me. . . . We were members of the youth movement, Maccabi, and after our parents saw what happened to the Jews throughout the world, and especially during the war, they sent the children. (Molkho, p. 13)

This first wave left Bulgarian Jewry largely bereft of its youth and soul.[22] But these were the trailblazers who would mark the way and set up camp in the new land for their parents and grandparents to follow: "Parents followed their offspring directly to Israel. Shiploads of Bulgarian Jews of all ages arrived monthly in Haifa. In the course of 1948–1949 successive waves of immigration brought into the State of Israel 45,000 of Bulgaria's 50,000 Jews."[23] Only a remnant of Bulgarian Jewry remained, which would become smaller with each passing year.[24] Those who stayed in Bulgaria were mostly Communists who believed that the solution of the Jewish problem lay not in Jewish nationalism but in the triumph of socialism, and the struggle to build socialism in Bulgaria was for them the primary task.[25] Avi Cordova described two groups of people who stayed behind:

> First they suffered from the Fascists, then the Communists. There was a very strong sense of community, and the Jews were closely tied to one another . . . and whoever didn't leave was the exception that proves the rule. Those who didn't leave fit into two categories; people very high up in the Communist Party . . . or people married to non-Jewish men or women, and even some of those emigrated. (Cordova, p. 4)

By 1949, all Zionist organizations in Bulgaria had dissolved themselves. In 1957, the Social, Cultural, and Educational Association of the Jews in the People's Republic of Bulgaria replaced the Central Consistory. In 1961, the Association handed over all property to the state.[26]

Within two years, the nexus of Bulgarian Jewish life moved from Sofia to Jaffa. This was the final act in a drama played out over fifteen hundred years, the climax of which began in 1876. From that date Bulgarian Jewry proceeded with single-minded determination toward its own chosen destiny. It would be difficult to name another ethnic group that transformed itself as swiftly according to a template of its own creation. The seventy years between independence and emigration was a period of metamorphosis in preparation for the final act of self-realization. It was a cocoon within which Bulgarian Jewry developed its wings for the final flight to the homeland.

> Bulgarian Jewry . . . was a very untraditional Jewry, the second generation cut off from religion. There were old people who went to synagogue, but among all the people national Jewish awareness was very developed. Most of the Jews whom I have met were active in the various parties; General Zionists, Maccabi, Po'alei Ziyon, Mapai, Ha-Shomer Ha-Za'ir. . . . The people who I knew were deeply aware that they were Jews, and it came to them as obvious that they go to Israel. (Cordova, p. 4)

The only Bulgarian synagogue in Jaffa is a storefront on Shderot Yerushalayim. Despite the presence of forty-five thousand Bulgarian Jews, this small sanctuary is more than adequate to hold the observant among them. Illustration by Cheri Haskell.

PART III

*The Jews of
Bulgaria in Israel*

CHAPTER 9

Theoretical Approaches

In the introduction to this book, several theoretical models were surveyed which have application to the study of the nature of the identity and ethnicity of Bulgarian Jews in Israel. The present work is predicated on the acceptance of the diachronic approach to the study of ethnicity and identity, an approach pioneered in Israel by Deshen, Shokeid, and Weingrod. In addition to this comprehensive orientation, several specific propositions developed by Israeli scholars were previously discussed which are pertinent to our examination of the Jews of Bulgaria in Israel. The following is an examination of three of the most promising of these approaches with an eye to their applicability to the present case: S. N. Eisenstadt's "Predisposition to Change"; Don Handelman's "Ethnic Group Types"; and Shlomo Deshen's "Cultural Paradigm."

S. N. Eisenstadt's "Predisposition to Change"

Shmuel Noah Eisenstadt recognized the Jews of Bulgaria and the Jews of Yugoslavia as being in a category by themselves. A comparison of these two communities would prove interesting, but is outside the scope of the present study. Here this distinct category will be examined in light of the historic and ethnographic data, and its applicability to the purpose of the present study.

Eisenstadt divided Jewish communities in the Diaspora into four types: the traditional, which includes Yemenite and some North African communities; the insecure transitional, which includes North African, Central, and Eastern European communities; the secure transitional, which includes the Bulgarian and Yugoslavian communities; and the inmates from displaced persons camps.[1]

Eisenstadt characterized his third category as follows:

> The secure, transitional sector . . . comprises Jewish communities
> settled within and approved by Gentile society. This group . . . is
> confined mainly to Serbian and Bulgarian Jewries, which consti-
> tuted, it seems, a unique type of Jewish society. Their most impor-
> tant characteristics are the following: (a) a small degree of social
> autonomy, mainly confined to family traditions and religious wor-
> ship; (b) strong primary identification with the general commu-
> nity and secondary, associational identification with the Jewish
> community; (c) acceptance of their Jewishness by the Gentile com-
> munity as a sub-system within the general social structure, their
> Jewishness, in consequence, usually fostering or emphasizing
> their social status.[2]

Eisenstadt further noted that this group was deported not because its members were Jews, but as the result of general political conditions. For him, "predisposition to change" was the most important factor in successful absorption:

> Positive predisposition to change was found mostly among those
> coming from countries where membership of the Jewish commu-
> nity constituted an approval of social status and/or a source of
> group cohesion against the outside world, namely the first and
> third sectors. Negative predisposition occurred mostly among
> those for whom being a Jew was a factor of insecurity and status
> anxiety—the second and fourth sectors. In the first case, uncon-
> ditional identification with the Jewish nation develops because
> membership in it is a positive in morale and in social security.[3]

There is certainly a great deal that rings true in Eisenstadt's analy-sis, and the fact that he recognized the distinctiveness of Bulgarian Jewry in the Israeli ethnic amalgam is a credit to his insight. The Jews of Bulgaria were not his main concern, of course, as he developed an encompassing framework for the study of immigration to Israel. Bul-garian Jews are the main concern of this study, however, and it is necessary to criticize his analysis carefully and refine it.

According to Eisenstadt, an important characteristic of the secure-transitional sector is its "small degree of social autonomy, mainly confined to family traditions and religious worship." In the case of Bulgarian Jewry this was clearly not so. We know now that the Jews of Bulgaria had established for themselves a high degree of social autonomy. They ran their own communities, schools, and banks, levied their own taxes and conducted their own affairs. It is true that these activities were not in conflict with the larger society, but they certainly show more than a "small degree" of autonomy.

Eisenstadt stated that the members of this sector had a "strong primary identification with the general community and a secondary, associational identification with the Jewish community." Here again the historic and ethnographic evidence clearly contradict this assertion. The sense of Jewish identity among the Jews of Bulgaria was absolute and not a matter of degree. Although citizens of Bulgaria, some even deriving pride and satisfaction from this fact, they were Jews first and last, and this point was emphasized by all informants and sources. Buko Lazarov, who left Bulgaria at age forty-eight, summed up his sense of identity: "I left in December '48. Even though it's thirty-two years, I have the closest relationships, friends whom I love personally. But I don't feel Bulgarian, I never felt like a Bulgarian, and I was always proud to be a Jew" (Lazarov, p. 10).

It is indeed true that the Jews were an accepted minority in Bulgaria; whether this fact played a role in "fostering and emphasizing their social status" is not entirely clear. It is clear that it served definitely to limit their rise in social status to positions of real power, through the gentlemen's agreements discussed in Part II. Whether this form of status ascription was viewed positively is questionable.

The concept of "predisposition to change" also creates some problems when applied to the Jews of Bulgaria. Indeed, they had undergone most of the changes necessary for accepting life in Israel prior to immigration: They had broken the bonds of traditional society and had become a largely secular, democratic community. They had undertaken the Jewish education of their children and provided a Zionist educational system and youth organizations modelled after those of the Yishuv. The war had wrenched them from their homes and businesses, impoverished them, and prepared them for the hardships which would await them in Israel. Most Jews were employed in trade or labor, both of which were in demand in Israel, and life in the labor battalions had accustomed many of the men to the hard work needed and admired in Israel. Finally, and most importantly, the Zionization of Bulgarian Jewry had been progressing steadily during the half century prior to immigration, and had become not only a "predisposing frame of reference" but an impelling motivation for many.[4] It is clear, then, that the Jews of Bulgaria were not only predisposed to adapt to the new country, they had adapted their own lives to the point where their community resembled the Yishuv in many important ways.

In sum, it can be said that Eisenstadt was on the right track in singling out the Jews of Bulgaria as belonging to a special category, but he failed to perceive much that was peculiar to them and, in fact, came to conclusions which were not derived from the reality of their lives in Bulgaria.

Don Handelman's "Ethnic Group Types"

The varieties of definitions of "ethnic group" are so broad as to include virtually any cultural or racial agglomerate. This diversity of definition leads to confusion in comparing characteristics of various groups called "ethnic." If the term is to be retained, further refinement of definition is necessary.

In Israel the problem is somewhat simplified, as the two main cultural groups have been designated by different terms. The non-Jews in Israel (Christians, Moslem and Druze Arabs, Circassians, Armenians, etc.) are designated "minorities" (*mi'utim*); Jews from a common place of origin are called "communities" (*edot*). Because of the social and political history of the Yishuv, *edot* usually refers to *edot ha-mizrah*, "communities of the East" (i.e., Afro-Asian Jewries). Thus, it would sound incongruous to the Israeli ear to call the Jews of Poland, for example, an *edah* (sg. *edot*).

These are *emic*, or native, categories. Don Handelman has taken up the question of definition refinement, and provides us with four *etic*, or scientific, categories to this end. These categories are useful in differentiating types of ethnic groups according to degree of "ethnic incorporation."[5] This is a valuable concept, for the degree of ethnic incorporation determines, or is an indicator of, cultural interaction and, ultimately, the degree of active ethnic identification. There is, however, a significant difference in interaction both within the group and with the larger society within each ethnic category. For example, a member of a Yemenite moshav and a Yemenite married to a Sabra living in Savyon, a wealthy suburb of Tel Aviv, will exhibit differing levels of ethnic incorporation. These categories, then, can rarely be applied to a group *in toto*. At the same time we recognize the value of differentiating ethnic affiliation on the basis of ethnic incorporation, one must avoid the temptation of designating individuals from the same country of origin with a specific ethnic group type. Although there are groups in Israel in which the majority of members live in homogeneous communities with a consistent degree of ethnic incorporation, there are always individuals who live with a greater or lesser degree of independence from that group. Ironic as it may at first appear, we have learned that ethnic incorporation, and indeed ethnic identity itself, must be viewed as an individual phenomenon, especially in pluralistic, highly mobile societies such as Israel.

Handelman's four categories, from lowest degree of ethnic incorporation to highest, are ethnic membership, ethnic network, ethnic association, and ethnic community. Without describing the details of these four categories, it is clear, especially from the folklorist's point of view, that they can be accepted only with further stipulation.

Since the late 1960s, the study of folklore has moved from a textual to a contextual orientation. Taking their lead from sociolinguistics and the ethnography of speaking,[6] folklorists sensitive to the social-scientific implications of their work have accepted the axiom that no product of human expression can be excized from its creator and interpreted correctly.[7] This fundamental reorientation had a profound effect on the study of ethnic folklore and the folkore of ethnicity.[8] Just as folkloric expression cannot be properly interpreted when divorced from the context in which it was created, so ethnic expression and behavior cannot be properly interpreted when divorced from the context in which it was produced. If one accepts the assumption that most forms of self-expression are produced for interpretation by others, then it becomes clear that they may be altered by their creators in order to elicit the desired reaction. The audience must always be taken into account.

This understanding of the nature of human self-expression has been largely accepted by students of ethnicity, and in the 1970s folklorists studying ethnic aesthetic expression produced a number of studies that recognize ethnicity not as an absolute but as a dynamic strategy of human interaction.[9] Just as there are individuals within a group who are more folkloristically creative than others (and even some who are not creative at all), there are differing degrees to which individuals have mastered the techniques of identity manipulation. In sum, the individual must be the basic unit in determining degree of ethnic incorporation. An individual may traverse all four of Handelman's "ethnic group types" within a single day, or even within a single event. Depending on the context of interaction, one may belong to an ethnic category, network, association, or group. Furthermore, in certain circumstances one may place oneself outside of any ethnic category altogether.

This phenomenon was evident in doing fieldwork for this study. Interviews were aimed at eliciting attitudes toward the old country, new home, other immigrants, use of folkloric expression and its preservation, and the concept of self. To be sure, there were certain neighborhoods and settlements in which individuals displayed a higher degree of ethnic incorporation. Immigrants from Bulgaria who live in Jaffa, who belong to one of the Bulgarian clubs and speak Bulgarian with family and friends, are certainly close to forming an ethnic community. Yet even among these individuals this is not seen as a desirable condition, but as the result of circumstances which did not permit their more complete assimilation into Israeli society. Such factors as immigration at an advanced age, inability to find housing outside of the neighborhood, inability to advance economically "up and out," or lack of fluency in Hebrew (which can be both the result of and the cause of the above) were often cited as inhibiting integration which, among the Jews of Bulgaria, is a universally held ideal. Such expressions regarding failure to more fully assimilate may have been encouraged, in part, by the desire of informants to explain their having remained in the ethnic community, which contradicted their self-proclaimed assimilationist ideology.

Handelman's concept of ethnic group types is useful given the two qualifications discussed; within a group of immigrants from a given country of origin there are sub-groups and individuals who exist within frameworks with greater or lesser degrees of ethnic incorporation, and an individual may traverse these four categories depending upon circumstances and context of daily interaction. This holds true in particular for the Jews of Bulgaria. Another question, however, need be asked: Is there not a core of consciousness, a cultural template that influences the behavior and choices of all immigrants from a given place of origin? This very question was addressed by Shlomo Deshen.

Shlomo Deshen's "Cultural Paradigm"

From his work with southern Tunisian immigrants, Deshen recognized what appeared to be a core of consciousness, perception, and attitude which weathered the trauma of transplantation and continued to manifest itself in many ways in the new country. This core he calls a "cultural paradigm."[10] The concept is not a new one, but Deshen presenting it in reference to his specific case is a valuable contribution to the ethnology of ethnicity in Israel.

One of the most persistent meta-problems in the study of culture is whether to approach the individual or the collective as the more fruitful subject of study. Generalizations must be made if science is to predict, but it is vital that they be made at the correct level of abstraction so that they neither include too few nor exclude too many. This problem was artfully addressed by anthropologist Ward H. Goodenough in his *Culture, Language and Society*:

> People learn as individuals. Therefore, if culture is learned, its
> ultimate locus must be in individuals rather than groups. If we

accept this, then cultural theory must explain in what sense we can speak of culture as being shared or as the property of groups at all, and it must explain what the processes are by which such "sharing" arises. It is not enough to deal with the problem by simply asserting that "shared culture" is an analytical constant as some anthropologists have done.[11]

Deshen's cultural paradigm is appropriate in that it recognizes shared attitudes and beliefs without excluding individual variation. The concept of cultural paradigm, template, model (or whatever term is used), is important in that it is the basis for determining individual variation. It is complementary to the contextual approach to behavior, for it determines the baseline for individual creativity and its manifestation, alteration, or even rejection, for its existence is not created in performance- or behavior-specific context. In a sense the concept of cultural paradigm can be criticized as being superorganic, a theoretical abstract. This criticism is valid, for no single individual will manifest all that is contained in the cultural template; in fact, that is the point. If carefully developed from the observation of individual behavior and recording of individual attitude, it is a useful construct. Thus, rather than being superimposed on the members of a group it must be derived from its individuals.

The cultural paradigm that informs Tunisian ethnicity in Israel exists whether or not its bearers are defending their ethnic identity, engaging in political activity, managing the impressions they make on others, employing their ethnicity for strategic gain in interpersonal relations, or simply expressing themselves on the basis of this shared paradigm. The presentation of this model was a clear break from the "absorption" and "modernization" models previously in vogue among Israel's social scientists. The precise mechanism for constructing such a paradigm, however, is not made entirely clear in Deshen's study.

A cultural paradigm is certainly easier to construct in the case of a homogeneous, traditional society than in a heterogeneous one in transition. In the case of the Jews of Bulgaria, the research has indicated that the core of "Bulgarianness" in Israel would be difficult to isolate in a static, paradigmatic model. The concept of cultural paradigm is valid, but is difficult to implement in isolating the salient cultural elements in the identity of the Jews of Bulgaria in Israel.

It was found helpful, then, to have an additional framework for viewing the development of ethnicity and identity, one that can be better tuned to groups which have adapted successfully to life in a new environment. Such an approach is suggested by the interview data through the consistency of informant response on several key issues. In the present research, certain historical events, persons, ideas and sentiments were brought up by informants in interviews with startling predictability. This consistency of response can be explained in part by the nature of the inquiry and interview format and process. It became clear, however, that these omnipresent topics, brought up independently, were the links of a chain which joined the Jews from Bulgaria in a common identity. To be sure, this is not their only identity, but it is the one they share. For some the links are strong, for others, weak. Still, even when individual informants had differing lifestyles, professions, political allegiances, and personalities, these were the images, symbols, ideologies and memories which created some sense of shared identity. I have termed these consistent foci of cognitive commonality "components of identity." The following is an examination of the most consistent and compelling of these components: Jewish identity in Bulgaria; Bulgarian-Jewish relations and the Holocaust; Zionism, education, and youth groups; and emigration and immigration.

CHAPTER 10

Components of Identity

My original research plan called for the collecting of folklore among Bulgarian immigrants through a combination of directed, open-ended interviews and participant observation. At the same time, these methods produced meager results; responses to questions regarding ideology and attitude toward the use and continuation of traditional Bulgarian forms of expression revealed a general apathy toward folkloric expression and an enthusiasm for cultural assimilation. This discovery, in turn, prompted an examination of Jewish ideological, social, cultural, educational, and political history far more detailed and in-depth than the summary originally planned.

It became clear that both folkloric competence and attitude toward folkloric expression could be explained only through diachronic analysis, through an understanding of the major themes of Jewish life in Bulgaria during the half century preceding immigration. The results of this historical analysis were retrofitted to the existing interview format. The original, naive but significant questions regarding folklore and identity were not, however, excised from the interview plan. They were retained in order to confirm the original conclusions which had led to the expansion and refining of the interview schedule. As a result of this process, the focus of the investigation shifted from *what kind of, how much, how transformed,* and *how transmitted was ethnic folkloric expression in the new country,* to *why was there so little of it?*

This lack of folkloric expression led to a necessary reorientation to the question of ethnicity. Documenting the scarcity among Bulgarian Jews in Israel, while revealing in itself, could be misleading if linked to the premise that such expression is a proportional measure of ethnic affect and identification. Furthermore, documenting lack without trying to explain it would hardly fulfill the intent of the study. The

original research plan envisioned using folklore as a window to immigrant attitudes and worldview. If this window was closed, it was important to know why in order to find another point of entry.

This point of entry was revealed by the direction in which informants consistently directed the interviews, a direction confirmed by
the data obtained through participant observation. This informant-
determined redirecting of the interviews can be seen in the sample
interviews included in Appendix C. The topics toward which the informants consistently redirected the interviews, those subjects which they
insisted on discussing in relation to their sense of self and place in
society, I have called "components of identity."

An interactive strategy was employed in directing the historical
research. At the same time that a more complete knowledge of Jewish
history in Bulgaria was required to understand attitudes in Israel, these
attitudes were keys to determining which aspects of that history were
salient. Thus, there is a correlation of topics discussed in Part II and the
components isolated here. The topics covered in this and the following
chapters are all components of identity. They have been divided into
categories to provide a clearer presentation of the material.

Jewish Identity in Bulgaria

In a static society, or in one undergoing a period of stasis, sense of
identity should also remain unchanged. Observers working over a
number of years would not have to be concerned that changes in the
social order would produce concomitant changes in individual perception of self and others. On the other hand, an observer working over a
period of time in a dynamic society will have to be acutely aware of the
effects of change on identity.

Israel has been just such a dynamic society. Because of this, our
study can hope only to identify, describe, and explain the components
of Bulgarian identity in Israel for the brief period during which the
data were collected. The variables are increased when one adds the
changes in attitude resulting from each individual's maturation to
those occurring in the group as a whole.

These problems are compounded when one tries to identify the
components of Jewish identity in Bulgaria. Bulgaria during the seventy years preceding emigration was a country in turmoil and a society in upheaval. There were dramatic differences in perception from
one generation to the next, more complex and profound than the
transient differences which separate generations in quieter times.
These differences often included language, religiosity, ideology, and
worldview. Thus, we cannot speak of Jewish identity in Bulgaria, for a

seventy-year-old and a thirty-year-old interviewed in 1938 would provide pictures of Jewish life in Bulgaria which would differ beyond the discrepancies produced by age, and both would probably express very different sentiments again in 1948.

Because of all this, generalizations made about Jewish identity in Bulgaria refer to a specific group at a specific time, although there are some generalizations that transcend these specifics. My interviews were with people aged fourteen to forty at the time of immigration. Most came between 1948 and 1950 with the mass wave after the war. Most were in their twenties and thirties when they arrived. Although aided by historical sources, much of our sense of how these Jews saw themselves in Bulgaria is retrospective. The distortions of memory and age are well known. Suffice it to say that interview data were triangulated whenever possible with historical data and data from other interviews, and discrepancies noted.

Throughout this study I have used the inelegant, cumbersome apellation "Jews of Bulgaria," rather than "Bulgarian Jews" or "Jewish Bulgarians." The connotations of these three combinations involve far more than nuance. They involve the most fundamental expression of self, of allegiance. They describe identity.

In "Bulgarian Jew" the individual so called is a Jew who is also a Bulgarian, or a type of Jew. This latter sense would be appropriate in a descriptive, etic sense, as certainly "Bulgarian Jews" have different cultural traits than "Italian Jews" or "Moroccan Jews." It is inappropriate in the emic, self-descriptive sense. Buko Lazarov, who as a tobacco buyer had many close contacts and friendships with Bulgarians, nevertheless felt his identity very strongly: "I was among many Bulgarians, both friends at work and outside of work. But I always felt like a Jew and not a Bulgarian. I never thought to change my religion, even though I had Bulgarian girlfriends as well . . . I was a Jew. Also in Israel when they say to me you're Bulgarian, I say I'm a Jew from Bulgaria, I'm not Bulgarian" (Lazarov, p. 10).

In "Jewish Bulgarian" the primary identification is with being Bulgarian, a Bulgarian of a certain type. This form is inappropriate to all societies that ascribe sub-groups specific minority status. It is more indicative of an ideological statement or a desired state than a reality, as in the implication that a "Jewish American" is equal to a WASP or "real American."

Neither of these combinations are appropriate in the present case, for they imply a social structure which did not and does not exist in Bulgaria. As seen in Part II, Bulgarian attitudes toward minority groups were shaped by a combination of historical experiences, the most important of which was the lengthy Ottoman domination with its millet system. This system benefited from and enhanced the Jews' own sense of separateness in Bulgaria. The introduction of social-democratic and pluralistic ideologies occurred simultaneously in Bulgaria with the spread of Zionist ideology, which became the dominant force in Jewish internal and external politics. Pluralism and social equality or even equivalence, which dominated Jewish relations with gentile society elsewhere in Europe, were preempted by the separatist doctrine of Zionism. The Jews of Bulgaria passed from the separatism of the millet system and traditional isolation to Zionism, strengthened by the rise of antisemitism. This resulted in a powerful sense of Jewish identity unparalleled in Europe.

A Bulgarian was a Christian and a Jew was a Jew. The sense of Jewish identity among the Jews of Bulgaria was absolute and not a matter of degree. This sense of self, or rather sense of community, is the core of all manifestations of ethnicity and identity. For the Jews in Bulgaria, self-governance and Zionist commitment were the logical sequiturs of Jewish existence. Because of this, the cultural and personal assimilation prevalent elsewhere in Europe did not exist in Bulgaria. In the final analysis, the inevitable result of this identity was immigration to the Jewish state at the first opportunity. Isidor Toliko spent most of his life in towns far from the centers of Jewish life, yet his sense of self was never in question: "I'm not Bulgarian. I have no sentiments. I'll tell you, in spite of the fact that it was not an ugly exile, our immigration to Israel was a step into freedom. Like when a man gets out of a concentration camp, or from prison, so he takes leave of it, he tries to forget it" (Toliko, p. 16).

The Jews of Bulgaria fall into what Walter Weiker, among the foremost students of contemporary Turkish Jewry, describes as a "middle category" in the Israeli system of ethnic categorization.[1] They are Sephardim, but from Europe. Furthermore, they are viewed positively by the dominant Ashkenazi establishment, "like us," as largely urbanized, educated, and westernized. Thus, they fall outside accepted stereotypes. Avi Cordova and Haim Molkho describe this situation:

> As you know the majority is Ashkenazi, and they think in stereotypes, naturally, about all the non-Ashkenazim, and that includes the Sephardim. So they have difficulty because that stereotype is incorrect because the Jews of Iran and Iraq (for example) are not Sephardim. Now the Bulgarians appear to them as Sephardim, but it's very difficult for them to accept that because they are Europeans like themselves. So there is a measure of ambivalence. In spite of this I appear to the Ashkenazim as a Sephardi even though (many of them) are far from me in education. That is, in general they see this group that made it in Israel

and integrated nicely, pleasant. It's not unusual for the dominant majority to behave in that way, there's something paternalistic in it, that is, "they're good because they're similar to us." (Cordova, p. 18)

I worked for many years in the Ministry of Agriculture, in central positions, and even when there was negative talk about Sephardim, they always said "Bulgarians aren't Sephardim." And I would say, "What does that mean, not Sephardim? Our origin is Sephardi." "No, not you, it's not exactly the same thing." Bulgarians are Bulgarians. It's a special people, something different, not Sephardim and not Ashkenazim, Bulgarians . . . for example look at Turkish and Greek Jewry. They are Sephardim. For them the business of Ladino was much stronger than it was with us. (Molkho, p. 18)

Zionism, Education, and Youth Groups

The pervasiveness of what may be called "Zionist culture" was discussed in Part II. The power of Zionist education in Bulgaria was naturally reinforced by Israeli ideology after immigration. This is an instance in which it may be suspected that the emphasis placed on the Zionist experience in Bulgaria by informants may have been inflated beyond reality by the process of reinforcement in Israel. Historical data, however, clearly demonstrate the power and pervasiveness of the movement in Jewish life in Bulgaria.

Israel is a youth-oriented country, and the Zionist movement has always been a youth-oriented movement. Since independence from Ottoman rule, the Jewish communities in Bulgaria invested their futures in their youth, and it was the youth that led the way, both to new ideas in Bulgaria and eventually to the new land of Israel. Lili Avrahami described her split loyalty to family and Zionism: "I said . . . it's the dream of my life to go, but how can I go without my family? Father said if you, the young ones go, if we want to go sometime we have to send the children first. If the children go we will go after them" (Avrahami, p. 21).

Since the consolidation of Zionist control of the Jewish community organizations in the 1920s, and the wresting of control from the "notables" this was not a rebellious youth. On the contrary, it was backed and encouraged by the community apparatus. Jewish youth could grow up entirely within the Zionist movement. In Sofia, where half of Bulgaria's fifty thousand Jews lived, a child could attend Hebrew elementary and high school, participate in the activities of a dozen different youth organizations, and graduate to a position of Zionist governance of the community.[2] A more comprehensive and encompassing Zionist framework existed nowhere else in the world outside of Israel.

From a tender age, the children were exposed both at home and at school to the myths and realities of Palestine. They studied non-Bulgarian subjects in Hebrew, were often taught by Jews from the Yishuv, studied the works of the Zionist thinkers, sang songs and danced dances of the Land of Israel, and many worked on special farms to train for the rigors of life in the agricultural settlements (*hahsharah*). The emotional surge toward Israel was so universal that even unenthusiastic parents were often swept up in the fervor. This surge eventually became the wave that would carry all but a few to the State of Israel. Yosef Eldzham described the influence the young generation had on its parents through personal experience:

> I'll tell you the truth, in the beginning I didn't think that I'd come to Israel, in spite of the fact that four groups already came to Israel. But one day my daughter came home and said, "Dad, you know what? I don't have any girlfriends left. All of them have left for Israel." And I said, "What shall we do?" And my wife said, "So what's the problem?" I got attacked from her side too. She said, "We can get along in Israel too." So I said OK, we'll go as well. (Eldzham, p. 13)

Elsewhere in Europe, Zionist youth groups had to operate clandestinely, under the threat of discovery and persecution. In Bulgaria, the youth groups marched in uniform down the main streets of the cities on both state and Zionist holidays, and participated in combined activities and sporting events with Bulgarian youth groups. As the Jewish community was fully identified with Zionist consciousness, these demonstrations of Jewish pride and strength were the antithesis of the anathema "Diaspora mentality" decried in Zionist doctrine. Indeed, long before reaching Israel's shores, the Jews of Bulgaria had developed values and an outlook more akin to the Israeli than to that of European Jewry as a whole.

The centrality of Jewish education and youth groups was emphasized by all informants who left Bulgaria in their teens and twenties. The impact of these factors was less personal in the lives of the older immigrants, but this did not seem to alter their ideology or attitudes toward Israel or Bulgaria. This centrality was not apparent only in the areas of education and ideology. In fact, discussions of language, song, dance, social and leisure activities, social relations, and religion all seemed to return to the influence of the Jewish schools and youth groups. These institutions provided the primary field for expressive behavior of all kinds. Both Zionist ideology and Hebrew culture and institutions during this period were emergent, progressive, and dynamic, oriented toward the youth and a brighter future. Thus they provided both motivation and fertile ground for a youth trying to express itself. This was largely at the expense of the past and tradition, although by its very nature reliant upon it.

Bulgarian-Jewish Relations and the Holocaust

In the discussion of S. N. Eisenstadt's work in relation to the Jews of Bulgaria it was noted that he linked "predisposition to change" in part to the status of the Jewish community in its country of origin and relations between Jews and non-Jews. The emphasis placed on Jewish-Bulgarian relations in the interviews reinforces this position and points to it as being a central component in identity. In this case the relationship is particularly fascinating due to three interdependent factors. These three factors also make the issue complex and difficult to interpret.

1. Antisemitic acts and attitudes were less severe in Bulgaria than elsewhere in Europe, but they still existed. Although legally granted full political and legal rights, Jews were excluded from positions of real power in the professions, government, and military.
2. Only the Jews of Bulgaria and Denmark were not deported to the death camps. Nevertheless, the Jews of Bulgaria suffered severe financial, legal, and social oppression during the war. Had the war continued another year it is likely they too would have been deported and killed.
3. Each and every informant depicted Bulgarian-Jewish relations in glowing terms, and minimized the catastrophe that befell them during the war.

This combination of seemingly contradictory factors points to the notion that the Jews of Bulgaria in Israel are using different criteria than those derived from an historical analysis in formulating attitudes toward their home country and its people. It seems that in retrospect they are in part comparing their relationship with the gentile majority and their fate during the war with those of Jewish communities elsewhere in Europe. Thus, in comparison with Polish, Romanian, or Czech Jews, for example, their situation was excellent indeed. How, after all, could the Jews of Bulgaria bemoan their fate when they survived in good health from a catastrophe which devoured six million of their people? In addition, it seems that their generally optimistic view of people and life predisposed them to view their past in a positive light.

There are additional factors which may help explain this apparent discrepancy between memory and reality. The Jewish community enjoyed the status of an established minority, one that, if not equal, was at least clearly defined and accepted. By and large the Jews of Bulgaria viewed Fascism as an alien ideology imposed from without, supported by a small minority of antisemites, and opposed by the majority of Bulgarians. In addition, their own strong sense of identity, established community organization, and ideological commitment provided them with a stable framework even in the most chaotic of times.

Studies of this period have shown that numerous factors combined to save the Jews of Bulgaria from the genocide wrought on their brothers in the rest of Europe. It is generally acknowledged that the lack of deep-rooted antisemitism on the European model, as opposed to institutionalized protected but inferior status, was one of the most important factors in avoiding catastrophe in Bulgaria. Informants were unanimous in praising their neighbors for their conduct during the War, even though they would at the same time describe antisemitic incidents. This relationship would seem to mitigate their decision to leave the country en masse.

Though saved from the death camps, the lessons of the Holocaust that had very nearly engulfed them were not lost on the Jews of Bulgaria. It was the gruesome fulfillment of Zionist predictions, and confirmed in the most horrible way the Zionist realization of the inviability of Jewish life in the Diaspora. The tolerant relationship between Jews and Bulgarians had permitted the flowering of Zionist schools and community organizations throughout the country. Thus, in a roundabout way, this good relationship fostered the development of an ideological and structural framework for its own dissolution.

The established, tolerant attitude toward the Jewish community on the part of the Bulgarian majority allowed for a strong, self-confident Jewish society with a confirmed sense of its own worth. It was this strength and confidence which girded them for the collective leap into an unsure future from a position of relative security, and was vital for the Jews of Bulgaria to overcome the tremendous social and economic difficulties they were to encounter in Israel.

In the following section we will examine specific cultural and folkloric traits which the Jews derived from their long association with the Bulgarian people. The area which informants consistently mentioned as being their most valued inheritance from this relationship,

however, lies in the less clearly definable realms of attitude and outlook. Mikha Kalev of Kibbutz Yad Mordekhai had some very definite
opinions in regard to culture and identity:

> I disagree with the notion of roots. Trees have roots, people
> don't. That's my thesis. There was a culture which I soaked up, I
> soaked up a cosmopolitan culture, which I don't regret for a
> moment. I don't deprecate another culture, and I don't think
> Jewish culture is the greatest in the world. That's chauvinistic
> and not correct, because there are other cultures equally worthy.
> I value and am part of Jewish culture, but I also know how to
> value the good things which I saw in other peoples, and also the
> Bulgarian people. They have a beautiful culture, beautiful prov-
> erbs, a sense of enlightenment, a strong work ethic, beautiful
> values, I think . . . there is some kind of foundation, and I didn't
> get that foundation here. I got it there. (Kalev, p. 35)

This inheritance is reflected in the general perception of the Jews
of Bulgaria by Israelis as an honest, hard-working, modest but confident immigrant group. Lidia Baruh, who runs a beauty shop in Holon, described the general opinion in Israel about the Jews from Bulgaria: "There is a special personality. Perhaps I exaggerate a bit but I
am proud of it. These are people who love to work. Perhaps you have
heard. They love to work. Honest people, who know that work is
work. And a good immigrant group. A very good immigrant group"
(Baruh, p. 19).

Informants overwhelmingly agreed with this perception, and
claimed these traits were learned from the Bulgarian people. These
were also the traits which, until recently at least, were most highly
respected in Israel. Thus, the Jews of Bulgaria arrived in Israel with
an ideological and pragmatic matrix which predisposed them to life in
the new country. They view this as their most important inheritance
from the people of Bulgaria.

Emigration and Immigration

By the time Israel gained her independence in 1948, approximately
seven thousand Jews from Bulgaria had already arrived in the country. Although there had been a Bulgarian presence in Israel since
1898,[3] most of these pre-state immigrants came to the country
through Aliyah Bet.[4] Most of these early immigrants were young and
came through the auspices of Youth Aliyah. Unattached, ideologically
committed, and mostly indoctrinated in the teachings of pioneering

Zionism, they settled on kibbutzim throughout the country. By the time of the mass influx, most Jews in Bulgaria had young relatives already in the country.

One of the most interesting questions that arose during the interviews for this study concerns the motivation for immigration. The pervasive Zionist atmosphere within the Jewish community was a factor. But a paradox still remains: if the Jews of Bulgaria had it as good as they claim, and if Bulgaria was such a fine place in which to live, was ideology enough to push them to an uncertain future in an unsettled, war-torn land? In countries where Jews suffered far more before, during, and after the Holocaust, a smaller percentage left for Israel. Why was this so?

Informants answered this question in different ways. It seems that the movement to emigrate was generated by a combination of ideological, historical, political, economic, and social factors. For some, it remains not truly explicable. Isidor Toliko, who retired from the postal service and now teaches yoga, turned the question back to me: "You study sociology. There are such moments in social movements which are not rational" (Toliko, p. 11).

By and large younger immigrants cited ideological reasons as being sufficient for immigration, although some felt more strongly than others. For many informants Zionism was a family tradition: "The main reason was ideological. The reason was that my family was a Zionist family. My brother was editor of one of the Zionist newspapers, *Ha-Shofar* . . . and was very active in Ha-Shomer Ha-Za'ir. My other brother was active in Maccabi. So that the entire family was a Zionist family, and the reason for aliyah was ideological" (Pasi, p. 12). This higher degree of ideological motivation combined with a youthful sense of adventure brought the young to Israel first. In addition, the British Mandatory Government was issuing entry permits to the young. Further, even when these few permits were obtainable, it was easier for Aliyah Bet to smuggle in the young and resilient.

With the establishment of the State of Israel, elimination of immigration quotas, and permission by the Bulgarian government for Jews to emigrate, thousands more young people left the country. The strong sense of family solidarity among the Jews of Bulgaria would not allow families to remain divided for long. Avi Cordova remembers:

> It was a general atmosphere in the streets where the Jews lived. That is very clear. At the moment they began speaking of the fact that it was possible to immigrate to Israel . . . there was a lot of competition to get those [immigration] certificates. And in actuality the division of the certificates was through the parties.

My father was active in Mapam and he really managed to get us on the first boat. (Cordova, p. 4)

Family solidarity was not the only factor for the older immigrants—community solidarity was also important. As comfortable as informants claimed to feel in Bulgaria among Bulgarians, and as little antisemitism as most informants felt existed, the primary field of affectual interaction was within the Jewish community: outside of work, Jews socialized with Jews.

As children, nieces and nephews, grandchildren, friends, business partners, and neighbors began to move, the temptation to remain quickly faded. It was soon obvious that Bulgarian Jewry would reestablish itself in Israel. The old country, or their part of it, would cease to exist in Bulgaria. In fact, the only place where Jewish Bulgaria would continue in some viable if fleeting form was Jaffa: "When there was a possibility of coming to Israel, there were families which were in general apathetic to the whole affair, but when the gates were opened, without exception, they rose as one man" (Toliko, p. 20).

Seen in this light, the decision on the part of the later immigrants was not only a leap into an uncertain future. It must also be seen as an attempt to preserve familial, associational, and perhaps even cultural ties. Many of the less ideologically motivated immigrants describe their emigration as going along with a "wave" whose force was irresistible. Viska Uziel, the only informant I spoke to who ever entertained the idea of returning to Bulgaria, described her emigration: "And there really was a wave, a kind of epidemic where everyone went, so we went also" (Uziel, p. 9).

The negative material and political factors which encouraged emigration must also be acknowledged. Bulgaria in 1948 was a very different place from Bulgaria in 1938. Despite partial reparations, the Jews' economic base was disrupted. Many could not recover their homes and businesses. Furthermore, prospects for a return to prosperity in trade and commerce faded as it became clear that the new regime was phasing out private enterprise. Politically, it did not take the Jewish leadership long to realize that the government had no intention of permitting the continuation of the internal democracy and self-rule which allowed the Jews to tend to their own affairs and the education of their children.

One can see with hindsight that, based on these facts, the Zionist predictions were correct. Private enterprise was abolished and Jewish autonomy banned. The Association of the Jews in the People's Republic of Bulgaria was a branch of the Bulgarian Communist Party, and it's main purpose was to phase out all remnants of an autonomous Jewish existence.

As grim as was the situation in post-war Bulgaria, conditions in Israel were worse. If the Zionist dream had painted a rosy picture of life in Israel, immigrants quickly discovered the harsh reality of life in the country during this period. The early arrivals were greeted by the pitched battles of the War of Independence, the later by the lack of housing, employment, food, and a government unprepared for and economically incapable of handling this first mass influx, an influx that would continue for more than a decade.

Many moved in with relatives in various parts of the country. Some of the younger immigrants joined kibbutzim. More often, however, young people who had previously joined kibbutzim came to the cities to help their parents and grandparents adjust, and few would later return. Haim Molkho described the situation on his kibbutz:

> I would say that everywhere the Youth Aliyah from Bulgaria was unusually successful, but the percentage which remained in the kibbutzim was small. The usual excuse was that when the parents came in 1948 the children left in order to help. . . . If we take the farm where I live, 'Urim, I imagine that at least five or six hundred members passed through who are of Bulgarian origin. Today only ten of us remain. (Molkho, p. 13)

Most immigrants were forced to live in shacks, tents, or inadequate housing, usually in Jaffa. Typically, immigrants would spend a few days or weeks in a transit camp (usually Pardes Hannah or Sha'ar Ha-'Aliyah) and then strike out on their own or stay temporarily with relatives. All, however, refused to remain in government camps and accept government dole or work for more than a short while. To this day they are proud of the fact that, unlike other immigrant groups, there were no Bulgarians in the *ma'abarot* (temorary government settlements). Haim Molkho expressed sentiments which were reported by all informants:

> I wanted to add something. Bulgarian Jewry came in 1948, together with all of the big aliyot, when there were ma'abarot and all those things. But they didn't stay in the ma'abarot, not for more than half a year. Not one Bulgarian Jew remained, all of them left for Jaffa, Ramle, Lod, each with his own valise, and nobody thought that the government has to provide for him or obtain things for him, and all of them got along well, and have apartments, and so forth. And that's due to their diligence. None of them remained as others did, thirty years in the ma'abarot. . . . There was nothing like that, the whole business of a handout. The

idea that the government would provide for you, and that you'd stand in line for food. And because of that they are distinctive, in their diligence, their honesty, and that's what I wanted to say. (Molkho, p. 19)

It was during these first, most trying years that the Jews of Bulgaria earned their reputation for hard work, modesty, stoicism, and "pulling themselves up by their bootstraps." Chepo Pasi, who worked for several years in Jaffa as a representative of his kibbutz movement, described the characteristics of the Bulgarian aliyah:

All of the people who came here in the liberal professions got along. The rest went to work, and it is recognized in Israel that the Bulgarian aliyah pulled up its sleeves and got to work. It wasn't a pampered aliyah, and that is one of the positive things. Secondly, it was always an optimistic aliyah, it never got depressed, it kept up cooperative endeavors, like the Tsadikov Choir and various organizations. I think that those are things that helped very much in their proper absorption, because they didn't wait for anybody else to help them, they helped themselves. And I think that as the years passed, each person found his own way. There are still some groups until today that seek each other out and continue the communal life they had outside Israel. I know that there are groups from Ha-Shomer Ha-Za'ir that meet every week, who get together every weekend, and they organize recreational activities together. But as for the Bulgarian aliyah as a whole, it was very different from other aliyot. (Pasi, p. 19)

The Community in Israel: Structure and Institutions

Within two years of the opening of the gates of immigration, the focus of life moved from Sofia to Jaffa. Bulgarian became the language of the streets, and shop signs in Bulgarian appeared almost overnight. Bulgarian branches of the major political parties were set up and a newspaper, *Far* ("Lighthouse"), was published daily in Bulgarian. The Tsadikov Choir was reestablished and a library of books brought from the old country was founded. Restaurants serving Bulgarian food appeared, and coffee shops and clubs for conversation and games opened along Shderot Yerushalayim, the main street of Bulgarian Jaffa.

All of these were only temporary support phenomena, and over the following twenty years Jaffa would serve as much as a sentimental center for the Jews of Bulgaria even as its Bulgarian population dwindled over the years. Jaffa was poor, and as the new immigrants became veterans, they moved up and out. Today, only a small community of mostly retirees and their social clubs remain.

Israelis from Bulgaria live throughout the country in cities, towns, kibbutzim, and moshavim although the largest single concentration is still in Jaffa. Many more live in the surrounding neighborhoods to which they moved as housing became available: South Tel Aviv, Bat Yam, Holon, Tel Baruh. Chepo Pasi describes the decline of Bulgarian Jaffa:

> I think that here it's not an ideological matter. Life in Jaffa can't fulfill the young people, and they feel as if they are in a kind of ghetto. In actuality Jaffa served as a kind of ma'abarah. The Bulgarians arrived and there were already Hungarians and Romanians and others. When they got settled they began to leave Jaffa, and then people came from the countries of North Africa. Jaffa was always used as a kind of ma'abarah, and when people became settled they left it. The young people left, after they got settled, had a trade, and left for Holon, Bat Yam, the surrounding areas. The older people remained, either because they didn't have the opportunity to find apartments in other areas, or because there is a concentration of retired people, who have all kinds of clubs and organizations, who share a common language and common experiences. (Pasi, p. 18)

As of 1970, about 80 percent of Israel's sixty thousand Jews of Bulgarian origin lived in the Tel Aviv-Jaffa area. Outside of Jaffa there are really no distinct Bulgarian neighborhoods in other towns, although there are some local concentrations. About seven thousand lived in Haifa, and the rest lived in Jerusalem, Ramle, Lod, Acre, Safed, and the settlements of Tel Hanan, Kfar Hittim, Zur Moshe, and the first Bulgarian settlement in Israel, Hartuv, which was founded in 1898.[5] There are also several kibbutzim with Bulgarian concentrations.

There is one official Bulgarian association in Israel, the Ihud Olei Bulgariyah (Bulgarian Immigrants Union). Its purpose is to expedite official business with the Bulgarian government, especially in regard to the financial holdings of former Bulgarian citizens now living in Israel. The Union also sends small monthly stipends to several former officials of the wartime Bulgarian government who were instrumental in preventing the deportation of Jews to the Nazi death camps. Its purpose served, its usefulness waning, the Union had become largely inoperative until the latest mini–immigration after the fall of totalitarian rule in Bulgaria in 1990. Yet even this is only a temporary reprieve (see Epilogue).

Sharing the office of the Union is the office of the Bulgarian old age home in Rishon Le-Ziyon. The only cultural institutions are several social clubs in Jaffa where old friends gather to drink coffee, play backgammon, dominoes, and cards, and celebrate holidays together on occasion, a small library sponsored by the Communists, and the Tsadikov Choir. The Maccabi Jaffa soccer team was once the focus of Bulgarian pride. As most of its players are now not of Bulgarian descent, and as it has been at the bottom of the national standings for several years, it has lost much of its former allegiance.

Bulgarian Jaffa has become the waiting room for the Rishon Le-Ziyon old age home, a fact attested to by the growing number of death notices in Bulgarian going up on the lamp posts, and the number of signs in Bulgarian coming down from the store fronts. Haim Belo, denizen of the Hayim Tovim (Good Life) Bulgarian game club, talked about the disappearance of the old way of life:

> What can I tell you, the old ones are going, fewer remain . . . the Bulgarian aliyah is already starting to go. The young ones, the Sabras who came aren't interested in the Bulgarian immigrants. For example, I came here in '48, I had children here, and I have grandchildren. The children hardly speak Bulgarian, but the Sabras, my grandchildren, not at all. You see notices that the old ones are already dead. This is the Bulgarian club, year after year the same people . . . the older ones are already gone. (Belo, p. 2)

CHAPTER 11

Folklore and Identity

The original intent of this study was, as seen in hindsight, a bit naive. It accepted the premise advanced by many folklorists that folklore is universally plentiful, that it has transformed itself and exists in profusion as great in modern industrial society as in peasant society. Thus, one can examine the folklore of an immigrant group and determine the transformations folklore underwent in the acculturation process, and utilize that information in analyzing the process itself.

One can see in the interview schedule (see Appendix C) that much time was devoted to the discussion of folklore in Bulgaria and Israel. Emphasis was placed on the informants' attitudes toward ethnic cultural expression, its transmission to the second generation, and preservation in the new country. In addition, participant observation was directed toward the documenting of folkloric behavior.

As consistent as were the responses which led to the formulation of the concept of components of identity, were the negative responses regarding ethnic folkloric behavior, its preservation and transmission. At first disturbing, these negative results led to an overall reassessment of research objectives, and the illumination of key areas of immigrant affect and attitudes. In other words, examining the reasons for the absence of ethnic folkloric expression and the negative or apathetic attitudes toward it was instructive in revealing the core of the ethnic identity of the Jews of Bulgaria in Israel. Accounting for this lack reshaped the parameters of this study.

The development of folkloristics in Israel from its origins in the 1940s until the present was traced in Part I. It was noted that the study of folklore in Israel has been a search for thriving traditions, almost exclusively among immigrants. Lacking thriving traditions, folklorists have been content to collect and analyze the remnants of once active repertoires. Because of the obsolescent theoretical basis of Israeli folkloristics until recently, negative findings cannot register as meaningful. They are regarded as the absence of folklore, rather than valuable evidence of changes in immigrant life and outlook. These findings are, however, of the greatest significance, for they help us to understand the acculturation process.

No attempt was made to elicit folklore in this study. I did not look for informants who were more proficient in folklore performance, nor did I attempt to jar folkloric memory during interviews, or serve as a catalyst for folkloric expressions during community events. Had I done this I am sure that passive repertoires could have been uncovered. This modus operandi, however, would not have served the purposes of this study. In fact, attitudes toward folklore proved as important as the folklore itself.

What follows is an examination of the role played by ethnic folkloric expression in four areas of social interaction, especially the nature of this expression and what it reveals about the ways in which the immigrants view themselves and their relationship to the larger society. These areas are language, holidays and celebrations, foodways, and performing arts.

Language

The Jews of Bulgaria have been linguistically bombarded over the past century. They emerged from the Ottoman period speaking Ladino at home and in their neighborhoods. For trade and official business they needed to know Turkish, Bulgarian and often Greek. Hebrew was taught to the boys sporadically for religious purposes.

The emergence of Bulgarian nationalism and independence reestablished the preeminence of the Bulgarian language in the country. Dormant for five centuries, Bulgarian was quickly re-equipped to serve as the official language. Soon all but the oldest Jews mastered the language, and for many it replaced Ladino as the first language at home. Ladino became the language of lower-class Jews, and only those informants with older parents or grandparents at home speak it fluently, though most can still understand it.

The schools of the Alliance Israelite Universelle in Bulgaria introduced French as the language of learning and culture for the Jews for a brief period. Several older informants had learned French in their youths. With the ouster of the Alliance and establishment of community controlled and administered schools, French soon disappeared from the Jewish neighborhoods. By 1920, its widespread instruction virtually ceased.

There was no equivalent in Bulgaria of the non-Zionist Jewish nationalist movements which existed in Eastern Europe. There was no movement to champion Ladino as the Bund championed Yiddish. As we have seen, Jewish nationalism in Bulgaria manifested itself in the Zionist movement, with Hebrew as its potent cultural symbol.

Hebrew was taught to all Jewish youngsters in school, and several societies were founded for its development.[1] Attempts to establish it as the first language of the Jews of Bulgaria failed. Nevertheless, it served as an important rallying point and, though not widely spoken, it was a focus of pride and identification. The rudiments of Hebrew gained in the Jewish schools of Bulgaria would certainly serve the immigrants well in Israel.

Bulgarian was the first language of the immigrant generation, but upon arrival in Israel it was largely abandoned and replaced with Hebrew. This was viewed as an ideological imperative by most immigrants, and competence in Hebrew is a source of pride and symbol of successful assimilation. Many informants whose Hebrew was less than fluent felt embarrassment at what they saw as a significant deficit in their "absorption." They often explained that in the early years they were so busy working to feed their families that they had no time for formal Hebrew training. Many felt that the hard times had interrupted their education.

What occurred, then, was a rapid linguistic shift from Ladino to Bulgarian to Hebrew. Most immigrants have some competence in all three. The least assimilated of the immigrants, the old folks who live in Jaffa, sometimes speak an ethnolect of Ladino, Turkish, Bulgarian, and Hebrew mixed together. Avraham Ofek, the Jerusalem sculptor, still enjoys going to Jaffa for an injection of Bulgarianness: "But you have to meet with the old folks, oh boy, you'll have a great time, you won't understand a thing; Turkish, Ladino, Bulgarian, they'll stick it in there, until you'll understand only one lonely Hebrew word" (Ofek, p. 7).

The Israeli-born generation usually knows little if any Bulgarian, and the third generation none at all. This was viewed as natural and proper by all my informants, and no attempt was made to encourage the use or learning of the language, either by the immigrants themselves or their children. When informants were asked whether they thought it important to preserve and pass on their language and culture, the responses were consistent—postal clerk, banker, kibbutznik, and professor all expressed similar sentiments:

> Under no circumstance. It would be a mistake to do that. That separates people, distances them. (Toliko, p. 16)

> It's not important to me. It was important to me to set them up here in Israel. My memories from Bulgaria are what remains

for them. But to influence them in that direction? No. (Eldzham, p. 20)

I don't see any point. I don't think that that has to be within any
particular framework. Each individual keeps his past in his own
little corner, but I don't think that there is any place because of
that for a revivalist organization. (Pasi, p. 21)

Nothing is important, actually it's not important to preserve anything, it happens naturally or it doesn't happen. Ideologically I
am opposed to the artificial preservation of tradition. There is
no such thing. (Cordova, p. 17)

There are no Bulgarian ethnic schools or courses in Bulgarian
language or culture in Israel. The Bulgarian library in Jaffa caters
exclusively to older immigrants who were unable to learn to read
Hebrew. Lili Avrahami meets many of the library's patrons in her role
as secretary of the old age home: "There's a library, some woman
brought books from home, and until today, the old Bulgarians, from
seventy years old up, go there all the time and read them a hundred
times" (Avrahami, p. 13).

Viska Uziel, who had trouble adapting to the decline in ideological
fervor after immigration, compared the atmosphere in the library in
its early days to the present nadir:

You should have seen and heard the library at one time. What a
life there was, intense. We used to, I don't know if you've heard
of him, there was an author, very very famous, Vaptsarov, who
was killed during the Fascist period, he was a Communist. We
used to have evenings with his poetry. Today if you go and try
to do something like that, who comes? I'm still young among
that group that studies there, all of the young people know
Hebrew and have no connection with Bulgarian culture and
sentiments. Of those who remain part come and part don't
come because it doesn't interest them and they're quite old.
(Uziel, p. 27)

The rapid decline of Bulgarian is evidenced in the fate of the
Bulgarian newspaper *Far*. Once a daily, it now appears twice a week.
Zhanti Zohar's son told the standard joke about the paper: "I want to
explain why they read it now. Everyone reads the Bulgarian paper in
the morning to see if he's not dead. You understand, if you see that you
don't appear there [in the obituaries], you're still alive" (Zohar, p. 3).

Nevertheless, the Bulgarian language can still function as a vehicle for ethnic interaction, even among the younger immigrants. Isidor Toliko, a firm believer in absorption, explained:

> Among ourselves we speak Bulgarian. It reminds us of the nostalgia of childhood. Among us are friends who came to Israel when they were very young. Their nostalgia is greater than mine. They are married to Israeli girls, speak Hebrew at home, but they enjoy it very much when we get together in a coffeehouse, they pop the cork of the past, and tell about how that was this way and this was that way, and that's it. (Toliko, p. 14)

Holidays and Celebrations

To both Bulgarian and non-Bulgarian Israelis, the Jews from Bulgaria were well-known for their secularism, and the notion of a religious Bulgarian is seen as being somewhat ludicrous:

> There is no such thing as a religious Bulgarian Jew. Very few were religious in the meaning of the word here. (Ofek, p. 7)

> On the Sabbath . . . there was a small group of older people who would visit the synagogue, but we were very far from that. Father used to say that if he went to synagogue the roof would fall in. (Uziel, p. 11)

> There are four types of Jews: Orthodox, religious, secular, and Bulgarian. (Nora Madjar, Plovdiv)

Several informants told of parents or grandparents who were religious and made them go to synagogue in their youth. Dan Ziyon, from Kibbutz Yad Mordekhai, was the son of the chief rabbi of Bulgaria. Not even these informants, who were brought up in religious families, continued religious observance after leaving home. Even the most religious Jews in Bulgaria cannot be compared with religious Jews elsewhere in Europe. The unique character of Bulgarian religiosity was described by Mikha Kalev and Lili Avrahami:

> It was a Jewry which was very open, very liberal, and there never was religious fanaticism. By the way, it was a shock for me to see Jews in their kaftans and earlocks and phylacteries, and all of those things which I saw when I was on the boat, that was a picture from another world. I know that there is not a single

Bulgarian in the National Religious Party. Not one Bulgarian, not one Jew from Bulgaria. (Kalev, p. 36)

In the school in which we learned Hebrew the books were from Poland. So there were all kinds of stories about Judaism we didn't quite understand. They didn't even know how to explain them to us. There were pictures with earlocks and *shtreymlakh* [traditional Eastern European Jewish fur hats] and we didn't know exactly what they were. We knew somewhere there were Jews like that, but I had never seen Jews like that except here in Israel when I came, in Jerusalem I saw them for the first time. So I don't really know if that Judaism, of Europe, had anything in common with us. (Avrahami, p. 10)

While worship in synagogue involved a minority of the Jewish population in Buglaria, this secularization did not diminish the observance of Jewish holidays and festivals in the home. Indeed, of all the affectual cultural areas discussed in the interviews, the holidays elicited the warmest memories, and continue to be the main focus of Bulgarian communal life in Israel.

The fact that the secularization of Jewish life in Bulgaria did not affect the celebration of religiously-based holidays may be explained in three ways. First, Jewish festivals are cultural as well as religious events (as are the festivals of most religions). Passover, for example, is celebrated by many secular Jews as a festival of freedom, marking the liberation of the children of Israel from bondage in Egypt, omitting the hand of God in the execution of the affair. As Bulgarian Jewry was a cultural as well as religious minority, both religious and secular Jews could continue to celebrate.[2] The few purely religious holidays, such as Rosh Ha-Shanah and Yom Kippur, suffered as a result of secularization. In Israel, they are observed by few Bulgarians. Lidia Baruh explained: "In Bulgaria there weren't many religious families.... However we kept the holidays, the holidays were very beautiful, if we had a holiday, it was a beautiful holiday, but the tradition to go and pray, no" (Baruh, p. 3).

Second, the wholesale adoption of Zionist ideology did not preclude the celebration of Jewish festivals. Although largely secular, the Zionist movement adapted much of Jewish symbolism to its cause, though Jewish history was seen in terms of human rather than supernatural forces. Furthermore, as the Jewish holidays are linked to the seasonal cycle in Israel, their meaning to Zionists is all the more potent. Thus, the celebration of Jewish holidays is sanctioned under the aegis of Zionist ideology, and they are national holidays in Israel.

Finally, most of the holidays are celebrated in the home, and are foci of family solidarity and community. They are accompanied by feasting, singing, and conversation. Many informants were enthusiastic in describing the joy of the celebrations at home, and songs were sung in both Bulgarian and Hebrew.

In addition to the Jewish holidays, most communities celebrated a purely Zionist holiday, Yom Ha-Shekel (Shekel Day). Yom Ha-Shekel was originally intended as a day to raise money for the Jewish National Fund, but it developed into much more. It became a nationalistic celebration of Jewish solidarity, which faced as much outward toward the Bulgarian majority as inward. Most cities and towns with a sizable Jewish population held marches down the main streets, which would include youth groups, scouts, bands, school groups, war veterans, and the community leadership. As was common in Bulgaria, all the youth and school groups would wear their distinctive uniforms and carry flags and banners. This public display of militant Jewish solidarity was unrivaled and unimaginable anywhere else in Europe. Of course, Yom Ha-Shekel was irrelevant in Israel, and with immigration passed one of the most overt symbols of community pride and solidarity for the Jews of Bulgaria. It passed without much regret, however, as the fulfillment of its own ideology, mizug galuyot.

Bulgarian Christian and national holidays were considered days off from work or school, little more. In Israel, the 9th of September, the day the Red Army entered Bulgaria in 1944, is celebrated by a few old Communists with a lecture or poetry reading in the Bulgarian library in Jaffa. Purim is celebrated in the Bulgarian clubs in Jaffa, usually with an Israeli band that knows some Bulgarian tunes. Fewer people go to synagogue in Israel than went in Bulgaria, and holidays are celebrated at home with family and friends in a way little different than that in which most secular Israelis celebrate. Haim Molkho echoed sentiments common to most of the informants: "If, for example, I would keep Yom Kippur in Bulgaria, here I don't. There I kept it to be a Jew. Here I am a Jew, and nobody cares if I keep the tradition" (Molkho, p. 15).

Holidays are a time when Bulgarian-Jewish culinary skills are at their finest, and it is in this realm that the culture of the Jews of Bulgaria manifests itself with the greatest persistance.

Foodways

The kitchen is the primary arena in Israel for the expression of Jewish-Bulgarian culture. It boasts a unique cuisine, a blending of Bulgarian, Turkish, and Spanish cooking, modified to comply with Jewish dietary law. It seems that the palates of the immigrants have been resistant to homogenization. The similarities in the produce available in Israel and Bulgaria have made the retention of Sephardic cuisine relatively easy.

When Bulgarian is no longer spoken in the home, when few physical vestiges of the old country remain, and contacts with other Bulgarians have become few, Sephardic dishes still appear on the table. Sephardic cookery has even become a symbol of Bulgarian ethnicity. Sammy Burekas is a fast-food chain serving Bulgarian specialties, and just as third and fourth generation American Jews will make Sunday pilgrimages to the few remaining kosher restaurants on the Lower East Side of Manhattan, so Bulgarian and non-Bulgarian Israelis make occasional pilgrimages to Jaffa to sample the food in the Bulgarian restaurants. Lili Avrahami described her feelings: "I get Bulgarian atmosphere in Jaffa. I do my shopping in Jaffa, they have Bulgarian cheese and so I go to Jaffa, take a walk around, meet everyone, hear some gossip, and with that I finish with my Bulgarianness" (Avrahami, p. 34).

Indeed, Sammy Burekas, Maccabi Jaffa, and the Tsadikov Choir are the only external symbols of Bulgarian ethnicity to remain in Israel. When asked, "Do you think there was a special Bulgarian-Jewish culture?" Avi Cordova, sociologist at Tel Aviv University, replied:

> There was. I assume these were transitional generations. But the culture was, on the one hand, very ethnic, but it's hard to say that the Jews had neighborhoods, and a traditional culture. In actuality, and here I'm speaking of the middle class, that class that existed among the Bulgarians which was totally involved in Bulgarian culture. My father, for example, spoke better Bulgarian than the Bulgarians themselves. And how shall I define the culture, it was expressed mainly in the foods. (Cordova, p. 12)

Performing Arts

The absence of unique folkloric forms of expression in other genres holds for the performing arts as well. In this area it is especially important to differentiate ethnic folklore from the folklore of ethnicity.[3]

It would be possible, if one were so inclined, for a researcher who wanted to emphasize the existence of ethnic folkloric behavior among the Jews of Bulgaria to find it. Acculturation does not erase the patterns imprinted in youth, nor does it destroy memory or nostalgia. Even among the most Israelicized of Bulgarian immigrants, phrases of Bulgarian will be spoken, songs occasionally sung or hummed, and stories from a common childhood told. The folklorist in search of expressions of ethnicity could lie in wait for such things, and probably come up with a respectable collection. This would not portray the reality of life in Israel for these immigrants, however, for when weighed against the norms of expression in daily life, these bits of ethnic folklore are limited and occasional. Furthermore, as we have noted, the attitude toward the cultivation and preservation of such expressions is largely negative, thus they would not represent an accurate picture of immigrant affect. Buko Lazarov, my oldest informant, spoke of the development of Israeli culture in halting Hebrew:

> What do we need Bulgarian culture for? We need Hebrew culture, native. I think that the culture will come from the kibbutzim, because they settled on the land. Look, if there is something original it's from the kibbutz. There is something that's not original, in every culture there is foreign influence. But that which is original is from the kibbutz. Our songs, our literature. Also our army. The best of our army comes from the kibbutzim, from the moshavim, from the workers, not from the bourgeoisie, from those scoundrels who only want to make money. (Lazarov, 27)

Ethnic folklore is very limited. When friends from the old country gather, a Bulgarian song will occasionally be heard. More frequently, Hebrew songs from the youth movements are sung. In fact, the culture of the youth movements is in general a more important source of "ethnic" folkloric expression than Bulgarian culture. Isidor Toliko described this paradox of ethnic folklore deriving from the new country rather than the old: "In the movement we would sing songs which we got from here. At home, the mothers and grandmothers would sing Sephardic songs, the sentimental romances. The young generation would sing Bulgarian songs, from the radio" (Toliko, p. 12).

Bulgarian folklore as such, that is, the folklore of the Bulgarian peasant, penetrated little into the lives of the urbanized, culturally autonomous Jews. Indeed, it was alien, as described by informants:

> Look, the truth is that the Jews in Bulgaria didn't particularly like the folk songs, they were a bit strange to them. But now it's a topic for memories. Now if some group arrives from Bulgaria, it's hard to find a place even if they sing folk songs. Now, for example, if I catch Bulgarian folk singing on the radio, I keep listening, but in Bulgaria if I heard those songs I'd switch stations. (Uziel, p. 28)

> Bulgarian folklore was very foreign to us. Here in Israel we are fascinated by performances, but it has no real basis. We didn't

absorb their folklore. That's a phenomenon which isn't unique to this ethnic group. Every ethnic group attempts to show, we are Romanians, so we dance Romanian dances, Argentinians, Argentinian dances. But to us it's quite distant, very distant. (Dagan, p. 17)

If we heard Bulgarian folk music, we would change the station on the radio and look for something else. Let's say it was folk music, which the peasants would sing. (Molkho, p. 11)

You remember that Molkho told you about Bulgarian music, that we used to turn off the radio when they played it in Bulgaria? Now when there are Bulgarian songs on the radio here in Israel translated into Hebrew, so we listen [laughs]. (Mrs. Molkho, p. 17)

The folklore of ethnicity retains some active expression. The Tsadikov Choir, founded in Bulgaria, was reestablished in Jaffa after immigration. Its repertoire is now largely Israeli, although a few Bulgarian songs are still included. Even these are sung mostly in Hebrew. Like the Maccabi Jaffa soccer club, most of the members of the Choir are now not of Bulgarian origin.

The most active locus of Bulgarian expression exists, naturally, in the least assimilated group, the old folks in Jaffa. The men still gather daily in the coffeehouse to be together, drink coffee, tea or Arak, and play cards, dominoes, and backgammon. They also get together in the clubs on holidays to celebrate.

Perhaps the most vivid picture of the nature of the ethnic identity and folkloric expression of the Jews of Bulgaria in Israel is drawn in the following descriptions of two public events. It should be remembered that those who attended, by their very presence, evidence a stronger link to the Bulgarian community than most immigrants from Bulgaria.

The following are excerpts from my fieldwork diary. The first describes an election rally for the Labor Party sponsored by the Union of Graduates of the Pioneering Zionist Youth Movements from Bulgaria. The second describes a performance by a small folk song-and-dance troupe from Bulgaria which was touring the country:

The conference was held at a large hall used by the Labor Party right off Dizengoff Circle. We weren't sure we had come to the right place because the poster in the arcade was in Romanian, and announced an almost identical rally for the Romanians.

As usual, at least 90 percent of the people were in their 50s to 70s and, as far as I could tell, all were Bulgarian (why would a non-Bulgarian want to attend such an event?). On the stage the Tsadikov Choir, youth division, was waiting. On both sides stood flags of Israel and the red flags of the Labor and Mapam parties.

Shimon Peres was to speak first, but as he had not yet arrived, the crowd was becoming restless, and the children's choir began to sing. Most of the songs were Israeli, most modern, with one Bulgarian song sung by the adult choir.

Finally Peres arrived to applause (not equal to that received by Victor Shemtov, Bulgarian-born chairman of Mapam), the choir was asked to sit, and Peres began his speech. He had to be brief as he was to speak at another rally that same evening. He had done his homework, and interspersed among the usual political remarks were comments on the history and positive nature of the Bulgarian aliyah—the same old cliches heard over and over about hard work, sweat of brow, honesty, up by the bootstraps—which were repeated by every speaker.

He was followed by about seven other speakers, active Bulgarians of one kind or another. Time dragged on, the crowd was restless, people began to leave. The emcee then cancelled the last couple of speakers, inciting a verbal duel on stage.

The actor Albert Cohen then got on stage and read a poem in Hebrew and Bulgarian by Simcho Isakov.[4] He was followed by an operetta-singing lady howling songs in Hebrew and Ladino. Finally, a man got on stage and held a sing-along, not of Bulgarian songs, but of Hebrew songs from the youth movements.

Some of those left sang and clapped, most sat and listened, until in mid-song he switched to Hatikvah, and that was that. The crowd mingled on the stairs and in the lobby—old home week. We wandered off toward Dizengoff Circle. (Fieldwork diary, June 20, 1981)

On Friday night I went to a performance of Aleko, the Bulgarian folk-dance-and song ensemble presently touring the country. It was in an old, rather degenerated movie house in Holon. The tickets cost fifty shekels, which is not cheap, but also not outrageous. There was quite a good crowd, almost filling the theater. The average age of the audience was about 60–70, with some younger and some older, but few under 40. I think I was the youngest by far.

Although most of the audience was Bulgarian, mostly Hebrew was spoken (in fact, almost exclusively). The troupe began with several Bulgarian folk songs and dances. Applause was polite. What really got the audience going was when the lead

singer, a woman, began singing popular schmalzy songs of the
30s and 40s. She obviously knew this would get them from past
experience, because she really schmiered it on. She encouraged
the audience to sing along, and many did. These popular hits of
youth brought a tear to many an eye. If there ever was a poignant example of the power of nostalgia over folklore for these
people, this was it. (Fieldwork diary, June 2, 1981)

The search for self has accompanied mankind since the development of human consciousness. From the earliest cave drawing up to
the latest philosophical treatise, the understanding of where one fits
in among others, what one's place might be within one's group and
without, has been a goal which seems to have seldom been fully
reached. The upheavals which have taken place in human society as
the result of the Enlightenment, Industrial Revolution, and technological and other social revolutions have, in many ways, made this
quest, at even the most elementary levels, more difficult than ever.
The creation of democratic societies with their ideologies of individual
rights and freedoms, racial, ethnic, and religious tolerance and equality, combined with the homogenizing influences of mass culture, make
the search for identity, which is in large part a function of the human
need to belong, that much more ephemeral.

Increasing numbers of the earth's people are being liberated from
the limitations of ascribed status, and enjoying the freedom and anguish of having the choice to achieve their status within the larger social
structure. One of the prices we pay for this freedom is a loss of certainty
as to who we are, and to whom we belong. Human beings seem to find it
difficult to derive much comfort from inclusion in large aggregates,
such as "the American people," or "humanity." We long for the warmth
and comfort of the solidary family, the clan, the tribe. Hence the periodic waves of collective root-seeking in modern industrialized nations,
as well as the bloodier inter-ethnic rivalries which consistently threaten
multi-ethnic states. Sometimes these searches are benign or constructive, at other times grotesque and horrific in the brutality of their
exclusion. In fact, by comparing the relative weight given to solidarity
versus exclusion in the ideology of identity of a given group, one may
be able to come to some conclusions regarding its malignancy. Yet here,
as in many other facets of identity, the relative weight ascribed to any
given measure of belonging tends to vary as a result of changes in the
wider contexts within which identity is formulated.

Because of this universal quest for self, for belonging, and its
poignant manifestations in modern multicultural societies, social scientists have made the study of identity one of the central themes in their
fields. Yet in open societies, such as contemporary America or Israel,

objective, quantifiable data on identity are hard to come by in all but the most unassimilated minorities and ethnic groups. For the majority of second, third, and fourth generations of immigrants, matters of ethnic identity tend to be subtle, fragmented, and manifest only in the area of linguistic, artistic, and culinary expression; in other words, identity is to be explored in the realm of folklore and sentiment.

For the Jews of Bulgaria who settled in Israel, this indeed proved to be the case; their sentiments toward their old and new homes, that is, their sense of self and identity vis-à-vis national origins and allegiances, were clearly manifested in their lore. Yet it was not only their sense of identity which was to be found in their lore, but the outcome of their history as well, for without an understanding of the recent events in the history of Bulgarian Jewry, the folklore would remain a puzzle. And it is in this realm that this research happened upon a remarkable symbiosis between history, ethnography, and folklore. All proved interdependent, and each helped inform the others.

With emphasis in Israeli social science almost exclusively focused on "exotic" or "problematic" immigrant groups, the study of an apparently well-adjusted and successful aliyah can teach us much about the social, economic, and cultural conditions which may either inhibit or assist in adjustment to life in the new country. For example, if we compare the recent influx of immigrants from the nations of the former Soviet Union with the immigration to Bulgaria, we may make several general observations.

In the material realm, both groups are European, economically stable, largely urban, and educated. Yet it is in the affective realm that there are significant differences. Whereas the Jews from Bulgaria had a high degree of Jewish identity, group solidarity, and Zionist commitment, most of the recent Soviet immigrants lack all of these. There are other differences, such as the relative sizes of the two groups, recent history, and social, economic, and political conditions in Israel during the period of their respective immigrations. As these conditions change, the reception of various immigrant groups changes as well. A case in point is the recent aliyah from Ethiopia.

The religiosity of the Ethiopian Jews has certainly been problematic for the Israeli Rabbinate, but it would have served as a social impediment during the early years of the state, when secular, socialist Zionism was the ideology of the ruling elite. With the rise to power of Israel's religious minority, however, and increasing value placed on traditional religious belief, important avenues have been opened to the Jews of Ethiopia which do not require the crippling devaluation of religious belief and practice, as was the case for traditional immigrant groups during the mass waves of immigration of the 1950s. It is, as of yet, too early to determine the long-term consequences of these changes, but they will certainly have an effect on the way in which more recent immigrants adapt to life in a still rapidly changing Israel.

In the case of the Bulgarian aliyah, this study has traced and analyzed various avenues in which there was a beneficial match between what Bulgarian Jewry had to offer and what Israel needed, and vice versa. This was an historical, social, and cultural fit that resulted in a positive image and a positive identity, both emically and etically.

At the time the gates to immigration were opened in Israel, Bulgaria opened her gates to emigration. At a time when housing in Jaffa was abandoned, the Jews of Bulgaria needed roofs over their heads. At a time when secular pioneering Zionism was the national ideology and passion, the immigrants were deeply ingrained with its message. At a time when adaptability and physical labor were required to build the country, they came inured to hard work and discomfort by years of war, displacement, and forced-labor battalions. At a time when privation was the norm in Israel, it had become old hat to the Jews from Bulgaria.

The success of the Bulgarian aliyah has become a cliché in Israel. Thus, in patriotic hindsight, it is easy to minimize the hardships the immigrants suffered, especially during the early years of the state. That the Bulgarian aliyah was "successful" should not imply that its experience was anything less than harrowing. For years, well into the 1950s, immigrants lived in inadequate housing without running water or electricity. Food was often scarce and work monotonous, backbreaking, and underpaid. There were inadequate health and education services, and even the rudimentary framework constructed for later aliyot was not in place. But their hardships are part of the mosaic of identity as well. For the Jews of Bulgaria in Israel, biography and history combine to tell the story of a people struggling to find meaning in the new nation they call home.

The old Turkish clock tower, one of the hallmarks of old Jaffa. Illustration by Cheri Haskell.

Epilogue

When I began the initial research for this study in 1974, I thought I would be able to write the final chapter on the topic. Over 90 percent of the Jews of Bulgaria had emigrated to Israel, there was no evidence of the survival of Jewish culture or community in Communist Bulgaria, and no evidence of significant ethnic identification among the children and grandchildren of the immigrants in Israel. It appeared to me that the Bulgarian community in Israel would dissolve into the emerging Israeli society, and the approximately three thousand Jews then thought to have remained in Bulgaria would assimilate and disappear as a distinguishable minority. Certainly the book on large-scale aliyas from Bulgaria was closed forever.

The dramatic fall of Communism in Eastern Europe led to a reawakening of Jewish consciousness in Bulgaria, as well as a resumption of aliya. Indeed, these unexpected events have caused a reevaluation of assumptions in all fields dealing with Eastern Europe, and made much of the current literature obsolete. In our case, too, a new chapter needed to be written.

Bulgaria has rarely been at the forefront of political and social change, and here too she has been among the last to change, led by her big Russian brother. She was the last to be freed from Ottoman rule, with Russia's intervention. She was brought under the Communist yoke by the Soviet Union, and she was among the last to free herself from totalitarian oppression. It was not until the winter of 1990–1991, after all other Eastern Block countries had ended Communist rule, that large crowds took to the streets of Sofia to demand change. During that icy January, over two hundred thousand Bulgarians took to the streets of Sofia to put an end to their present system, exchanging the "Internationale" for the Beatle's "All We Need Is Love." Although debate is common as to whether those presently in power have done much more than change their names from Communist to Socialist, totalitarian rule has ended, and the country is floundering somewhere between the old system and and an undefined and uncertain new political and economic structure.

The loss of a guaranteed Soviet market for Bulgarian products and of discounted Soviet supplies of fuel and other essential commodities, along with general economic confusion and dislocation, has hit Bulgarians hard. Although the bread lines and hunger of the first post-Communist year have eased, the standard of living has plunged from already low pre-1990 levels, and people on fixed incomes are unable to make ends meet. This very difficult economic situation has had a profound effect on Jewish identity in Bulgaria.

In the summer of 1992 I returned to Israel to speak with new immigrants from Bulgaria, and to Bulgaria to speak with Jews emerging from forty-five years of repression. I traveled with my father, who was born in Bulgaria and left at age fifteen in 1932. We roamed throughout both countries, talking to people of various walks of life, visiting institutions, trying to make some sense out of a rapidly changing reality. The observations I make here are not the result of systematic research, but I hope they will give the reader a sense of general trends and attitudes, often conflicting, of the resurgence of Jewish life in Bulgaria.

The most striking feature of this reawakening of a dormant identity is that it revolves exclusively around the official organizations, and is almost entirely absent from the personal and family sphere. Unlike the Soviet Union and other Eastern Block countries, Bulgaria had no clandestine Jewish movement under Communist rule. There were no secret prayer meetings or Hebrew classes, few refuseniks or dissidents. This may be due to three factors: the small number of Jews remaining after the mass exodus of 1948–1950, the nature of those left behind, and the character of Jewish society before the advent of Communist rule. Estimates of those who remained in Bulgaria after the mass emigration range from three to five thousand, or about 10 percent of the total Jewish population. The concentration of Jews in any given town, then, was quite small, and the effect of the departure of 90 percent of the community was devastating for the retention of any kind of communal life.

Some of those who remained were committed Communists and supporters of the new regime. Some were married to Bulgarians who were unwilling to leave. Some were assimilated and engaged in Bulgarian national life as writers, artists, and professionals. Some were elderly and without families.

Finally, the lack of traditional Jewish religious identification prior to the exodus, a lack which has been discussed extensively in previous chapters, dictated the way in which this identity would manifest itself. It may be assumed that those few who remained in Bulgaria identified least with the Jewish community as a whole. Thus, they lacked both the motivation and the knowledge to find in Jewish tradition a source of strength in maintaining an independent existence. In fact, since Zionism replaced traditional Judaism as the primary ideology of Bulgarian Jewry, the mass exodus to Zion provided its ultimate fulfillment. Those who stayed behind, then, in a sense rejected their Jewish identity as it was currently constituted. With neither Judaism nor Zionism as the foundation of identity, all they had left was a notion of solidarity with the Bulgarian people in the struggle against fascism. It is easy to understand, then, why at least 90 percent of their children married Bulgarians. The lack of knowledge and understanding of even the most basic elements of Jewish tradition is startling today among both Jews remaining in Bulgaria, as well as recent Bulgarian immigrants to Israel.

The only official Jewish organization permitted to function under Communist rule was the Social Cultural and Educational Association of the Jews in the People's Republic of Bulgaria, located in a large, square building on the corner of 50 Stamboliski Boulevard in Sofia. Its main function was to house a permanent exhibition celebrating an exaggerated role for the Communists in saving the Jews of Bulgaria from the Nazi concentration camps. It also published a yearbook containing a variety of articles on Jewish history, language, and culture in Bulgaria. Today, the Beit Ha-'Am (National Home) remains the focus of Jewish identification and activity in the country.

The name of the central organization has been changed to the Organization of the Jews of Bulgaria "Shalom," but much of its leadership remains the same. The building now houses the offices of all of the organizations involved in Jewish life in the country: the Women's International Zionist Organization (WIZO), the Maccabi Sports Organization, Youth (World Union of Jewish Students), the Jewish Agency, a Sunday school attended by approximately one hundred eight-to-sixteen-year-olds (Wednesdays, Fridays, and Sundays), a chamber orchestra, choir, bridge club, and restaurant/social club. It sponsors the reestablished weekly *Evreiski Vesti* (Jewish News, the former Jewish Communist organ), ten-day summer camps for youth, and organizes study tours to Israel. It is also the address for Jews hoping to reclaim property confiscated during and after the Second World War.

There is another Jewish organization, Zion, which is anti-Communist and in opposition to Shalom. It is reported to have approximately fifty members, is mostly politically-oriented, and as far as we could tell has no office and sponsors no regular activities. We were unable to contact any of its members during our stay.

Fifty Stamboliski Boulevard has become a beehive of activity. Besides the Sunday school and youth groups, Jews come to the various offices to seek solutions to the widest variety of problems. This is understandable, as the state bureaucracies and economy have broken down, people all over the country are seeking personal, ethnic, and religious connections to external agencies and organizations through which they can receive aid. They come to get information on Israel and aliyah, property distribution, travel and educational opportunities, and community holiday celebrations. Foreign Jewish aid is channeled through the building, and pensioners may receive supplements to their thirteen dollars of monthly government allowance.

I spent several days at the Beit Ha-'Am and was impressed by the level of apparent energy of the place, as people raced down the halls with briefcases and file folders, rushing back and forth to offices and meetings. Yet the most striking feature of the place was the seeming lack of individual initiative and spontaneity. All activity gave the impression of having been organized and presented from above. This impression was reinforced in discussions with three Israelis; a couple from a kibbutz movement in Israel who were completing a year in Bulgaria with Project Arevim of the World Union of Jewish students, and a teacher from Israel whose mother was born in Bulgaria and decided to devote a sabbatical to teaching Hebrew in the country.

These three volunteers were frustrated by what they saw as a lack of initiative on the part of those seeking their assistance. They complained of having to organize every detail of programs and activities for the community, and the failure of people to follow up on or continue their programs without direct supervision. They were also upset by the "complaining" attitude they found among many Bulgarians, both Jews and gentiles, who, they said, attributed all of their difficulties and shortcomings to forces outside of their control. They also voiced a complaint I heard from many of those attempting to help the community, both in Bulgaria and in Israel; that much of the interest in identifying oneself as a Jew at the present time is the result of economic rather than spiritual or communal motivation. Indeed, many Bulgarians are seeking outside intervention in alleviating their plight. We heard this theme repeated throughout Bulgaria, as people hoped that Soviet aid would be replaced by Western. Talk of "biznis" was everywhere, and people seemed to feel that one could get rich simply by making the right deal rather than producing the right product, a lesson most likely learned from the U.S. government with its encouragement of hostile takeovers, junk bonds, and corporate bailouts.

This attitude is not surprising, considering the relationship of dependence fostered by the former Communist government, and the Ottoman Empire before it. Individual initiative, independent thinking, and creativity were indeed discouraged under these governments, and it is no wonder that it is difficult for Bulgarians to learn them today. In the case of the Jews, this attitude is reinforced in a number of ways, including assistance from the Joint Distribution Committee and other agencies, stipends for students and new immigrants equal to several years of work at Bulgarian salaries, and emissaries from abroad who plan and organize activities. Passivity, dependence, and timidity are all legacies of Bulgarian history, but as one Israeli volunteer put it, "if they blame one more thing on five hundred years of Turkish oppression, I'm going to explode!" Another suggested that the best thing Jews could do to aid the Bulgarian Jewish community was to stop helping them and let them figure it out for themselves.

Yet there are wonderful bright spots throughout the country, as mostly young people work to reclaim a history, culture and tradition until very recently totally unknown to them. The youth counselor in Sofia works to organize Sunday school, outings, and camps for the children, providing an organized celebration to learn about each holiday. Although still bewildered by the strangeness of it all, children study Hebrew language and songs, and dance Israeli dances. In Plovdiv, the second largest Jewish community, with about five hundred Jews, two young volunteer teachers, with little institutional support, are determined to share what knowledge they have gained in a year of intensive self-teaching with the children of the community. About thirty children of all ages come to the Jewish center twice a week for classes and games. Even gentile children ask to come; games, singing, and dances are not part of the Bulgarian school curriculum, but are used extensively in Jewish education.

The decline of Jewish religious tradition which began with the end of Ottoman rule, or perhaps even as far back as the debacle of Shabbatai Zevi, was completed during forty-five years of Communism. The revival of Jewish life in Bulgaria has had little religious impact, despite the public celebration of holidays. Friday night services at the central synagogue in Sofia are held in a small chapel off the side of the main sanctuary, which has been under "renovation" for decades. On the Friday evening we attended services, there were about fifteen men and fifteen women, mostly in their fifties or older. Afterwards, the restaurant/club in the Beit Ha-'Am was filled with over fifty young people, from their teens to forties, eating, smoking, and drinking in a manner reminiscent of no particular Jewish celebration. In Plovdiv, the synagogue has been closed since the 1960s, and there has been no apparent need or attempt to re-open it. There is little interest in reclaiming the synagogues for worship, but a great deal of excitement about other Jewish property. Plans are under way to reclaim Jewish holdings throughout the country which were confiscated first by the fascists and later by the Communists. These properties are worth millions of dollars, and many speculate that one of the reasons the number of people currently claiming to be Jewish in Bulgaria has reached about six thousand is that many hope this reclaimed real estate will be distributed among the Jewish community as a whole (see Table 2).

One reason the economic situation in Bulgaria has hit Jews particularly hard is that the majority live in the cities and have no family in the villages. When times get hard and food is scarce, many urban dwellers go to relatives in the countryside where food and shelter are more readily available. Many Jews are also employed in the arts, which have suffered from the lack of government funds. Finally, older people on fixed pensions make a large part of the Jewish population, especially as more and more young people are moving to Israel.

Between 1990 and 1991, one to two thousand Jews have immigrated to Israel. Although precise statistics are not available, informants stated that many have returned, and of those quite a few have gone back to Israel again in the face of the difficult economic situation in Bulgaria. Just as among the Bulgarian Jewish population as a whole, over 90 percent of the Jewish immigrants are married to non-Jews, and a large percentage are also the children of one Jewish parent or even grandparent. Both the immigrants themselves and those dealing with immigrants agree that, unlike the mass immigration of 1948–1950, the primary impetus is economic.

The Ikhud 'Olei Bulgariyah (Union of Bulgarian Immigrants), moribund and fading during the period of my primary fieldwork in the early 1980s, has risen from the ashes on the breeze of the new aliyah. Physically, it has moved from the dingy, cramped office it inhabited near the Central Bus Station in Tel Aviv, back to its roots in Jaffa in a bright, air-conditioned office on Shderot Yerushalayim, the heart of the old Bulgarian community.

Like the reawakened Beit Ha-'Am in Sofia, the Ihud has found a new breath of life, if only temporary. Both immigrants and Bulgarian guest-workers come to the office with the widest possible variety of questions and problems: housing, work, permits, visas, insurance. All problems are dealt with or referred by the small staff and volunteers, mostly veterans of the old aliyah. Lili Avrahami, for years the heart of the Ikhud, has been replaced as secretary by a young woman herself recently arrived fro Plovdiv. Yet Lili continues to provide aid, advice, and solace to the new immigrants lost not only in the new country, but among a new people to which only half of them belong, and those often only nominally.

At breakfast the day after our arrival in Israel, my father and I discovered that our waitress, a charming woman in her thirties, had arrived from Plovdiv a year and a half before. A Bulgarian married to a Jew, she already had a good command of conversational Hebrew, spoke of her son who was entering the army, and of the apartment she and her husband had just purchased with a low-interest government loan in Ashdod. She had been a nurse in Bulgaria, and was to enter an eight-month retraining course to obtain her Israeli nursing license. Yet she complained of loneliness, not fitting in, lack of friends, and the hardships of life in her new home.

Indeed, even though most of the new immigrants we spoke to had jobs and apartments, and many had even purchased new cars using their immigrant deduction on import taxes, they almost all complained of the difficulty of adjusting to life in Israel, for various reasons. One young woman, an actress in Bulgaria married to a Jew, could not comprehend a country where buses would not run on the Sabbath: "This is the twentieth century!" she exclaimed. As Lili would often say, "these are not Jews, not the Jews we knew." Although referring to those who were Jews by birth, in fact, half the new immigrants are non-Jewish spouses, making her statement not only metaphorically true, but often ethnically accurate.

I cannot say with certainty that this, any more than the last, is truly the final chapter in the history of the Jews of Bulgaria. History in general, and Jewish history in particular, has a way of contradicting certitude. Yet I do not see the events described in this epilogue as fundamentally altering my earlier conclusions. The numbers are too small, their impact too minimal, and their content too diluted to alter the trend toward ethnic entropy. Without a significant influx of Jews into Bulgaria from elsewhere, I do not believe a grass-roots resurgence of Jewish life there will last for more that a short time, especially if economic incentives to Jewish identification are removed.

As for the new immigrants, some will stay, but as conditions in Bulgaria improve over time, many will return. Here again, the small numbers will have little effect on the fading away of a distinct Bulgarian cultural element in the mosaic of Israeli ethnicity.

Appendix A
Statistics

Table 1. Immigration to Israel from Bulgaria by Year.

1919–1948	7,057
1948–1951	37,260
1952–1960	1,680
1961–1964	460
1965–1971	334
1972–1979	118
1980–1984	48
1985–1989	132
1989	85

Source: Statistical Abstract of Israel, 1990 (Jerusalem: Israel Central Bureau of Statistics, 1990).

Table 2. Age and Sex Distribution by Geographical Region— Bulgaria, 1992.

City	0–6		6–12		12–18		18–35		35–65		65+		Total
	M	F	M	F	M	F	M	F	M	F	M	F	
Blagoevgrad	1	1	1	1	3	2	2	3	3	2	5	2	26
Burgas	4	6	11	7	7	6	18	21	15	12	31	34	172
Varna	8	8	15	17	13	15	31	34	34	41	42	51	309
Vidin	2	1	2	2	1	2	6	8	5	8	10	13	60
Dupnitza	8	9	11	8	6	9	16	14	21	19	24	30	175
Kyustendil	3	3	4	6	4	5	10	11	12	12	14	16	100
Lom	—	1	7	5	1	1	6	7	5	8	7	8	56
Pazardjik	2	1	2	2	—	1	5	5	5	5	5	7	40
Pleven	6	8	8	7	7	7	15	16	16	15	19	22	146
Plovdiv	20	32	15	28	33	39	30	34	169	190	90	131	811
Russe	—	4	5	5	5	9	22	20	40	39	25	36	210
Samokov	1	1	1	—	2	2	4	3	3	3	2	2	24
Sliven	2	1	3	4	3	3	6	7	8	5	11	9	62
Sofia	60	63	54	61	61	70	309	284	611	682	421	460	3136
Stara Zagora	4	4	9	8	4	5	13	13	13	12	10	11	106
Haskovo	3	3	4	3	3	4	9	6	11	12	14	16	88
Shumen	2	1	1	1	3	2	3	4	2	3	4	5	31
Jambol	9	6	10	13	11	9	13	11	20	22	19	20	163
Total	135	153	163	8	167	191	518	501	993	1090	753	873	5715

Source: Unofficial Jewish Agency survey of individuals identifying themselves as Jewish, June 1992.

Appendix B
List of Informants

The following is a list of key informants, in alphabetical order, with a brief description of each informant as of 1982.

LILI AVRAHAMI. Born in Pazardzhik in 1924, her father was a lawyer and mother a housewife. She came to Israel in 1944 and worked as a prison guard. She is divorced, has two sons, lives in an apartment in Bat Yam, and works in the office of the Bulgarian old age home in Jaffa.

LIDIA BARUH. Born in Vidin in 1926, she came to Israel in 1952. Lidia has two daughters and lives in a small house with her husband in Tel Giborim, near the beauty shop which she runs.

HAIM BELO. Born in Sofia in 1928, he came to Israel in 1948, and has worked as a truck driver and driving instructor. Now retired, he spends his days at the Good Life Club. Haim's wife owns a beauty shop, and they have three children and seven grandchildren.

AVI CORDOVA. Born in Sofia in 1938, Avi left Bulgaria with his family and came to Israel at age ten. He is now assistant professor of sociology at Tel Aviv University, and lives in Ramat Aviv. He is unmarried, and his parents live in Jaffa.

SHLOMO DAGAN. Born in Sofia in 1923, son of a leather merchant, Shlomo came to Israel in 1947 with his group as a leader in the Zionist youth movement. He settled on Kibbutz Yad Mordekhai, where he lives with his wife.

YOSEF ELDZHAM. Born in Kyustendil in 1902, Yosef's family moved to Sofia in 1908. He then lived in Pazardzhik for twelve years, Plovdiv for nine years, and Sofia for twenty years, moving frequently for his work with a large bank. Yosef's father was a sandal maker, and Yosef married in Bulgaria and moved to Israel in 1949 with his wife and daughter.

MIKHA KALEV. Born in Plovdiv in 1923, the son of a laborer. An activist in the Zionist movement, Mikha came to Israel in 1947 and settled with his group at Yad Mordekhai, where he lives with his wife.

BUKO LAZAROV. Born in Kyustendil in 1900, Buko has spent his life as a buyer in the tobacco industry, but hopes to write on the Jews of Bulgaria. He came to Israel with his wife in 1948, is now widowed and lives in a small house in Tel Baruh.

HAIM MOLKHO. Born in Plovdiv in 1927, Haim came to Israel with his youth movement group in 1946 and settled with his wife on Kibbutz Urim, where he is one of the few Bulgarian members left today.

AVRAHAM OFEK. Born in Burgas in 1935, Avraham's family moved to Sofia in 1937, to Ferdinand (Mikhailovgrad) in 1942, then back to Sofia in 1945 where they lived until they immigrated to Israel in 1949. His father was a small merchant and his mother a housewife. Avraham lives in Jerusalem where he earns his livelihood as a sculptor, and is married to a Sabra.

CHEPO PASI. Born in Plovdiv in 1923 to a lower class family, Chepo was a Zionist activist. He arrived in Israel in 1947, and married in Yad Mordekhai in 1952, where he lives today. He is head of the kibbutz electronics workshop.

ISIDOR TOLIKO. Born in 1907 in Nikopol, Isidor was the son of a grain merchant. He moved to Ruschuk at age twenty-five where he worked as a clerk in a transport office. He married in 1933 and came to Israel in 1948. He tried to found an agricultural settlement until 1954, when he took a job as a postal clerk. He is now retired, teaches yoga, and lives with his wife in an apartment in Holon.

DAN ZIYON. Son of the chief rabbi of Bulgaria, Dan was born in Sofia in 1921. His parents came from Solonika. He was sent to the Samovit camp with his family during the World War II. They left in 1947, and Dan joined Kibbutz Yad Mordekhai, where he lives with his wife.

YAEL ZIYON. Wife of Dan, Yael was born in Stara Zagora in 1929, daughter of a small merchant. Yael arrived in Israel in 1947 and joined Kibbutz Yad Mordekhai with her husband.

VISKA UZIEL. Born in Pleven in 1930, Viska was brought up by institutions and family members after her mother died. She came to Israel in 1949. She is widowed, has two married daughters, works in an office, and lives in an apartment in Bat Yam.

ZHANTI ZOHAR. Born in Sofia in 1921, Zhanti's father was a salesman, his mother a seamstress. She came to Israel in 1948 and lives with her husband in Tel Aviv.

Appendix C
Two Interviews

The following are transcripts of two complete interviews. They are provided to show the reader how the interviews were conducted. The interviews were conducted in Hebrew and Bulgarian, and translated into English by the author. In the transcripts that follow, "G" designates the author; interviewees are designated by their first initial. The first interview is with a member of a kibbutz, the second with a denizen of the Bulgarian club in Jaffa. These individuals represent opposite ends of the acculturation spectrum; most Jews from Bulgaria lie somewhere in between.

Chepo Pasi, July 16, 1981, 1:00 P.M., Kibbutz Yad
Mordekhai electronics workshop

> G: Where were you born in Bulgaria?
> C: I was born in Plovdiv, in 1923, in the month of January.
> G: Until which year did you live in Plovdiv?
> C: I lived in Plovdiv until 1947.
> G: In what type of neighborhood did you live in Plovdiv?
> C: In Plovdiv I lived in the Marasha neighborhood, which was a neighborhood in which there were many Jews, and it was in the heart of the Jewish neighborhood next to the Jewish school and the synogogue.
> G: Were there also non-Jews who lived there?
> C: There were also non-Jews but their number was very small.
> G: And were there relations between you and your family and non-Jews in Plovdiv?
> C: Very little. We had neighbors with whom we had good relations, but not many.
> G: And who lived at home?
> C: Father and mother, two other brothers and a sister.
> G: And did your grandmother and grandfather live elsewhere?
> C: No, when I was born they were no longer alive.

G: Did you marry in Bulgaria or in Israel?

C: No, I got married in Israel.

G: What did your father do?

C: My father was a laborer, and he worked primarily in the export of eggs. There was, actually you can't call it an industry, but an occupation which was concentrated mainly in the hands of the Jews, and they were involved in the export of eggs to Germany and Europe, and he worked in one of the warehouses where they collected the eggs.

G: And your mother?

C: My mother was a housewife.

G: Did you go to the Jewish school?

C: I studied in the Jewish school and afterwards continued in high school.

G: Was the Jewish school of the community or of the Alliance or what?

C: No, when I went the Alliance wasn't there, because among Bulgarian Jews there was a struggle against the Alliance, and they closed the schools of the Alliance, and from that time they were Zionist schools.

G: Belonging to which . . .

C: To the community, and I studied there for seven years, that was the framework of the Jewish school. Four years of elementary school, and three years preparation for high school.

G: The high school was government-run.

C: Yes, government-run. I studied in a government-run high school.

G: In which year did you finish high school?

C: I finished just before the outbreak of the war, in '41. I finished and took my matriculation exam in '41.

G: The Fascists were already in power.

C: Yes they already were, there were already restrictions imposed on the Jews, but the war between Germany and the Soviet Union hadn't begun, in July the war began, a few weeks after we finished our studies.

G: What happened to you and your family during the period of the war and the Fascists?

C: During the Fascist period my father stopped working, he was an old man and that affected him badly. There was a kind of momentum in his work. Old people like him who stop working begin to fall apart. A year or two after that he died.

G: Did they force him to stop work?

C: There was no other choice because there was . . .

[interruption]

G: You were telling me about what happened to your family.

C: In the meantime, my two brothers died.

G: Not from anything connected with . . .

C: No. Actually there is something which is related to it. One of my brothers died from a kidney disease when he had to come to Plovdiv. The other brother, all of his friends had finished army service, and there was a round of *aliyah*, and they had already made *aliyah*, and he went into a depression, and he had to go and serve in the Bulgarian army, and he killed himself. That's not the central reason but was one of the contributing factors. I had to provide for the family in spite of the fact that I didn't have a profession, but they say that I have good hands, I worked in electronics. I would fix electric appliances for acquaintances and neighbors, because I couldn't study further because the regime which came to power after the Germans entered Bulgaria imposed a curfew, and the Jews were allowed outside only during specific hours during the day. And so I couldn't go to school. So I had to provide for the family in that way.

After that I was able to work in a workshop which gave me a good living, both for me and my family. And in that way we made it through the war. All those who had finished school were conscripted in the work camps. Not only those. They conscripted them in the work camps, and in '41 I went to the camp. We worked during the summer months. We paved roads. Or repaired railway tracks. In the winter we would return home. In the summer they would conscript us again. The battalions were made up of Jews with Bulgarian officers. And that's how I got through the war years.

G: What were the conditions in the camp where you served?

C: In the camp in which I was for four years, every year it was different. But mostly it was hard forced labor, especially when there were sadistic officers. And in order for them to look good in the eyes of their superiors, they pressured the Jews to work a great deal. And it was clear that it was the result of pressure and punishment, and in addition those years were difficult: there was no food in Bulgaria, and for many months there was food of only one kind, and that was beans. Six months I worked on beans in one of the camps. There was also malaria, and to a man we were sick perhaps like in Auschwitz. They used to give drugs which would weaken a man. In the camp about which I'm telling you now, where there was malaria in southern Bulgaria, the conditions were very hard.

G: Do you think that that was out of the ordinary? Because I've heard from several people that they actually enjoyed the camps.

C: That camp, as far as the conditions which we created; we had a choir, and there were all kinds of activities, and from that point of view we tried as hard as we could to create some kind of life within the camp, but as far as the conditions themselves, it was very hard.

G: And what did you do after the war?

C: I worked in the trade I began during the war. But most of my work was in Zionist activity. I hardly looked at my work in the shop. I left it to my sister, and she took care of opening the shop, and I was active in Ha-Shomer Ha-Za'ir.

G: Did you begin to be active in Ha-Shomer Ha-Za'ir only after the war?

C: No, I was a member before the war. Before the outbreak of the war, all of the leadership went to Israel, and I had to take over . . .

G: In which year did you come to Israel?

C: In '47. Because they were afraid that the Nazis would enter Bulgaria, the leadership was afraid that they'd be sent to the camps, so the leadership decided that younger men would take over the management of things in case something like that would happen. So I was a member of the leadership, in spite of the fact that at that time the movement was split up, it hardly was able to exist, and there were centers in various cities.

G: You were able to continue to work during the war, and start a shop, and after the war continue to make a living, so why did your family leave Bulgaria?

C: The main reason was ideological. The reason was that my family was a Zionist family. My brother was one of the editors of the Zionist newspapers, *Ha-Shofar*. He was one of the newspaper's editors, and was very active in Ha-Shomer Ha-Za'ir. My other brother was active in Maccabi. So that the entire family was a Zionist family, and the reason for *aliyah* was ideological.

G: You said that one brother was in Maccabi and you were in Ha-Shomer Ha-Za'ir, and the third also, why did one brother go to Maccabi and you to Ha-Shomer Ha-Za'ir, was it an ideological difference or what?

C: In general at a young age ideological differences weren't very important, and people go more according to where their friends are. It's clear that later, all of those things take on an ideological significance. I couldn't be a General Zionist. The socialist elements which were part of Ha-Shomer Ha-Za'ir intrigued me more.

G: And your brother, why Maccabi?

C: His friends were in Maccabi, and his group of friends began to slowly take on elements of Ha-Shomer Ha-Za'ir, and they were in Ha-Maccabi Ha-Za'ir afterwards. But many of them had a Marxist orientation as well, and became leftists.

G: Which languages did you speak at home?

C: At home we spoke Ladino. Among my brothers we spoke Bulgarian. Usually, with the older generation, with the older people, we spoke Ladino, and among the brothers I spoke Bulgarian.

G: Do you think that the generation of your parents was the last generation to speak Ladino daily?

C: Yes.

G: And in which language did you feel more comfortable?

C: I felt more comfortable in Bulgarian. There was a hesitance to speak Ladino. In general the younger people felt embarassed to speak Ladino, and they felt that in the spirit of the times they should speak Bulgarian.

G: Were your parents traditional, religious?

C: My father, you can't say, like all of the Jews of Bulgaria actually. He would go to synagogue on Yom Kippur.

G: But not on the Sabbath . . .

C: No, he didn't keep any of the particulars.

G: And which holidays did you celebrate at home?

C: All of the holidays. All of the holidays and in a beautiful way. Passover, Hanukah, Yom Kippur.

G: But that was in the synagogue.

C: Yom Kippur was in the synagogue. Passover was celebrated within the extended family, not only our family, but with the families of my mother's brothers, the families of my father's brothers. But we celebrated all of the holidays.

G: This is a slightly more theoretical question. Do you think that Judaism was an important part of your Jewish identity in Bulgaria?

C: Without a doubt.

G: And you thought of yourself as a Zionist.

C: Yes.

G: Ha-Shomer Ha-Za'ir, you were active I understand.

C: Yes.

G: And when did it occur to you seriously to make *aliyah*?

C: I always saw the continuation of my life, and of my friendships in Ha-Shomer Ha-Za'ir in *aliyah*. When the war broke out, opportunities for *aliyah* appeared very far off, I entered a period of very deep depression. It wasn't a matter of pressure from the war, it was my worldview.

G: Did your parents also have a Zionist worldview?

C: Theoretically.

G: And do you think that if the Fascists hadn't taken power they would have come to Israel in the end? Theoretically.

C: Yes yes, that's clear. I think that, like all of the Zionists in Bulgaria, they found Zionist ideology very compelling, but when their sons wanted to make *aliyah*, they recoiled, because they thought that in

Israel life would be difficult, malaria, bad economic conditions. They were able to be Zionists outside of Israel. That their sons should go and make *aliyah* caused them to recoil, but as far as my parents are concerned, I don't think they would have tried to prevent their children from coming to Israel.

G: Were most of your friends also Zionist?

C: Yes, most of my friends.

G: Outside of Zionism, were you active in any other kind of political activity in Bulgaria?

C: During the war there was a strong conflict within Ha-Shomer Ha-Za'ir. Are we to stand on the side when there is such a difficult struggle between the forces of fascism and the democratic forces in Bulgaria? And so, Ha-Shomer Ha-Za'ir decided to join the Communist Youth. There was a decision in the movement after very lengthy negotiations, that we would join the Communist Party, the Communist Youth, get through the war, and after the war refound Ha-Shomer Ha-Za'ir. So I was active in the partisan cadres, cadres which operated in secret.

G: But within that framework you were still within the framework of Ha-Shomer Ha-Za'ir?

C: It was clear that, I was known as a member of Ha-Shomer Ha-Za'ir, but I was active within the framework of the Communist Youth as well.

G: So that was the only Bulgarian organization to which you belonged?

C: No.

G: Did you feel more Bulgarian or Jewish?

C: More Jewish.

G: Was the atmosphere at home different from the atmosphere in other homes? That is, was there a Jewish atmosphere at home?

C: Yes.

G: Did you celebrate any non-Jewish holidays, Bulgarian or Zionist, at home?

C: No.

G: And were most of your friends Jews?

C: Yes, most of my friends were Jews.

G: Did you feel proud to be a Bulgarian?

C: A Bulgarian? No. In spite of the fact that I loved Bulgarian culture, I loved the Bulgarian poetry.

G: Folk poetry?

C: No, the poetry.

G: Khristo Botev . . .

C: Khristo Botev, and Slaveikov, the famous authors.

G: Were you proud to be Jewish?

C: Without a doubt.

G: Do you think that as a people the Bulgarians were antisemites?

C: It is impossible to say about an entire people that its antisemitic or not antisemitic. I think that there were antisemitic elements, but not a high percent.

G: And do you think that there was a large part of the population which opposed the Fascists?

C: There was a part which opposed the Fascists, in spite of the fact that it wasn't expressed as in other countries, such as Denmark when the underground took all of the Jews to Sweden. It didn't reach those proportions, but all of the groups which were allied with the Communist Party fought the Fascists, and they were pro-Jewish. And the radio station of the underground tried to explain to the Bulgarians that the anti-Jewish policies were policies which helped only the Germans.

G: Do you recall instances when the gentiles helped the Jews during the Fascist period?

C: I didn't have any personal experience, but there were instances. I can't point to instances within my family.

G: Before the Fascist period do you think that Bulgaria was a good place for Jews?

C: Yes, I think that the Jews had a good life, because they lived, in actuality, in a ghetto. A spiritual ghetto. In general they lived within Jewish neighborhoods, there was a Jewish school, and there were Jewish youth movements which were very active. So that I think that Jewish life, which was active, gave the Jews fulfillment, and it was concentrated around the synagogue, school, and the Jewish community.

G: Did you visit Bulgarian homes freely?

C: No. I didn't have friends who were that close.

G: What kind of food did you eat at home?

C: The well-known Sephardi cuisine. A cuisine with many vegetables, with many fried foods.

G: Different from Bulgarian cuisine.

C: Without a doubt. In spite of the fact that there was mutual influence, but Jewish cuisine was different.

G: Do you remember that your parents sang Jewish songs at home? Or Bulgarian songs?

C: Yes.

G: Which?

C: Mostly Bulgarian songs. After my brothers joined the youth movements there were more movement songs, and not folk songs.

G: What about dance. Were there times when you danced Jewish folk dances or Bulgarian folk dances?

C: Mostly Bulgarian.

G: In what context?

C: Within the youth groups. They danced also hora, but within the clubs, within the movement. Younger people danced social dances, but we didn't associate with those kids.

G: Would you say that Jewish culture played a more important role in your daily life or Bulgarian?

C: I think that, except for the holidays, we were very aware of Bulgarian literature, Bulgarian poetry, and I think they were dominant.

G: So you left in '47.

C: Yes.

G: By ship?

C: By ship.

G: Which?

C: There were two large ships, Pan York and Pan Christian.

G: Like all the others here. And where did you live when you first arrived in Israel?

C: I was sure that I would go to a kibbutz. My friends who came before the war from Ha-Shomer Ha-Za'ir were in Kibbutz Evron, near Nahariya. I requested to remain in Bulgaria in order, in spite of the fact that my friends made *aliyah*. I asked to stay so that I could organize the members of Ha-Shomer Ha-Za'ir, and I stayed in Bulgaria for several years, and we organized Ha-Shomer Ha-Za'ir anew, and the movement developed into a large movement. When I made *aliyah*, my *gar'in* [cadre] was already settled with families. They were already settled in Evron, with families and children. And when I arrived there I felt that the years that had passed had made a distance between us, and I preferred to be with my friends with whom I had arrived later. I preferred to be with them, and we were in Kibbutz Eilon. Afterwards we requested to refound Yad Mordekhai.

G: I heard that you had requested to form a Bulgarian kibbutz?

C: We wanted to found a Bulgarian kibbutz, but the movement didn't allow it, because the conditions in Yad Mordekhai after the war were very tough, everything had been destroyed, many members were killed in the war, many members left, and they wanted to introduce a strong body to help them. And they saw in our *gar'in* a group which could contribute to the rebulding.

G: Was it important for you to remain within the group which came from Bulgaria?

C: Without a doubt.

G: Why?

C: It's a matter of a shared past, mentality.

G: Language also?

C: No. Very soon we all spoke Hebrew, and we spoke Bulgarian only in order to hide something from others. The spoken language was Hebrew.

G: When did you marry?

C: I married quite late. I married in '53.

G: Here in Yad Mordekhai.

C: Here in Yad Mordekhai.

G: Is your wife also from Bulgaria?

C: My wife is also from Bulgaria.

G: Which language do you speak among yourselves?

C: Between us we speak Hebrew. Very seldom, when there is something connected with the past, because until today we love Bulgarian poetry. Seldom when we look through books, here and there there is a word in Bulgarian, but in general Hebrew.

G: Was there a time when you read the Bulgarian newspaper?

C: Never.

G: And do your children know Bulgarian?

C: No. My older daughter, because of her grandmother when she'd come would speak Bulgarian, she catches individual words, but you can't say that she knows Bulgarian.

G: In which language do you prefer to read?

C: Hebrew.

G: And among your friends, you said that only when you wanted to hide something . . .

C: Yes . . .

G: Until today?

C: Until today.

G: Even when only Bulgarians get together?

C: Yes.

G: And it wasn't important to you to teach your children about Bulgaria and . . .

C: They like to hear about Bulgaria. When I tell them it sounds to them like a fairy tale, and they love to hear it. If someone enters the conversation in the middle of a story, they shut him up, a sign that they really like to hear, but I had no desire to teach them Bulgarian. I didn't see any point.

G: As far as Judaism here in Israel, do you practice anything?

C: I in particular. Every time there were elections in Israel, I went to campaign in Jaffa, because I had connections with those who had left the *gar'in*, and also with people who used to belong to the party. And because there was a high concentration of Bulgarians in Jaffa, I went to Jaffa before every election, three months before. There was a period when I was in Jaffa for three years, and I brought out the Bulgarian paper which is published there.

G: Which?

C: *Al Ha-Mishmar*. We brought out *Ha-Mishmar* in Bulgarian. I edited it for almost three years, and that was in '54–'55. The editor was Victor Shemtov. He got a leadership position and wanted to handle that, so I took the editorship for three years.

G: And during that time you lived in Jaffa.

C: I lived in Jaffa except for the Sabbath.

G: But you didn't want to remain in that framework?

C: When I would return home I felt that I was returning to a different world.

G: But you said something about religion. I asked you if Judaism played a role here in Israel?

C: I thought you meant Bulgarian Jewry . . .

G: Oh! No I meant about the Sabbath, or something connected with the Jewish religion.

C: No, no. In the kibbutz we celebrate all of the holidays, and we furnished them with different content and different context.

G: Were you in Mapam all these years?

C: Until today.

G: And I understand that you were active. Are you active till today?

C: Not all the time. With breaks. That is, I was active on the kibbutz, when I fill a position on the kibbutz I'm active in the kibbutz. There were several years when I was active outside, and afterwards with very important events, but not as a general thing.

G: It interests me that you were active in Jaffa for several years, and active here and there where there was a group of Bulgarians, what are the differences between the Bulgarians who remained within the Bulgarian context in Jaffa, in Ramle, and those who left it? Do you think there is something special in those people, why did they stay there?

C: I think that here it's not just an ideological matter. Life in Jaffa can't fulfill the young people, and they feel as if they are in a kind of ghetto. In actuality Jaffa served as a kind of *ma'abarah*. The Bulgarians arrived, and there were already Hungarians and Romanians and others. When the Romanians got settled the Bulgarians came. When they got settled they began to leave Jaffa, and they came from the countries of North Africa. Jaffa was always used as a kind of *ma'abarah*, and when people became settled they left. The young people left. After they got settled, after they got a trade, they left for Holon, for Bat Yam, to the surrounding areas. The older people remained, either because they didn't have the opportunity to find apartments in other areas, or because there is a concentration of retired people, who have all kinds of clubs and organizations, who share a common language and common experiences.

G: Do you think there is something special in the Bulgarian *aliyah* which differentiated it from other *aliyot*?

C: I think so. First of all the Bulgarian *aliyah* was one which didn't go with the current, it didn't seek the protection of the large parties, in spite of the fact that they had the right to receive some rewards for their activism. I didn't feel that I needed that because I was a kibbutz member, but activists from Bulgaria were disappointed because the government didn't receive them and appreciate their efforts outside of Israel, because many of them had been in prison, and were being pressured by the new government. When they arrived in Israel they had to get along like everyone else, and they received no help as other groups received. But they passed that over quietly, and they got along.

All of the people who came who were in the liberal professions got along somehow. The rest went to work, and it is recognized in Israel that the Bulgarian *aliyah* pulled up its sleeves and got to work. It wasn't a pampered *aliyah*. And that is one of positive things. Secondly, it was always an optimistic *aliyah*, it never got depressed, it kept up cooperative endeavors, like the Tsadikov Choir and various organizations, I think that those are things which helped very much in their proper absorption, because they didn't wait for anybody else to help them, they helped themselves. And I think that, the years passed, and each person found his own way. There are groups, until today, who seek each other out and continue the communal life which they had outside of Israel. I know that there are groups from Ha-Shomer Ha-Za'ir which meet every week, who get together every weekend. They organize recreational activities together. But as for the Bulgarian *aliyah*, it was very different from other *aliyot*.

G: Do you value your Bulgarian past, your Bulgarian roots?

C: Without a doubt, yes.

G: In what way?

C: First of all, there were two periods. Both before and after the war were stormy periods. Before the war was the struggle against the Fascist government, and after the war was the stormy struggle with the Communists. Those periods were periods of conflict, and they left deep scars on me.

G: But as far as Bulgarian culture, Bulgarian society, and all of those things. That is, you mentioned things which were out of the ordinary, which occurred because of the war, but I mean that which is based on Bulgaria.

C: Yes, I'll tell you. We loved Bulgarian poetry like I told you, Bulgarian literature. We also loved the Bulgarian landscape. Within the framework of the youth movements we used to take many hikes in summer in the mountains, we loved Bulgaria altogether, the literature, the poetry, the dances, the landscape, its nature, and of course it is one of the primary elements of my entire personality.

G: Are most of your good friends today from Bulgaria?

C: Yes.

G: Do you think that Bulgarians should preserve aspects of Bulgarian culture?

C: I don't see any point. I don't think that that has to be within any particular framework. Each individual keeps his past in his own little corner, but I don't think that there is any place because of that past to form a revivalist organization.

G: Tell me in order of preference for you. Do you feel Bulgarian, Israeli, Jewish, Sephardi. Put them in order.

C: Israeli, first. Jew. I don't know if Sephardi is something which applies to me, because it has no significance for me.

G: So Israeli and Jew, but Sephardi and Bulgarian don't . . .

C: No, no.

G: Do you miss Bulgaria?

C: No. I don't miss it, but recently, because there is a steady stream of people who visit Bulgaria there is some, but I don't have any nostalgia for Bulgaria. In spite of the fact that I love the landscape as I said. I would gladly visit.

G: Do you have any plans in that direction?

C: Yes.

G: When you eat at home, not in the dining room, do you still eat things which you ate in Bulgaria?

C: I would gladly eat them.

G: But do you?

C: Not very often. Because that type of cooking requires much more time, preparations, and at home we usually prepare things which can be done quickly. All of those foods need a lot of preparation, but when I go to Tel Aviv, when I have to go to a restaurant, I prefer to go to a Bulgarian restaurant.

G: Are there occasions when you still sing the Bulgarian songs together?

C: Yes.

G: In what context?

C: Within the framework of a birthday, or the anniversary of our *aliyah*, because that was exactly on New Year's. We left in '47 at the end of December, and we got on the boat on New Years. We usually get together in one of the members' rooms, and once in a while someone will remember a song. Also on other occasions. Two days ago there was a wedding, so we sang Bulgarian songs.

G: Do you have any Bulgarian records at home, that you listen to?

C: Maybe one record, one or two.

G: If there is s Bulgarian performance or group, do you try to go?

C: Yes, gladly.

G: When was the last time that you actually went?

C: Many years ago.

G: Because for example, a few months ago, Aleko was here.

C: Yes, but I heard that it was a small group and not so good.

G: Is there anything else from Bulgarian folklore which is still preserved here? That you keep or that there are times when it enters your life?

C: When something comes which is connected to Bulgaria I read it, but I don't especially look for it. There is a newspaper from Bulgaria which the Consistory publishes, and when it comes I try to get a hold of it.

G: I meant more about culture, folklore, songs, dances . . .

C: No.

G: How do you think that Israelis view the Bulgarians, the Bulgarian *aliyah*?

C: I think that, I think that it identifies with the way in which I see the Bulgarian *aliyah*, because those things were expressed in many different circumstances. I have the feeling that because the Jews of Bulgaria attained an honorable position in medicine and science, and as laborers, in all of the areas, I think that the way I felt is shared by the Israelis.

G: How many children do you have?

C: I have three children.

G: Where was your father born?

C: My father was born in Plovdiv.

G: And your mother too?

C: My mother was born in Pazardzhik.

G: And the previous generation?

C: I tried to find out, and I wasn't able to complete anything, but I have the impression, through rumors, that our roots are from Soloniki, from Greece, in Greece there was a very large Jewish community, and my roots from my mother's side are from Greece.

G: And from your father's side?

C: From Bulgaria.

G: That's it. I'm finished. I thank you very much.

C: You're welcome.

Haim Belo, January 6, 1982, 11:00 A.M., Mo'adon Bulgariyah, Jaffa

I took a day trip from Kibbutz Be'eri to Jaffa to snoop around, and went to the Mo'adon Bulgariyah. The club is a coffee shop in a dilapidated building in the heart of Jaffa, with a long narrow outside staircase. The club was filled on this weekday morning. Most of the clientele was old, but there were some young men as well. Everyone was drinking tea or coffee, smoking, talking, staring, or playing backgammon or dominoes. I asked around, was directed to Haim, was given a cup of coffee, and conducted the interview with a crowd looking on and participating. This is the other side of the Bulgarian *aliyah*: those who adjusted to life in Israel by continuing life from Bulgaria.

G: How long has this place been here, do you know?

H: This place as existed many many years. Now it's up here, but before it was also downstairs. They sold the downstairs to a plastics factory so we came upstairs. But it's been here for about twenty-five years.

G: Is it less active all the time or . . .

H: What can I tell you, the old ones are going, fewer remain. It's usually full. But what can I tell you, the Bulgarian *aliyah* is already starting to go. The young ones, the Sabras who come, aren't interested in the Bulgarian immigrants, they're Sabras. For example I came here in '48, I had children here, and I have grandchildren. The children hardly speak Bulgarian, but the Sabras, my grandchildren not at all. You see notices that the old ones are already dead. There is hardly any other Bulgarian place, here it's almost full. This is the Bulgarian club, year after year the same people, and sometimes younger ones come, young, they're now older, they come, the older ones are already gone.

G: Do young ones ever come who never came before, and start to be interested in . . .

H: Hardly. For example the young man sitting by the wall, his father was here, he almost never came, but now he started to come.

G: Was he born in Bulgaria?

H: He came at a very young age. But his children are Sabras, and I don't think they will come in twenty years, if it will still exist.

G: Do they speak Bulgarian?

H: He speaks Bulgarian because he came with Bulgarian parents, who used it from the beginning, his parents still don't know Hebrew, they don't know another language. But he still speaks because he came at a young age and they only spoke Bulgarian at home.

G: Do you speak here only Bulgarian or also Hebrew?

H: I came at a young age, I came here at age twenty, and we learned some Hebrew, and now at home we speak Hebrew.

G: I mean here at the club.

H: Here almost all Bulgarian.

G: Ladino?

H: Ladino sometimes, there are older ones who use Ladino. We speak it a little, we speak more Bulgarian, and all of those who are sitting here, sometimes strangers come who aren't Bulgarian, so we speak Hebrew, so they'll understand too. But in general we speak Bulgarian.

G: Besides playing cards and backgammon and sitting and talking, does the club have any activities?

H: We play cards and backgammon, it's a games club. But it's a closed club. It's not for everyone.

G: But every Bulgarian who comes . . .

H: That's because of the police, they don't want to have games, so it's a closed club, and every one of us has a membership card, so there's no problem. Downstairs there's a sign that it's a closed club.

G: But you don't say, for any Bulgarian who wants . . .

H: He comes, there isn't any check, why don't you have a card, but if the police comes to check 90 percent have, but if they ask you and you don't have, so you came to visit. It's not a problem.

G: So it's all for the police.

H: Yes, because they don't allow the games. Here we pass the time, we play.

G: Do most of the people work here in the area?

H: Here in the big room most of the people are pensioners. The young ones play but there aren't many.

G: Do you come every day?

H: Almost every day. I used to work, so after work I used to come. Now I left work I have nothing to do in the morning.

G: Can you compare this to a place you had in Bulgaria, a club?

H: In Bulgaria there were many coffee shops. But what can I tell you, the Communists, and I left the country. What's going on there now I don't know.

G: No I meant . . .

H: Yes, in my time when I was in Bulgaria, during the Fascist period, there were many places.

G: Does this remind you of anything there?

H: Yes, because when I was there we used to go, so that like we come here every day we used to go there every day. But those places, when the Russians came, the Communists, they began to close them. And I don't think they continued, maybe here and there, to drink coffee, but maybe there still are places like that. Like there are here, like there were in my time before the Communists, I don't think there are any more.

G: Where were you born in Bulgaria?

H: Sofia.

G: And until age twenty you were there?

H: Until age twenty I was there, and at age twenty I came here with two children, and afterwards I had three children, and I have seven grandchildren. But the Bulgarians are slowly going, the young ones remain.

G: Are you sad that the children who went to school here didn't learn about Bulgarian culture and language?

H: It's their own life. Just as my life was in Bulgaria, here the children have their own lives as Sabras, they have a different life, not the same life as ours. And one can't do anything against that.

G: But does that hurt you that . . .

H: No, what is there to hurt? Everyone has his time and everyone has his age, there is no reason to hurt. I brought them here, I came here, so one has to accept the fact that they're Sabras and not Bulgarians.

G: Did you live in the Jewish quarter in Sofia?

H: No, we had gentile friends also but most of my friends were Jews, and we would sit together in a Bulgarian coffee house.

G: Why did you come to Israel?

H: To tell the truth I don't know if everyone came because of this, but because of the Communism which I didn't like.

G: Not because of Zionism?

H: There was something in my heart but, for example if Americans had come to Bulgaria and not the Russians, I wouldn't have come to Israel. But there in the Jewish school there was Maccabi, and all kinds of Jewish parties, we used to get together, dance the khoro, sing Jewish songs, we had something in our hearts, but I'll tell you the truth, I didn't come because I was such a good Zionist, but I didn't like my life there, in Bulgaria, with the Communists, I didn't like it, I love freedom, and there there is no freedom. I had to do things which I didn't like, and if you refuse you have a lot of serious problems. So I said O.K. I'll go to my own country, there there will be freedom. I came because of that, if everyone came for that reason I don't know.

G: There are all kinds of reasons.

H: There are all kinds of reasons. There are those who came before the Germans, before the problems with the Communists and the problems with the Germans. They came as Zionists. When I was a child I didn't think of coming.

G: You weren't in a movement?

H: Yes, I was in Maccabi there, there were others in Ha-Shomer Ha-Za'ir and others in Betar, there were all kinds of parties there. But I myself, if you ask me, I fled the Communists, I didn't like that regime.

G: Did you suffer during the time of the Fascists?

H: Look, I suffered as every Jew suffered, but I am not sorry, it was the best experience in my life. At that time I was exactly fifteen, sixteen. At the same time that mother and father had to beg for bread, and they threw us out by force from Sofia to another city in order to take, in order for the Germans to take us to Auschwitz, I didn't have worries like those, I was too young, things were good, personally.

G: Where did they send you?

H: From Sofia, they sent me to Shumen, like from here if they send you to Hadera or Haifa, or Natanya. From there they were going to send us on the trains to Germany and make soap out of us, or burn us up.

G: Did you have to work in a labor camp?

H: No, but many of my friends had to. And besides that, during the time of the Germans, my father and older men than I, there was a labor camp to which they would take the Jews, some for the Germans, some for the state. Those were not good things, but at age fifteen everything was good.

G: Here you are involved in Bulgarian life, you come to the coffee house.

H: Those are my surroundings.

G: When you came to Israel, did you come directly to Jaffa?

H: No. I was in Pardes Hannah. There we had tents. They gave us food to eat, until one day they brought us to Jaffa. I got an apartment, had children, and afterwards we began to progress, and bought a house together, and every person got settled according to his needs.

G: If they had taken you somewhere else, other than the Bulgarian street, would you have continued . . .

H: I wanted to be with the Bulgarians, Jaffa was, until today Bulgarian, I wanted to be, and I was, nobody bothered me.

G: What did you do?

H: First of all when I came as a new immigrant in diapers, from Pardes Hannah, they took me to work in an orchard. To spray fertilizer on the oranges there. He [the boss] was very satisfied, he wanted to give me an apartment and everything, and work six months with a salary, without paying rent for the apartment, it was his house. He said I'll give you an apartment without paying. And when the season comes you'll work for six months, I'll pay you, and when you don't work and don't earn money it will be enough for you to live. I told him I didn't want it, I have to go with the Bulgarians, almost everyone left. I took what was coming to me and came here to Jaffa. I came to a small apartment, and I didn't live poorly! Until we got up in the world. Afterwards I was a driver, I was a driving instructor, afterwards in charge of a truck. I always stayed around driving but I had many jobs, until I retired.

G: Do you think that the Bulgarians, the gentiles were mostly antisemites?

H: I'll tell you, I love the Bulgarians. They always behaved well, until today when you go there as a guest, but despite that there was antisemitism. It happens. During the German period, they helped us, and understood us. But besides that, there was a jealousy, there were antisemites which is natural, I'm not talking about them I'm talking about the majority.

G: Did they help the Jews during the Fascist time?

H: There were those who helped, there were those who came here as gentiles who couldn't stand Communism, they came here to join us because they were used to us, there are those.

G: Still today?

H: Yes, there's one here who is almost more important than the owner, he lived there for many years without us, and even had a good job under the Communists, with good pay. He fled illegally from there and came here, to be with us.

G: And you said that you had two children when you came here from Bulgaria.

H: I came here with one boy age three, the two girls I had here. What's your family name?

G: Haskell, my father was born in Plovdiv, afterwards was in Pordim, and after that was in Samokov.

H: By the way I was born in Bulgaria and lived all the time in Sofia, from Sofia I came here, but my father was from Greece, and he married my mother, I am half Bulgarian and half Greek. I don't know Greece, don't know how to speak Greek.

G: Today in Jaffa are there Bulgarian organizations?

H: Of course, for example I am a member of the Good Life Club [Agudat Hayim Tovim]. That's a Bulgarian club.

G: What do you do?

H: We get together, put together evenings, and often donate money that we collect to the Soldier's Welfare Organization.

Unknown: There are performances, fundraisers.

H: We put on benefits for underprivileged children. What can I tell you, we have folk dances.

G: Yes?

H: Yes.

G: Where?

H: There is a club, our club is across the street, but it's not open, it's open once a week, when all the members get together, and we also play cards, dominoes and backgammon, drink Arak and beer, get together to be together to see each other, not to grow apart. We give special evenings. Sometimes we give evenings just for members, sometimes for members and strangers, we give money to the Soldier's Fund . . .

G: On which day?

H: We just got together on Hanukah, the first of January which was the gentile New Year, so we have a tradition from Bulgaria, so we celebrate it. We get together, have a good time, eat, drink. Not bad! But there are several clubs here. There is a club of the French Hospital, and there are several pensioners clubs, and this coffee house.

G: Besides the clubs you mentioned are there any political clubs?

H: No no. But there is a club, not big and not small, and sometimes the Communists want rent for it, with us each member pays every month, we have to pay for electricity, water, rent.

G: How many members are there?

H: There are about eighty members.

G: And here?

H: Here also about one hundred people.

G: The same people who are in the club?

H: There are those like myself who are from the club, and there are those, and many of them, who aren't in the club anymore.

G: I heard that there is also a library.

H: No, we used to have a library, but it's not used any more.

G: No, of the Mapam.

[Onlooker describes the Mapam library, mostly unintelligible]

G: And is it open all the time?

Onlooker: All the time.

H: And they have books in Bulgarian?

O: Yes.

H: Where is it?

O: I'll show you.

G: I'd like to see it too. There is an image of the Bulgarians that they are a good aliyah, and working people.

H: The old age home is for old people who don't have anyone to look after them, so they go there, they take care of them, almost all Bulgarians, I don't think there are also others.

G: I'm going there on Sunday, I have an interview with Albert Beni, do you know him?

H: Possibly. There there are only old people, who can hardly function, they eat and drink there, sleep there, live there until they die. They're already too old.

G: Now Ihud 'Olei Bulgariyah [Bulgarian Immigrants Association] . . .

H: That's something else.

G: What's that?

H: It's an organization of the Bulgarians.

G: Do they do anything?

H: Maybe they do something. For example there were compensations from the Germans, who they gave to those who suffered, so there they took care of that.

G: So it only deals with those kind of problems.

H: It takes care of the Bulgarians' problems. Is there something else you want to know?

G: I'm just looking to see.

H: Look, walk around, see, speak, ask.

G: About the holidays. Are there Bulgarian holidays, you mentioned Silvester, are there other hoidays?

H: We don't celebrate Silvester, no gentile holidays, Bulgarian. We celebrate our own holidays. Hanukah, Purim . . .

G: Do you celebrate in a Bulgarian way?

H: Yes, in the club, ours. For example we had two nights of Hanukah: one night for members, and one night for members and strangers, almost all Bulgarians. But besides Silvester, no.

G: The Ninth of September or . . .

H: Are you kidding? We aren't Communists. There are those who celebrate things like that, and among them there are maybe Bulgarians, I don't know.

G: For example on Hanukah, what do you do? Sing in Bulgarian, or in Hebrew, or . . .

H: Sing, talk, have a good time, light Hanukah candles, good food, do what we have to do for Hanukah.

G: Are there religious Bulgarians in Jaffa, who go to synagogue?

H: There aren't many among the Bulgarians. There are perhaps a few among the old people who are more religious, but in general, we have communities, and a synagogue, and everything, but something strong of the religious, I don't think so. There are those who keep the Sabbath, don't eat on Yom Kippur, there are those, and there are those who don't keep anything. There are all kinds.

G: In Bulgaria did you go to synagogue . . .

H: In Bulgaria we were better Jews than we are here.

G: On the Sabbath or only the holidays?

H: On the Sabbath no, the Sabbath wasn't a holiday. We used to celebrate Sunday because Sunday was their holiday, the Sabbath was the Jews holiday, but everything was open, there. Here, the Sabbath is the Sabbath. There the Sabbath was work day, a regular day, Sunday was the holiday.

G: If I ask you how you see yourself, in order, tell me: Israeli, Bulgarian, Jew . . .

H: Jew, first of all Jew. I love Bulgaria, and I dream all these years to be in Bulgaria and remember the life that I lived there, but first of all I am a Jew.

G: Then Bulgarian or Israeli?

H: Israeli, 100 percent Israeli. Bulgarian? Bulgaria, that's the place I was born, but I'm a Jew in Israel. I suffered there because I was a Jew.

G: Have you gone to visit Bulgaria?

H: No. I would go, but here almost everyone has gone.

G: Would you like to visit?

H: Very much. That's a money matter, it costs a lot of money, and it's a matter of time. My wife can't allow herself a month, month and a half, without working here. She has a shop, a beauty salon, and in order to keep her clients, she could lose them after so much time. And it's also a problem of money. It costs a lot of money.

G: In Bulgaria did you feel more Bulgarian or Jewish?

H: Jew. And I suffered like a Jew. And I had Bulgarian friends who were very good to me, and there were antisemites, so how could you not be a Jew?

G: Were most of your friends Jews or non-Jews there?

H: I had both, I had Jews and also Bulgarians, but good friends. Besides the fact that there were many antisemites, because they were jealous, because the Jews used to go with gentile girls, beautiful girls. A Jew had a better chance of taking a girl to the coffee shop, to take her out, to take her to nice places, the gentiles didn't have it and it used to eat them up. Look, it's natural that there are also antisemites. Many times I had problems, they used to ask, are there no more gentiles that you have to go with Jews? There were questions like that. But in general, Bulgarians and Jews used to get together, we used to have a good time. But as far as what I felt, I felt only Jewish, I couldn't feel otherwise. They didn't give you the opportunity to feel otherwise. On the contrary. When the Germans came and we began to suffer and they kicked us out of the city in order to kill us, to convert, to make yourself, that also didn't occur to us. Because we felt Jewish in our blood. There were some shitty Jews who became Christians in order to save themselves. I don't know if it helped them much.

G: Did you speak Bulgarian with your children?

H: I didn't have any children, I myself was a child.

G: When you came here with your children.

H: Age seven months. They speak Bulgarian, but they're almost Sabras, the others came here, were born here.

G: But at home . . .

H: At home, Bulgarian and Hebrew and Ladino, it depends.

G: To which party do you think most of the Jews in Jaffa belong? In there anything like that, that most belong to Mapai, or most belong to Labour?

H: What can I tell you, I can't tell you that.

G: There is an image of the Bulgarians that they're leftists.

H: If you ask me, for example, I was always with Herut, I always liked Begin, and I personally, there are those who are against that, there are all kinds.

G: But you said that you miss Bulgaria.

H: Yes!

G: What do you miss?

H: I miss the good life I had as a child, as a young man, the girl friends I had there, the friends I had there, the houses in which we lived. I miss it!

G: So it's more a matter of your age . . .

H: Yes. And I'm sure that if I go to Bulgaria it will break it because I won't see that which I left, I'll see something completely different.

G: Maybe it's better to leave it as a memory . . .

H: Better to leave it as a good memory than destroy it. What I left won't exist.

G: Is there anything of Bulgarian folklore which you keep here? You mentioned that you dance khoro.

H: Listen, we do that in the club because of tradition, because of the fact that we lived in Bulgaria, and we learned how to dance there the folk dances, but we still use that, it's beautiful. If Bulgarians in the city or outside of the city do something so they invite our group.

G: There's a group?

H: There's a group, but now, what can I tell you, the guy who used to beat the drum died, he died a year ago, and since then there's hardly a group. There were costumes, and women and men, and we would play the khoro, so that for the person who knew it would have tears in his eyes. But slowly slowly they are getting old, and drummer died, and another who was a good dancer also died, so with the years everything goes.

G: How do you think Israelis view the Bulgarian aliyah?

H: How do the Israelis see? I don't think we have a bad name. I think that they view the Bulgarians positively. I heard many times people who love Bulgarians. They are a people who work, don't live from crime, a good people, I hear in the street all the time, I love the Bulgarians, they are good material. Maybe there is bad material among us, but in general I think that they think well of us. There were times in my life when I said, I'm Bulgarian, then if you're Bulgarian we can get along. What can I tell you, maybe there are those who hate Bulgarians.

G: Good. That's what I had to ask. You gave me a lot.

H: I told you what I could tell you and I hope I helped you.

G: You helped me.

[unintelligible]

H: What I read there are things which I've read in the other papers already, so there's not much to read there.

G: I've been told that people read it to know if they're dead or alive.

H: They buy it to see who went. In the newspaper there are always notices. But the Bulgarian newspaper has started to go down, and I think it only comes out once or twice a month now. It used to come out every day but now it doesn't come out every day.

G: Is the newspaper office near here?

H: Yes, the *Far* office is on Giv'at Herzl and Salame, on the corner, just across the gas station on Giv'at Herzl.

Notes

Introduction

1. See Robert A. Georges and Stephen Stern, *American and Canadian Immigrant and Ethnic Folklore: An Annotated Bibliography* (New York and London: Garland Publishing, 1982), pp. 3–23; and Stephen Stern, "Ethnic Folklore and the Folklore of Ethnicity," in *Folklore and Ethnicity*, ed. Larry Danielson (Los Angeles: California Folklore Society, 1977), pp. 7–32.
2. See Eli-Kaija Kongas Miranda, "Finnish-American Folklore: Quantitative and Qualitative Analysis," (Ph.D. diss., Indiana University, 1963); Robert A. Georges, "Greek-American Folk Beliefs and Narratives: Survivals and Living Traditions" (Ph.D. diss., Indiana University, 1964); Frank Paulsen, "Danish American Folk Traditions: A Study in Fading Survivals," (Ph.D. diss., Indiana University, 1967); Linda Degh, "Survival and Revival of European Folk Cultures in America," *Ethnologia Europea* 2–3 (1968–1969), pp. 97–108.
3. Linda Degh, "Approaches to Folklore Research among Immigrant Groups," *Journal of American Folklore* 77 (1966), pp. 551–556; Richard M. Dorson, "Concepts of Folklore and Folklife Studies," in *Folklore and Folklife*, ed. Richard M. Dorson (Chicago: University of Chicago Press, 1972), p. 44.
4. See Robert Klymasz, "Ukranian Folklore in Canada: An Immigrant Complex in Transition," (Ph.D. diss., Indiana University, 1970); Babro Sklute, "Legends and Folk Beliefs in a Swedish American Community: A Study in Folklore and Acculturation (Ph.D. diss., Indiana University, 1970); Kenneth A. Thigpen, "Folklore and the Ethnicity Factor in the Lives of RomanianAmericans," (Ph.D. diss., Indiana University, 1973).
5. See Américo Paredes and Richard Bauman, eds., *Toward New Perspectives in Folklore* (Austin: American Folklore Society, 1972).
6. See, for example, Richard Bauman, *Verbal Art as Performance* (Romley, Massachussetts: Newbury House Publishing, 1977); and Dan Ben-Amos, "Toward a Definition of Folklore in Context," in *New Perspectives in Folklore*, ed. Américo Paredes and Richard Bauman (Austin: University of Texas Press, 1972), pp. 3–15.
7. Linda Degh, *Folklore and Society* (Bloomington: Indiana University Press, 1969); "Prepared Comments by Linda Degh to Richard M. Dorson's 'Is There a Folk in the City,'" in *The Urban Experience and Folk Tradition*, ed. Americo Paredes and Ellen J. Stekert (Austin: University of Texas Press, 1971), pp. 54–55; "Ethnicity in Modern European Ethnology," *Folklore Forum* 7 (1974), pp. 48–55; *People in the Tobacco Belt: Four Lives*, National Museum of Man Mercury Series, Canadian Center for Folk Culture Studies, Paper No. 13 (Ottawa, 1975).
8. Dorson, "Concepts of Folklore and Folklife Studies," p. 44.
9. See Stern, "Ethnic Folklore and the Folklore of Ethnicity."

Chapter 1

1. Leonard Weller, *Sociology in Israel* (Westport: Greenwood Press, 1974); Harvey Goldberg, "Anthropology in Israel," *Current Anthropology* 17 (1976), pp. 119–121.

2. Raphael Patai, *Israel between East and West* (Philadelphia: Jewish Publication Society of America, 1953).
3. For a description of his childhood and youth in Hungary, see Patai's autobiography, *Apprentice in Budapest: Memories of a World that Is No More* (Salt Lake City: University of Utah Press, 1988).
4. Patai, p. xiii.
5. Patai, pp. xii–xiii. Among Brauer's important works are *Ethnologie der jemenitischen Juden* (Heidelberg: Ca. Winter, 1934); *The Jews of Kurdistan: An Ethnological Study*, [Yehudei Kurdistan: Mehkar Etnologi]. Sifriyah Le'folklor Ve'etnologiyah, vol. 2, completed, edited, and translated by Raphael Patai (Jerusalem: Palestine Institute of Folklore and Ethnology, 1947. Reprint, Detroit: Wayne State University Press, 1993).
6. Patai, p. xiii.
7. Patai, p. xiii.
8. Patai, pp. 306–340.
9. See Patai, ed., *Encyclopedia of Zionism*, vol. 2, p. 1192; see also G. Cyderovitch, "The Living Standards of the Jewish Community at the End of the War," *Bulletin of the Economic Research of the Jewish Agency* 10, no. 2 (1946).
10. S. N. Eisenstadt, *Israeli Society* (London: Weidenfeld and Nicolson, 1967), p. 63.
11. For a detailed statistical discussion of immigration to Israel during this period, see Moshe Sicron, *Immigration to Israel 1948–1953* (Jerusalem: Falk Institute, 1957) (repr. in '*Olim Be-Yisrael* [Immigrants to Israel], ed. Moshe Lissak, Beverly Mizrahi and Ofrah Ben-David (Jerusalem: Akadmon, 1969), pp. 105–121).
12. Ephraim Dekel, *B'riha: Flight to the Homeland*, trans. Dina Ettinger (New York: Herzl Press, n.d.). For a discussion of "illegal" immigration from Bulgaria, see Baruch Confino, *Aliyah Bet Mi-Hofei Bulgaria 1938–1948* ["Illegal" Immigration from the Shores of Bulgaria], trans. Sason Levi (Jerusalem-Tel Aviv: Akhiyasaf Publishing House, 1965).
13. Judith T. Shuval, *Immigrants on the Threshold* (New York: Atherton, 1963), p. 7.
14. *Immigration and Settlement*, pp. 52–56.
15. *Dhimmi* is the Arabic term referring to Jews and Christians, the non-Moslem "People of the Book." For a description of Jewish life under Moslem rule, see Andre N. Chouraqui, *Between East and West: A History of the Jews of North Africa* (Philadelphia: Jewish Publication Society of America, 1968). For a discussion of the function of Zionist ideology in the acculturation of immigrants to Israel, see Judith T. Shuval, "The Role of Ideology as a Predisposing Frame of Reference for Immigrants," *Human Relations* 12 (1959), p. 52.
16. See Elihu Katz and S. N. Eisenstadt, "Some Sociological Observations on the Response of Israeli Organizations to New Immigrants," *Administrative Science Quarterly* 1 (1960), pp. 113–133 (repr. in *Olim Be-Yisrael* [Immigrants in Israel], ed. Moshe Lissak, Beverly Mizrahi, and Ofrah Ben-David [Jerusalem: Akadmon, 1969], pp. 395–417).
17. Louis Guttman, Introduction, *Immigrants on the Threshold*, by Judith T. Shuval (New York: Atherton Press, 1963), pp. vii–xiii.
18. Judith T. Shuval, "The Role of Class in Structuring Inter-Group Hostility," *Human Relations* 10 (1957), pp. 61–75.
19. The questionnaire used in the fieldwork appears in Shuval, *Immigrants on the Threshold*, pp. 195–209.
20. Shuval, *Immigrants on the Threshold*, p. 10.
21. Guttman, Introduction, in Shuval, *Immigrants of the Threshold*, p. xi.
22. Ibid., p. ix.
23. Weller, *Sociology in Israel*, p. 27.
24. Shuval, *Immigrants on the Threshold*, pp. 178–179.
25. Shuval, "The Role of Ideology as a Predisposing Frame of Reference for Immigrants," and *Immigrants on the Threshold*, pp. 43–78.
26. Weller, *Sociology in Israel*, pp. 27–28.
27. Shuval, *Immigrants on the Threshold*, pp. 184–185.
28. Yosef Ben-David, "Ethnic Differences or Social Change?," *Megamot* (1952), pp.

171–183; Y. Isaacs, "Israel—A New Melting Pot," in *The Cultural Integration of Immigrants*, ed. W. D. Borrie (Paris: UNESCO, 1956), pp. 234–266; Hagit Reiger, "Some Aspects of the Acculturation of Yemenite Youth Immigrants," in *Between Past and Future*, ed. Carl Frankenstein (Jerusalem: The Szold Foundation, 1953), pp. 82–108; Abraham Shumsky, *The Clash of Cultures in Israel* (New York: Columbia University Press, 1955).

29. Ben-David, pp. 171–183.
30. Judith T. Shuval, "Emerging Patterns of Social Strain in Israel," *Social Forces* 40 (1962), pp. 323–330; Percy Cohen, "Ethnic Hostility in Israel," *New Society* 22 (1963), pp. 14–16.
31. Harvey Goldberg, Introduction, "Culture and Ethnicity in the Study of Israeli Society," *Ethnic Groups* 1 (1977), pp. 163–186.
32. Harvey Goldberg, Introduction, p. 169.
33. For a full description of the Institute and its character, see Dan Ben-Amos, "Folklore in Israel," *Schweizerisches Archiv für Volkskunde* 59 (1963), pp. 19–20.
34. Ibid., pp. 18–24.
35. Ibid., p. 21.
36. "As long as tradition remains there are endless opportunities to study and research the culture of these folk groups. Yet there is little time, and the day not far off, when a new Israeli culture will come into being, assimilating everything within it." Elisheva Schoenfeld, "Jüdische-orientalische Märchenerzahler in Israel," *Internationaler Kongress der Volkserzählungen in Kiel und Kopenhagen* (Berlin, 1961), pp. 385–390.
37. Dov Noy, "The First Thousand Folktales in the Israel Folktale Archives," *Fabula* 4 (1961), p. 109.
38. Ben-Amos, "Folklore in Israel," p. 23.
39. Exceptions may be found in the pages of *Yeda' 'Am* and *Mahanayim* by such authors as Yom Tov Lewinski and Dov Sadan. Of value in their own right, these studies do not, however, represent a methodological, scholarly approach. See Galit Hasan-Rokem and Eli Yassif, "The Study of Jewish Folklore in Israel," *Jewish Folklore and Ethnology Review* 11 (1989), pp. 4–5.
40. Eisenstadt, *Absorption of Immigrants*, p. 54.

Chapter 2

1. *American Anthropologist* 64 (1962), pp. 115–131.
2. Weingrod, "Reciprocal Change," p. 119; for a description of the classic moshav structure, see pp. 115–119. Israeli sociologists have long been interested in the economic and structural role of the moshav in immigrant absorption; see S. N. Eisenstadt, "Sociological Aspects of the Economic Adaptation of Oriental Immigrants in Israel: A Case Study of Modernization," *Economic Development and Cultural Change* 4 (1956); J. Goren *The Villages of the New Immigrants in Israel* [in Hebrew] (Tel Aviv: Ministry of Agriculture, 1960), pp. 269–278; Yonina Talmon-Garber, "Social Differentiation in Cooperative Communities," *British Journal of Sociology*, 3 (1952), pp. 339–357; Dov Weintraub, "Patterns of Social Change in New Immigrants' Smallholders' Cooperative Settlements," diss., Hebrew University, 1962; Dov Weintraub, Moshe Lissak, and Yaakov Azmon, eds., *Moshava, Kibbutz and Moshav: Patterns of Jewish Rural Settlement and Development in Palestine* (Ithaca and London: Cornell University Press, 1969), pp. 122–158, 275–313; Weintraub, et al., *Immigration and Social Change: Agricultural Settlements of New Immigrants in Israel* (New York: Humanities Press, 1971). Much of the preliminary work by the authors cited above, as well as the work of researchers not cited, first appeared in mimeographed reports for the Jewish Agency Settlement Department. See footnotes in Shlomo Deshen, *A Case of Breakdown of Modernization in an Israeli Immigrant Community: An Essay in Applied Sociology* (Kiryat Gat: Lachish Regional Administration, Jewish Agency Land Settlement Department, 1964).

3. Don Handelman and Shlomo Deshen, *The Social Anthropology of Israel: A Bibliographical Essay with Primary Reference to Loci of Social Stress* (Tel Aviv: Tel Aviv University Institute for Social Research, 1975), p. 39.

4. Max Gluckman, Introduction, *Immigrant Voters in Israel: Parties and Congregations in a Local Election Campaign*, by Shlomo Deshen (Manchester: Manchester University Press, 1970), p. xx; Emmanuel Marx, "Anthropological Studies in a Centralized State: Max Gluckman and the Bernstein Israel Research Project," *Jewish Journal of Sociology* 17 (1975), pp. 31–50; Marx, *A Composite Portrait of Israel* (London: Academic Press, 1980).

5. Handelman and Deshen, *Social Anthropology of Israel*, p. 21.

6. Erik Cohen, *The City in Zionist Ideology*, Jerusalem Urban Studies, Report no. 1, Institute of Urban and Regional Studies (Jerusalem: Eliezer Kaplan School of Economics and Social Sciences, 1970).

7. Shlomo Deshen, "Conflict and Social Change: The Case of an Israeli Village," *Sociologia Ruralis* 6 (1966), pp. 31–35; "Non-Conformists in an Israeli Immigrant Community," *Mankind Quarterly* 9 (1969), pp. 166–177.

8. Raanan Weitz, "The Sociologists and the Policy Makers: A Case Study of Agricultural Settlements in Israel," *Transactions of the Fifth World Congress of Sociology* 1 (1962), pp. 59–75; Jeff Halper, "The Persian Jews of Nevei Shalom: A Study in Mobility," *Ariel* 53 (1983), pp. 34–50.

9. Moshe Shokeid, "Old Conflicts in a New Environment: A Study of a Moroccan Atlas Mountains Community Transplanted to Israel," *Jewish Journal of Sociololgy* 9 (1967), pp. 191–208; "Immigration and Factionalism: An Analysis of Functions in Rural Israeli Communities of Immigrants," *British Journal of Sociology* 19 (1968), pp. 385–406.

10. Harvey Goldberg, "Acculturation, Continuity and Youth in an Israeli Immigrant Village," Ph.D. diss., Harvard University, (1966).

11. Harvey Goldberg, "FBD Marriage and Demography among Tripolitanian Jews in Israel," *Southwestern Journal of Anthropology* 23 (1967), pp. 179–191.

12. Harvey Goldberg, "Egalitarianism in an Autocratic Village in Israel," *Ethnology* 8 (1969), pp. 54–75.

13. Harvey Goldberg, "Domestic Organization of Wealth in an Israeli Immigrant Village," *Human Organization* 28 (1969), pp. 58–63.

14. Alex Weingrod, *Israel: Group Relations in a New Society* (Westport: Greenwood Press, 1965); and *Reluctant Pioneers: Village Development in Israel* (Ithaca, NY: Cornell University Press, 1966).

15. Ruth Rubin, "First World Conference on Jewish Folklore Research," *Journal of American Folklore Supplement* (April 1960), pp. 18–20. For a discussion of other folklore conferences held in Israel during this period, see Haim Schwarzbaum, *Studies in Jewish and World Folklore* (Berlin: Walter De Gruyter, 1968), pp. 3–4; "The Seventh Annual Hebrew Folk-Narrative Conference," *Fabula* 6 (1963), pp. 180–181, gives a particularly vivid portrait of the Thompsonite collection and analysis in which Israel's folklorists were, and to a large extent still are, engaged.

16. Dov Noy, Introduction, *Folktales of Israel*, ed. Dov Noy with the assistance of Dan Ben-Amos, trans. Gene Baharav (Chicago: University of Chicago Press, 1963), p. 9.

17. Dov Noy, ed., *Moroccan Jewish Folktales* (New York: Herzl Press, 1966), p. 9.

18. Dov Noy, *Jefet Schwili erzählt: Hundertneunundsechzig jemenitische Volkserzählungen aufgezeichnet in Israel 1957–1960* (Berlin: Walter De Gruyter, 1963).

19. Patai, "Jewish Folklore and Jewish Tradition," p. 21.

20. See William R. Bascom. "Folklore and Anthropology," *Journal of American Folklore* 56 (1953), p. 289; and "Verbal Art," *Journal of American Folklore* 68 (1955), pp. 245–252.

21. Moshe Shokeid, "A Case of Ethnic Myth Making," *Cross-Currents in Israeli Culture and Politics*, ed. Myron Aronoff (New Brunswick: Transaction Books, 1984), pp. 39–50; Shlomo Swirsky, "The Oriental Jews in Israel: Why Many Tilted Toward Begin," *Dissent* (winter, 1984), pp. 71–91.

22. Alex Weingrod, "Recent Trends in Israeli Ethnicity," *Ethnic and Racial Studies* 2 (1979), pp. 55–65.

23. Shlomo Deshen, "Varieties of Abandonment of Religious Symbols," *Journal for the Scientific Study of Religion* 11 (1972), pp. 33–41; "Ethnicity and Citizenship in the Ritual of an Israeli Synagogue," *Southwestern Journal of Anthropology* 28 (1972), pp. 69–82; "Political Ethnicity and Cultural Ethnicity in Israel during the 1960s," in *Urban Ethnicity*, ed. Abner Cohen (London: Tavistock, 1974), pp. 281–309; "Ritualization of Literacy: The Works of Tunisian Scholars in Israel," *American Ethnologist* 2 (1975), pp. 251–260; Moshe Shokeid, "Cultural Ethnicity in Israel: The Case of Middle Eastern Jews' Religiosity," *AJS Review* 9 (1984), pp. 247–271; Shlomo Deshen and Moshe Shokeid, *The Predicament of Homecoming: Cultural and Social Life of North African Immigrants in Israel* (Ithaca, NY: Cornell University Press, 1974); Harvey Goldberg, *Cave Dwellers and Citrus Growers: A Jewish Community in Libya and Israel* (Cambridge: Cambridge University Press, 1972); "The Social Context of North African Jewish Patronyms," in *Folklore Research Center Studies*, vol. 3, ed. Dov Noy and Issachar Ben-Ami (Jerusalem: The Magnes Press, 1972); "Culture Change in an Israeli Village: The Twist Came to Even Yosef," *Middle Eastern Studies* 9 (1973), pp. 73–80; "The Mimouna and the Minority Status of the Moroccan Jews," *Ethnology* 17 (1978), pp. 75–87.
24. Harvey Goldberg, Introduction, "Culture and Ethnicity in the Study of Israeli Society," *Ethnic Groups* 1 (1977), pp. 163–186.
25. Yoram Bilu, "The Benefits of Attenuation: Continuity and Change in Jewish Moroccan Ethnopsychiatry in Israel," in *After the Ingathering: Studies in Israeli Ethnicity*, ed. Alex Weingrod (New York: Gordon and Breach, 1985), pp. 297–315; "Dreams and Wishes of the Saint," in *Judaism Viewed from Within and From Without: Anthropological Studies*, ed. Harvey Goldberg (Albany: State University of New York Press, 1987), pp. 285–313; Issachar Ben-Ami, "Relations between Jews and Muslims in the Veneration of Folk Saints in Morocco," *International Folklore Review* (1983), pp. 93–105.
26. Solomon Poll and Ernest Krausz, eds., *On Ethnic and Religious Diversity in Israel* (Ramat Gan: Institute for the Study of Ethnic Relations and Religious Groups, 1975); Michael Inbar and Chaim Adler, *Ethnic Integration in Israel: A Comparative Case of Two Moroccan Brothers Who Settled in France and Israel* (New Brunswick: Transaction Books, 1977); Ernest Krausz, ed., *Migration, Ethnicity and Community*, Studies in Israeli Society, vol. 1 (New Brunswick: Transaction Books, 1980).
27. Sammy Smooha, *Israel: Pluralism and Conflict* (London: Routledge and Kegan Paul, 1978).
28. Don Handelman, "The Organization of Ethnicity," *Ethnic Groups* 1 (1976), pp. 187–200.
29. Shmuel Noah Eisenstadt, Preface, *The Predicament of Homecoming: Cultural and Social Life of the North African Immigrants in Israel*, by Shlomo Deshen and Moshe Shokeid (Ithaca: Cornell University Press, 1974).
30. Dov Noy and Issachar Ben Ami, eds., *Folklore Research Center Studies*, vol. 1 (Jerusalem: Magnes Press, 1970).
31. Abraham Stahl, "Hishtanuto shel ha-Sipur ha-'Amami shel Yehudei ha-Mizrah le-ahar 'Aliyatam 'Artsah," [The change in the folk tale of Oriental Jewry following their immigration to Israel], pp. 344–349; Harvey Goldberg, "From Sheikh to Mazkir: Structural Continuity and Organizational Change in the Leadership of a Tripolitanian Jewish Community," pp. 29–41, and "The Social Context of North African Jewish Patronyms," pp. 245–258.
32. Américo Paredes and Richard Bauman, eds., *Toward New Perspectives in Folklore* (Austin: University of Texas Press, 1972).
33. See, for example, the journal *Mekhkarei Yerushalayim be-Folklor Yehudi* [Jerusalem studies in Jewish folklore], which is edited by Galit Hasan-Roken and Tamar Alexander.

Chapter 3

1. Sammy Smooha, *Social Research on Jewish Ethnicity in Israel 1948–1986: Review and Selected Bibliography with Abstracts* (Haifa: University of Haifa Press, 1986).

2. Hanna Herzog, "Ethnicity as a Product of Political Negotiations," *Ethnic and Racial Studies* 7 (1984), pp. 517–533.
3. Sara Hershkovitz, "Spatial Segregation Trends in the Tel-Aviv Metropolitan Area, Israel," *Geographical Research Forum* 6 (1983), pp. 50–71; Shlomo Hasson, "The Emergence of an Urban Social Movement in Israeli Society: An Integrated Approach," *International Journal of Urban and Regional Research* 7 (1983), pp. 157–172.
4. Yehuda Amir, Shlomo Sharan, and Rachel Ben-Ari, eds., *School Integration: Cross-Cultural Perspectives* (Hillsdale, New Jersey: Lawrence Erlbaum, 1984); Orit Ichilov and Miri Shacham, "Interethnic Contacts with Gifted Disadvantaged Students: Effects on Ethnic Attitudes," *Urban Education* 19 (1984), pp. 187–200; Abraham Stahl, "Introducing Ethnic Materials to the Classroom: Problems and Challenge," *Urban Education* 20 (1985), pp. 257–271; Shalva Weil, "The Effect of Ethnic Origin on Children's Perceptions of Their Families," *Journal of Comparative Family Studies* 16 (1983), pp. 348–366.
5. See, for example, Yochanan Peres, "Why Is It Difficult to Cope with Ethnic Pluralism in Israel?" in *On the Difficulty of Being an Israeli*, ed. Alouph Hareven (Jerusalem: The Van Leer Jerusalem Foundation n.d.), pp. 77–89; Eliezer Ben-Raphael, *The Emergence of Ethnicity: Cultural Groups and Social Conflict in Israel* (Westport, Connecticut: Greenwood Press, 1982); Moshe Semyonov and Vered Kraus, "The Social Hierarchies of Communities and Neighborhoods," *Social Science Quarterly* 63 (1982), pp. 780–789.
6. Chicago: University of Chicago Press, 1989.
7. Chicago: University of Chicago Press, 1990.
8. Philadelphia: ISHI, 1980. See also Goldberg's "Historical and Cultural Dimensions of Ethnic Phenomena in Israel," in *Studies in Israeli Ethnicity*, ed. Weingrod, pp. 179–200.
9. Goldberg, *Jewish Life in Muslim Libya*, p. ix.
10. Shlomo Deshen, "Varieties of Abandonment of Religious Symbols," *Journal for the Scientific Study of Religion* 11 (1972), pp. 33–41; "Ethnicity and Citizenship in the Ritual of an Israeli Synagogue," *Southwestern Journal of Anthropology* 28 (1972), pp. 69–82; "Ritualization of Literacy: The Works of Tunisian Scholars in Israel," *American Ethnologist* 2 (1975), pp. 251–260.
11. Albany, New York: State University of New York Press, 1987.
12. An exception in this case is Percy Cohen, who predicted mizrahi identification with the political right as early as 1962. See "Ethnic Hostility in Israel," *New Society* 22 (1963), pp. 14–16, and "Ethnicity, Class and Political Alignment in Israel," *Jewish Journal of Sociology* 25 (1983), pp. 119–130. As a non-Israeli, Cohen may have had greater objectivity.
13. Menachem Friedman, "Life Tradition and Book Tradition in the Development of Ultraorthodox Judaism," in *Judaism Viewed from Within and from Without*, ed. Harvey Goldberg, pp. 235–256.
14. Shlomo Deshen, "Religion among Middle Eastern Immigrants in Israel," in *Israel: A Developing Society*, ed. Asher Arian, (Assen: Van Gorcum, 1980), pp. 235–246; Moshe Shokeid, "Cultural Ethnicity in Israel: The Case of Middle Eastern Jews' Religiosity," *Association of Jewish Studies Review* 9 (1985), pp. 247–271.
15. Moshe Shokeid, "Cultural Ethnicity in Israel: The Case of Middle Eastern Jews' Religiosity."
16. Eli Yassif, "Storytelling in the 'Repentance' Movement: Rhetoric, Folklore and Cultural Debate in Contemporary Israel," *Jewish Folklore and Ethnology Review* 14 (1992), pp. 26–31.
17. Percy S. Cohen, "Ethnicity, Class and Political Alignment in Israel," *Jewish Journal of Sociology* 25 (1983), p. 124.
18. Judith T. Shuval, "Class and Ethnicity: A Study in Community Structure and Interpersonal Relations," Ph.D. diss., Radcliffe College, 1955; S. N. Eisenstadt, "Sociological Aspects of the Economic Adaption of Oriental Immigrants in Israel: A Case Study of Modernization," *Economic Development and Cultural Change* 4 (1956), pp. 269–278.
19. Deborah Bernstein, "Immigrant and Society: A Critical View of the Dominant

School of Israeli Sociology," *British Journal of Sociology* 31 (1980), pp. 5–23; "Immigrant Transit Camps: The Formation of Dependent Relations in Israeli Society," *Ethnic and Racial Studies* 4 (1981), pp. 26–43; "Conflict and Protest in Israeli Society: The Case of the Black Panthers of Israel," *Youth and Society* 16 (1984), pp. 129–152; Deborah Bernstein and Shlomo Swirski, "The Rapid Economic Development of Israel and the Emergence of the Ethnic Division of Labor," *British Journal of Sociology* 33 (1982), pp. 64–85.

20. Deborah Bernstein, "Immigrant Transit Camps: The Formation of Dependent Relations in Israeli Society," p. 41.
21. Yosef Ben-David, "Ethnic Differences or Social Change?" p. 33.
22. Hannah Ayalon, Eliezer Ben-Raphael, and Stephen Sharot, "Variation in Ethnic Identification among Israeli Jews," *Ethnic and Racial Studies* 8 (1985), pp. 390–391.
23. Ibid., p. 403.
24. Haifa: Haifa University Press, 1987.
25. London: Routledge and Kegan Paul, 1978.
26. Smooha, p. 17.
27. New York: Gordon and Breach, 1985.
28. Weingrod, *Studies in Israeli Ethnicity*, pp. xv–xvi.
29. In ibid., pp. 179–200.
30. Goldberg, "Historical and Cultural Dimension," p. 198.
31. *Israel Social Science Research* 3 (1985); revised and reprinted as *Ethiopian Jews and Israel*, ed. Michael Ashkenazi and Alex Weingrod (New Brunswick: Transaction Books, 1987).
32. Ashkenazi and Weingrod, eds., *Ethiopian Immigrants in Beer Sheva*, p. 49.
33. *Israel Social Science Research* 3 (1985), pp. 112–149. For a recent survey and bibliography, see Shalva Weil, "Ethiopian Jews in Israel: A Survey of Research and Documentation," *Jewish Folklore and Ethnology Review* 11 (1989), pp. 28–32.
34. Aliza Shenhar, *The Jewish and Israeli Folklore* (New Delhi: South Asian Publishers, 1987).
35. Aliza Shenhar and Haya Bar-Itzhak, *Folktales from Beit She'an* (Haifa: Haifa University Press, 1981); and *Folktales from Shelomy* (Haifa: Haifa University Press, 1982)
36. Yoram Bilu, "Demonic Explanations of Disease among Moroccan Jews in Israel," *Jerusalem Studies in Jewish Folklore* 2 (1986), pp. 89–103; and "The Moroccan Demon in Israel: The Case of Evil Spirit Disease," *Ethos* 8 (1980), pp. 24–38.
37. Issachar Ben-Ami, *Saint Veneration among the Jews of Morocco* (Jerusalem: Magnes Press,, 1984); Yoram Bilu and Issachar Ben-Ami, " 'Saints' Sanctuaries in Israeli Development Towns: On a Mechanism of Urban Transformation," *Urban Anthropology* 16 (1987), pp. 243–272.
38. Moshe Shokeid, *Children of Circumstances: Israeli Emigrants in New York* (Ithaca and London: Cornell University Press, 1988).
39. Alex Weingrod, *The Saint of Be'er Sheva* (Albany: State University of New York Press, 1990).

Chapter 4

1. See Thomas Butler, Introduction, *Bulgaria Past and Present*, ed. Thomas Butler (Columbus, Ohio: American Association for the Advancement of Slavic Studies, 1973), p. xiv; and Guy H. Haskell, "Bulgarian Folklore and Ethnography: A Bibliographical Essay," *East European and Slavic Folklore Newsletter* 1, no. 3 (autumn, 1980), pp. 1–10.
2. Binyamin Arditti, "Purvite Evrei v Bulgariya," [The first Jews in Bulgaria], in *Evreite v istoriyata, literaturata, i politikata—Sbornik na evreiskiya naroden universitet* [Jews in history, literature and politics: Symposium of the Jewish Peoples' University] (Sofia: n.p. 1933). See also Haim Keshales, "Dorot Ha-Rishonim" [The first generations], in *Yahadut Bulgaria* [Bulgarian Jewry], ed. Albert Romano, et al. (Jerusalem-Tel Aviv: Encyclopedia of the Jewish Diaspora, 1967), pp. 27–36.

3. Tamir, pp. 3–7; Simon Marcus, "Romaniots," *Encyclopedia Judaica* (Jerusalem: Keter, 1973), vol. 14, p. 231. See also Andrew Sharf, *Byzantine Jewry: From Justinian to the Fourth Crusade* (New York: Shocken Books, 1971); and Joshua Starr, *The Jews in the Byzantine Empire: 641–1204* (New York: Burt Franklin, 1939).
4. See Robert F. Byrnes, ed., *Communal Families in the Balkans: The Zadrugas* (South Bend, Indiana: University of Notre Dame Press, 1976).
5. David Marshall Lang, The *Bulgarians: From Pagan Times to the Ottoman Conquest* (London: Thames and Hudson, 1976), pp. 21–42.
6. Tamir, p. vii.
7. Nissan Oren, "Bulgaria," *Encyclopedia Judaica* (Jerusalem: Keter, 1973), vol. 2, pp. 1480–1481.
8. Tamir, pp. 14–15.
9. Keshales, "Dorot Ha-Rishonim," p. 30.
10. Tamir, pp. 41–42.
11. Solomon Rosanes, *Korot Ha-Yehudim Be-Turkiyah Ve-'Artsot Ha-Kedem* [History of the Jews in Turkey and ancient lands] (Tel Aviv: Dvir, 1930), p. 220.

Chapter 5

1. Arlene Malinowski, "A Report on the Status of Judeo-Spanish in Turkey," *International Journal of the Sociology* (1982), p. 10; see also Keshales, "Dorot Ha-Rishonim," pp. 37–62.
2. These Moslem Bulgarians are called Pomaks and were especially numerous in the Rhodope region. They constituted a not insignificant portion of the population until 1949. See Tamir, p. 50.
3. Nikolai Todorov, "Evreiskoto naselenie v Balkanskite provintsii na Osmanskata Imperia prez XV–XIX vek [The Jewish population of the Balkan provinces of the Ottoman Empire from the XV–XIX centuries], in *Prouchvaniya za istoriyata na Evreiskoto Naselenie v Bulgarskite zemi XV–XX vek* [Studies in the Jewish population of the Bulgarian lands: XV–XX centuries] (Sofia: Bulgarian Academy of Sciences, 1980), pp. 7–21.
4. Oren, "Bulgaria," p. 1482.
5. Tamir, p. 54.
6. Oren, "Bulgaria," p. 1482.
7. Yosef Yerushalmi, "Coping with Catastrophe: Jewish Reactions to the Expulsion from Spain," Sydelle Lewis Lecture in Jewish Studies, March 5, 1984, Indiana University.
8. Ibid.
9. Cited in Tamir, p. 56.
10. Tamir, p. 57.
11. The census of 1897 recorded a minority population of 120,000: 75,000 Jews (62.5 percent), 14,000 Greeks, 11,000 Slavs, 20,000 Turks, and small numbers of Vlachs, Albanians, and Gypsies.
12. Oren, "Bulgaria," p. 1482.
13. Nikolai Todorov, "The City in the Bulgarian Lands from the Fifteenth to the Nineteenth Century," in *Bulgaria: Past and Present*, ed. Thomas Butler (Columbus, Ohio: American Association for the Advancement of Slavic Studies, 1973), pp. 15–30.
14. Tamir, p. 71.
15. Mair Jose Benardete, *Hispanic Culture and Character of the Sephardi Jews* (New York: Hispanic Institute in the United States, 1952), p. 72.
16. Tamir, p. 66. Documentation on the religious and cultural life of Balkan Jewry during this period is varied and extensive, but does not bear directly on the present study. See Tamir, pp. 66–74, and Benardete, *Hispanic Culture and the Character of the Sephardi Jews.*
17. For a detailed description of this system, which continued well into the nineteenth

century, see R. J. Crampton, "Bulgarian Society in the Early 19th Century," in *Balkan Society in the Age Of Greek Independence*, ed. Richard Clogg (Totowa, New Jersey: Barnes and Noble Books, 1981), pp. 157–204.

18. For example, Joseph Caro, author of the *Shulkhan Arukh*, "Code of Jewish Law," was active in Nikopol in the sixteenth century.
19. Tamir, p. 76.
20. Ibid., pp. 76–77.
21. Ya'akov Nitsani, "Kehilat Plovdiv: 'Em Ha-Tsiyonut Be-Bulgariya" [The Jewish community of Plovdiv: Mother city of Zionism in Bulgaria] *Reshumot*, n.s. 5 (1953), p. 30.

Chapter 6

1. C. E. Black, *The Establishment of Constitutional Government in Bulgaria* (Princeton: Princeton University Press, 1943).
2. Stanley G. Evans, *A Short History of Bulgaria* (London: Laurence and Wishart, 1960), p. 129.
3. For a vivid description of such a community structure in Plovdiv, see Nitsani, pp. 25–33.
4. Marcel Kalev, "Yahadut Bulgariyah ve-Tnu'atah ha-Ziyonit," in *Aharon Ben-Yosef*, ed. Yosef Shapira (Tel Aviv: The Aharon Ben-Yosef Committee, 1953–1954), p. 138.
5. Tamir, p. 99.
6. Aharon Zwergbaum, "Zionism," *Encyclopedia Judaica*, vol. 16, p. 1108.
7. Gedalyah Elkoshi and Hugo Valentin, "Marcus Ehrenpreis," *Encyclopedia Judaica*, Vol. 6, pp. 509–510.
8. Nitsani, pp. 25–50.
9. Binyamin Arditti, "Yosef Marko Baruh," in Shapira, pp. 159—169.
10. Nitsani, p. 26.
11. Zwergbaum, p. 1108.
12. William F. Russel, *Schools in Bulgaria* (New York: Teachers College, Columbia University, 1957), p. 33.
13. L. A. D. Dellin, ed., *Bulgaria* (New York: Frederick A. Praeger, 1957), p. 229.
14. Stoyan Omarchevsky, "The Jews in Bulgaria," *Reflex* 4, no. 5 (May 1929), p. 49.
15. Nitsani, pp. 48–49.
16. Benardete, pp. 130–131.
17. Tamir, p. 108.
18. Nitsani, pp. 48–49.
19. Stoyan Omarchevsky, "The Jews in Bulgaria," *Reflex* 4, no. 5 (May, 1929), p. 48.
20. Nitsani, p. 33.
21. Tracy K. Harris, "The Decline of Judeo Spanish," *International Journal of the Sociology of Language* 37 (1982), pp. 82–85; and Malinowski, p. 17.
22. Aron Rodrigue, *French Jews, Turkish Jews* (Bloomington: Indiana University Press, 1990), pp. 170–171.
23. See Albert Versano, "Hitakhdut Makabi," [The Maccabi union] in Shapira, pp. 170–175.
24. See Nisim Kohen, "Ha-Shomer Ha-Tsa'ir," in Shapira, pp. 179–186.
25. See Jean Daniel, "Kavim le-Toldot Po'alei Tsiyon," [Approaches to the history of Po'alei Tsiyon] in Shapira, pp. 187–202.
26. Tamir, p. 155.
27. Nissan Oren, *Revolution Administered: Agrarianism and Communism in Bulgaria* (Baltimore and London: Johns Hopkins University Press, 1973), p. 123.
28. Albert Versano, ed., *Maccabi Bulgariyah* (Tel Aviv: The Albert Kiyoso Circle, 1976), p. 8; see also Albert Romano, " 'Agudot 'Maccabi' Be-Bulgariyah" [The Maccabi organizatons in Bulgaria], in his *Yahadut Bulgariyah*, pp. 319–356.
29. Nitsani, p. 38.

30. Zevi Einfeld, "Batei Sefer Ha-'Ivriyim Be-Sofia" [Hebrew schools in Sofia], *Ha-'Olam* (London) 17, no. 4 (January, 1929), p. 74; Nitsani, p. 40.
31. Omarchevsky, p. 50.
32. Ibid., p. 51. For a complete set of statistics on the enrollments and budgets of the Jewish schools in Bulgaria, see Romano, et al., pp. 643–661.
33. Einfeld, p. 74.
34. Nitsani, p. 35.
35. Haim Vital, "The Jews of Bulgaria: A Survey of Jewish Ruin," *Congress Bi-Weekly* 8, no. 37 (1941), p. 12.
36. Versano, *Maccabi Bulgariyah.*
37. Kalev, p. 138.
38. Nitsani, p. 27.
39. Harris, "Reasons for the Decline of Judeo-Spanish," *International Journal of the Sociology of Language* 37 (1982), pp. 74–76.
40. Simon Marcus, *Ha-Safah Ha-Sfaradit-Yehudit*, p. 57.
41. Harris, "Reasons for the Decline," p. 73.
42. See Albert Kalev, pp. 175–178.
43. Leon Sciaky, *Farewell Solonika* (New York: Current Books, 1946), quoted by Benardete, p. 167.
44. Harris, pp. 72–73.
45. Joseph Rothschild, *The Communist Party of Bulgaria: 1883–1936* (New York: Columbia University Press, 1959), p. 5.
46. Rothschild, p. 8.
47. *Encyclopedia Judaica*, vol. 11, pp. 1565–1566.
48. N. M. Gelber, "Jewish Life in Bulgaria," *Jewish Social Studies* 8 (1946), p. 108.
49. Gelber, pp. 109–111.
50. Haim Vital, "The Jews of Bulgaria," p. 12. A monograph was published by Binyamin Arditi in 1968 about his own community, entitled *Yehudei Bulgariyah: Kehilat Shumlah* [The Jews of Bulgaria: The community of Shumla] (Holon, Israel: the author, 1968).
51. Anastas Totev, "Characteristic Demographic Features of Bulgaria, 1880–1980," in *Bulgaria: Past and Present*, ed. Thomas Butler (Columbus, Ohio: American Association for the Advancement of Slavic Studies, 1973), p. 33.
52. Nitsani, p. 43.
53. Ibid., pp. 43–44; Krispin, pp. 224–227.
54. Arditi, *Yehudei Bulgariyah*, pp. 44–48.
55. Ibid., pp. 102–104.
56. Nitsani, p. 42.

Chapter 7

1. Nissan Oren, "The Bulgarian Exception: A Reassessment of the Salvation of the Jewish Community," *Yad Vashem Studies* 8 (1968), pp. 83–106.
2. Oren discusses the first three trends and their proponents in his article, "The Bulgarian Exception," pp. 83–85. The final and most remarkable approach is Vicki Tamir's, p. 217. See especially her chauvinist anti-Bulgarian polemic, "The Bulgarian Psyche," pp. 233–251.
3. Frederick B. Chary, "Bulgaria and the Jews: The Final Solution, 1940–1944, diss., University of Pittsburgh, 1968; published as *The Bulgarian Jews and the Final Solution: 1940–1944* (Pittsburgh: University of Pittsburgh Press, 1972).
4. See also Binyamin Arditi, *Yehudei Bulgariyah Ba-Shnot Ha-Mishtar Ha-Nazi: 1940–1944* [The Jews of Bulgaria during the years of Nazi rule] (Tel Aviv: Israel Press, 1962); and Albert Beni, *Yehudei Bulgariyah Ba-Ma'avak Neged Ha-Nazim* [The Jews of Bulgaria in the struggle against the Nazis] (World Zionist Organization: Depart-

ment of Zionist and Social Activity among Sephardic Communities and Immigrants from Oriental Countries, 1980).

5. Peter Meyer, "Bulgaria," in his *The Jews of the Soviet Satellites* (Syracuse, New York: Syracuse University Press, 1953), pp. 122–123.
6. Nissan Oren, *Revolution Administered: Agrarianism and Communism in Bulgaria* (Baltimore and London: Johns Hopkins University Press, 1973), pp. 122–123.
7. Oren, "The Bulgarian Exception," pp. 88–89.
8. Quoted in Matei Yulzari, "The Bulgarian Jews in the Resistance Movement," in *They Fought Back: The Story of the Jewish Resistance in Nazi Europe*, ed. and trans. Yuri Suhl (New York: Crown Publishers, 1967), p. 278.
9. J. P. Brown, *Bulgaria under Communist Rule* (New York: Praeger, 1970), p. 3.
10. Meyer, 567–568. For a discussion of the various antisemitic organizations in Bulgaria, see Binyamin Arditi, *Rolyata na Tsar Boris III pri izselvaneto na Evreite ot Bulgaria* [The role of King Boris III in the deportation of the Jews of Bulgaria] (Tel Aviv: n.p., 1952), pp. 24–35, and Dimo Kazasov, *Burni Godini* [Stormy years] (Sofia, n. p., 1949), pp. 643–645. These groups produced their share of antisemitic propaganda; see Binyamin Arditi, *Ha-Sifrut Ha-Antishemit Be-Bulgariyah: Reshimah Bibliografit* [Antisemitic literature in Bulgaria: A bibliography], (Holon, Israel: the author, 1972).
11. *The Jewish Communities of Nazi Occupied Europe*. The Research Institute on Peace and Post War Problems of the American Jewish Committee, 1944 (rpt. New York: Howard Fertig, 1982), p. 1.
12. Chary, "The Bulgarian Jews and the Final Solution," p. 37.
13. *The Jewish Communities of Nazi Occupied Europe*, p. 4.
14. Yulzari, p. 277.
15. Chary, "The Bulgarian Jews and the Final Solution," p. 33; see Buko Piti, ed., *Bulgarskata obshtestvenost za rasizma i antisemitizma* [Bulgarian public opinion on racism and Antisemitism] (Sofia: n.p., 1937); Piti later wrote *Te, spasitelite* [They, the rescuers] (Tel Aviv, n.p., 1969).
16. Yulzari, p. 226.
17. The American and other schools sponsored by organizations in the Allied nations, which had become important and influential in Bulgarian education and had numerous Jewish students, were also forced to close. See Floyd H. Black, *The American College in Sofia* (Boston: Trustees of the Sofia American Schools, 1958), pp. 77–90.
18. For vivid descriptions of life in the battalions, see Eli Baruh, *Iz istoriyata na Bulgarskoto evreistvo: nashite stradaniya v Evreiskite trudovi lageri prez fashistkiya rezhim v Bulgaria: 1941–1944* [From the history of Bulgarian Jewry: Our suffering in the Jewish labor camps during the Fascist regime in Bulgaria: 1941–1944] (Tel Aviv: Yafor Printing House, 1960); and Reuven (Doti) Benaroyo, *Nedovursheniyat put na Negovo Velichestvo: iz spomenite na edin ot mnogoto evreiskite trudovi lageri* [His majesty's unfinished road: Recollections of one of many Jewish labor camps] (Tel Aviv: n.p., 1975).
19. Yulzari, p. 279.
20. Ibid., p. 277.
21. See Alexander Matkowski, "The Destruction of Macedonian Jewry in 1943," *Yad Vashem Studies* 3 (1959), pp. 203–258; *Tragedijata na Evreite ot Makedonija* [The tragedy of the Jews of Macedonia] (Skopje: Kultura, 1962); and Nadejda Slavi Vasileva, "On the Catastrophe of the Thracian Jews: Recollection," *Yad Vashem Studies* 3 (1959), pp. 295–302.
22. Oren, "The Bulgarian Exception," p. 96.
23. Oren, "The Bulgarian Exception," pp. 96–98.
24. Meyer, p. 573.
25. Oren, *Revolution Administered*, p. 124.
26. Reuben Ainsztein, *Jewish Resistance in Nazi-Occupied Eastern Europe* (New York: Barnes and Noble, 1974), p. xxi.
27. Stephane Groueff, *Crown of Thorns*.

28. See Arditi, *Rolyata na Tsar Boris*; Marshall Lee Miller, *Bulgaria during the Second World War* (Stanford, California: Stanford University Press, 1975)), pp. 135–150; Helmut Heiber, "Der Tod des Zaren Boris," *Vierteljahrshefte fur Zeitgeschichte* 9 (1961), pp. 384–416; Chary, *The Bulgarian Jews*, pp. 157–166.
29. Meyer, p. 573.

Chapter 8

1. Yulzari, pp. 279–281.
2. Oren, *Revolution Administered*, p. 124.
3. Ibid.
4. Quoted in Ora Alcalay, "Bulgaria," *European Judaism* 3, no. 2 (winter 1968–1969), p. 26.
5. Oren, *Encyclopedia Judaica*, p. 1489.
6. Tamir, p. 222.
7. Baruch Hazzan, "The Jewish Community of Bulgaria," in *The Balkan Jewish Communities*, ed. Daniel J. Elazar (Lanham, Maryland: University Press of America, 1984), p. 73.
8. Oren, *Encyclopedia Judaica*, p. 1490.
9. Hazzan, p. 79; Zwergbaum, p. 1109.
10. *Izgrav* (February 18, 1945), quoted in Emanuel Margalit, "Ha-Ma'avak Ha-Ziyoni shel Yehudei Bulgariyah 'im Hishtaltut Ha-Komunistim" [The Zionist struggle of the Jews of Bulgaria with the communist regime], *Gesher* 3, no. 2 (July 1957), p. 98.
11. *Po'alei Ziyon* (December 15, 1944), quoted in Margalit, p. 98.
12. *Po'alei Ziyon* (March 30, 1945), quoted in Margalit, p. 98.
13. Oren, *Encyclopedia Judaica*, p. 1490.
14. Tamir, p. 219.
15. Oren, *Encyclopedia Judaica*, p. 1490.
16. Margalit, pp. 97–98.
17. Tamir, p. 221.
18. Hazzan, p. 75.
19. Oren, *Encyclopedia Judaica*, p. 1490.
20. Ibid., p. 1491.
21. Ibid., p. 1490.
22. Barukh Konfino, *Aliyah Bet Mi-Hofei Bulgariyah, 1938–1940, 1947–1948: Hisul Galut Bulgariya, 1948–1949* [Illegal immigration from the shores of Bulgaria, 1938–1940, 1947–1948; Dissolution of the Bulgarian community, 1948–1949], trans. Sason Levi (Jerusalem-Tel Aviv: Ahiyasaf Publishing House, 1965), pp. 12–90.
23. Tamir, (p. 230; Konfino, pp. 93–135.
24. For a description of Jewish life in Bulgaria following the mass immigrations, see Hazzan, pp. 79–101.
25. Alcalay, p. 31.
26. Ibid., p. 29.

Chapter 9

1. Eisenstadt, *The Absorption of Immigrants*, pp. 118–119.
2. Ibid., p. 119.
3. Ibid., pp. 119–120.
4. Judith T. Shuval, "The Role of Ideology as a Predisposing Frame of Reference for Immigrants," *Human Relations* 7 (1959), pp. 51–63; *Immigrants on the Threshold* (London: Prentice-Hall International, 1963), pp. 139–155.
5. Don Handelman, "The Organization of Ethnicity," *Ethnic Groups* 1 (1977), pp. 187–200.

6. See bibliography in Dell Hymes, *Foundations in Sociolinguistics: An Ethnographic Approach* (Philadelphia: University of Pennsylvania Press, 1974), pp. 210–231.
7. See Américo Paredes and Richard Bauman, eds., *Toward New Perspectives in Folklore* (Austin and London: University of Texas Press, 1972).
8. The most comprehensive discussion of this reorientation in folkloristic approaches to ethnicity is Stephen Stern's "Ethnic Folklore and the Folklore of Ethnicity," in *Folklore and Ethnicity*, ed. Larry Danielson (Los Angeles: California Folklore Society, 1978), pp. 7–32; see especially the large number of dissertations produced by students at Indiana University since the early 1970s concerning folklore and ethnicity—this study is a legacy of and, hopefully, a contribution to these earlier works.
9. Stern, pp. 7–32.
10. Shlomo Deshen, "Ethnic Boundaries and Cultural Paradigms: The Case of Southern Tunisian Immigrants in Israel," *Working Papers in Sephardic and Oriental Jewish Studies* 2 (New York: American Sephardi Federation, 1976).
11. Ward H. Goodenough, *Language, Culture, and Society* (Addison-Wesley Modular Publications, module no. 7, 1971), p. 20.

Chapter 10

1. Walter F. Weiker, "Stratification in Israeli Society: Is There a Middle Category?" *Israel Social Science Research* 1 (1983), pp. 30–56.
2. Zevi Einfeld, "Batei Ha-Sefer Ha-'Ivriyim Be-Sofia," *Ha-Olam* (London) 17, no. 4 (January, 1929), pp. 73–75.
3. Avraham Bahar, *Zihronot Har-Tuv* [Memories of Har-Tuv] (Jerusalem: Published by the family, 1970; repr. 1990).
4. Barukh Konfino, *Aliyah Bet Mi-Hofei Bulgariyah, pp. 5–90.*
5. Avidan Mashiah, "Bulgarian Jews in Israel," in *Encyclopedia of Zionism and Israel*, ed. Raphael Patai (New York: Herzl Press/McGraw Hill, 1971), vol. 1, p. 169.

Chapter 11

1. Albert Kalev, pp. 175–178.
2. Romano, "Ha-Yahadut Ve-Ha-Tnu'ah Ha-Ziyonit Be-Bulgariyah," pp. 455–459.
3. Danielson, p. 1.
4. Jewish poet from Bulgaria, who often wrote on Zionist themes; see *'Andarta: Mehaber Shirim* [Memorial to a poet], trans. Rafa'el Eli'az (Tel Aviv: Committee for Publishing the Works of Simcho Isakov of the Union of Bulgarian Immigrants, 1973); and *Alfred Sason* (Tel Aviv: Albert Beni, 1980).

Bibliography

Social Scientific Works

Abarbanel, Jay S. *The Cooperative Farmer and the Welfare State: Economic Change in an Israeli Moshav.* Manchester: University of Manchester Press, 1974.
———. "The Dilemma of Economic Competition in an Israeli Moshav." In *Symbol and Politics in Communal Ideology*, edited by S. F. Moore and B. G. Meyerhoff, pp. 144–165. Ithaca, New York: Cornell University Press, 1974.
Abramovitch, Henry, and Yoram Bilu. "Visitational Dreams and Naming Practices among Moroccan Jews in Israel." *Jewish Journal of Sociology* 27 (1985), pp. 13–21.
Adler, Israel, and Robert Hodge. "Ethnicity and the Process of Status Attainment in Israel." *Israel Social Science Research* 1 (1983), pp. 5–23.
Altman, Y., and G. Mars. "The Emigration of Soviet Georgian Jews in Israel." *Jewish Journal of Sociology* 26 (1984), pp. 35–45.
Aronoff, Myron. *Frontiertown: The Politics of Community Building in Israel.* Manchester: Manchester University Press, 1974.
Ashkenazi, Michael, and Alex Weingrod. *Ethiopian Immigrants in Beer Sheva: An Anthropological Study of the Absorption Process.* Highland Park, Illinois: American Association for Ethiopian Jews, 1984.
———, eds. *Ethiopian Jews and Israel.* New Brunswick, New Jersey: Transaction Books, 1987.
Avrukh, Kevin. *American Immigrants in Israel.* Chicago: University of Chicago Press, 1981.
Ayalon, Hanna, Eliezer Ben-Raphael, and Stephen Sharot. "Variations in Ethnic Identification among Israeli Jews." *Ethnic and Racial Studies* 8 (1985), pp. 389–407.
Barth, Frederick, ed. *Ethnic Groups and Boundaries.* London: Allen and Unwin, 1969.
Bar Yosef, Rivka Weis. "Desocialization and Resocialization: The Adjustment Process of Immigrants." *The International Migration Review* 2 (1968), pp. 19–38.
Bascom, William R. "Folklore and Anthropology." *Journal of American Folklore* 56 (1953), pp. 283–290.
———. "Verbal Art." *Journal of American Folklore* 68 (1955), pp. 245–252.
Bauman, Richard. *Verbal Art as Performance.* Rowley, Massachussetts: Newbury House Publishers, 1977.
Ben-Ami, Issachar. *He-Arazat ha-Kdoshim ba-kerev Yehudei Moroko* [Saint veneration among the Jews of Morocco]. Folklore Research Center Studies 8. Jerusalem: Magnes Press, 1984.
Ben-Amos, Dan. "Folklore in Israel." *Schweizerisches Archiv für Volkskunde* 59 (1963), pp. 14–24.
Ben-David, Yosef. "Ethnic Differences or Social Change?" *Megamot* (January, 1952), pp. 171–183. (Rpt. in *Between Past and Future*, edited by Carl Frankenstein, pp. 33–52. Jerusalem: Henrietta Szold Institute, 1953, and in *Olim be-Yisrael* [Immigrants in Israel], edited by Moshe Lissak, et al., pp. 74–61. Jerusalem: Akadmon, 1969.)
Ben-Raphael, Eliezer. *The Emergence of Ethnicity: Cultural Groups and Social Conflict in Israel.* Westport, Connecticut: Greenwood Press, 1982.
Ben-Raphael, Eliezer, and Stephen Sharot. "Ethnic Pluralism and Religious Congrega-

tions: A Comparison of Neighborhoods in Israel." *Ethnic Groups* 7 (1987), pp. 65–83.

Ben Zvi, Yitzhak. *The Exiled and the Redeemed.* Philadelphia: Jewish Publication Society, 1957.

Bernstein, Deborah. "Conflict and Protest in Israeli Society: The Case of the Black Panthers of Israel." *Youth and Society* 16 (1984), pp. 129–152.

———. "Immigrants and Society: A Critical View of the Dominant School of Israeli Sociology." *British Journal of Sociology* 31 (1980), pp. 246–264.

———. "Immigrant Transit Camps: The Formation of Dependent Relations in Israeli Society." *Ethnic and Racial Studies* 4 (1981), pp. 26–43.

Bernstein, Deborah, and Shlomo Swirsky. "The Rapid Economic Development of Israel and the Emergence of the Ethnic Division of Labour." *British Journal of Sociology* 33 (1982), pp. 64–85.

Bernstein, Judith, and Aaron Antonovsky, "The Integration of Ethnic Groups in Israel." *The Jewish Journal of Sociology* 23 (1981), pp. 5–23.

Bilu, Yoram. "The Benefits of Attenuation: Continuity and Change in Jewish Moroccan Ethnopsychiatry in Israel." In *Studies in Israeli Ethnicity: After the Ingathering*, edited by Alex Weingrod, pp. 297–316. New York: Gordon and Breach, 1985.

———. "The Moroccan Demon in Israel: The Case of Evil Spirit Disease." *Ethos* 8 (1980), pp. 24–38.

Bilu, Yoram, and Henry Abramovitch. "In Search of the Saddiq: Visitational Dreams among Moroccan Jews in Israel." *Psychiatry* 48 (1985), pp. 83–92.

Bonne, Alfred. "The Adjustment of Oriental Immigrants to Industrial Employment in Israel." *International Social Sciences Bulletin* 8 (1956), pp. 12–35.

Brauer, Erich. *Ethnologie der jemenitischen Juden.* Heidelberg: Ca. Winter, 1934.

———. *Yehudei Kurdistan: Mehkar Etnologi.* Sifriyah le-Folklor ve-Etnologiyah [The Jews of Kurdistan: An ethnological study]. Folklore and Ethnology Library], vol. 2. Completed, edited, and translated by Raphael Patai. Jerusalem: Palestine Institute of Folklore and Ethnology, 1947. (Rpt. Detroit: Wayne State University Press, 1993.)

Carmin Karpman, I. J. *Who's Who in World Jewry.* New York: Pitman Publishing Corporation, 1973.

Chouraqui, Andre N. *Between East and West: A History of the Jews of North Africa.* Philadelphia: Jewish Publication Society, 1968.

Cohen, Erik. "The Black Panthers and Israeli Society." *Jewish Journal of Sociology* 14 (1972), pp. 92–109.

———. *The City in Zionist Ideology.* Report no. 1. Jerusalem Urban Studies. Institute of Urban and Regional Studies. Jerusalem: Eliezer Kaplan School of Economics and Social Sciences, 1970.

———. "Ethnicity and Legitimation in Contemporary Israel." *The Jerusalem Quarterly* 28 (1983), pp. 111–124.

———. "Recent Anthropological Studies of Middle Eastern Communities and Ethnic Groups." *Annual Review of Anthropology* 6 (1977), pp. 315–347.

———"Social Images in an Israeli Development Town." *Human Relations* 21 (1968), pp. 63–176.

Cohen, Percy S. "Alignments and Allegiances in the Community of Sha'arayim in Israel." *Jewish Journal of Sociology* 4 (1962), pp. 14–38.

———. "Ethnic Group Differences in Israel." *Race* 9 (1968), pp. 303–310.

———. "Ethnic Hostility in Israel." *New Society* 22 (1963), pp. 14–16.

———. "Ethnicity, Class and Political Alignment in Israel." *Jewish Journal of Sociology* 25 (1983), pp. 119–130.

———"Leadership and Politics amongst Israeli Yemenites." Diss., University of London, 1961.

Curtis, Michael, and Mordecai Chertoff. *Israel: Social Structure and Change.* New Brunswick, New Jersey: E. P. Dutton and Co., 1973.

Cyderovitch, G. "The Living Standards of the Jewish Community at the End of the War." *Bulletin of the Economic Research Institute of the Jewish Agency* 10, no. 2 (1946), pp. 36–45.

Danielson, Larry. Introduction. *Studies in Folklore and Ethnicity*, edited by Larry Danielson, pp. 1–5. Los Angeles: California Folklore Society, 1978.

Datan, Nancy, Aaron Antonovsky, and Benjamin Maoz. *A Time to Reap: The Middle Age of Women in Five Israeli Subcultures*. Baltimore: Johns Hopkins University Press, 1981.

Degh, Linda. "Approaches to Folklore Research Among Immigrant Groups." *Journal of American Folklore* 77 (1966), pp. 551–556.

———. "Ethnicity in Modern European Ethnology." *Folklore Forum* 7 (1974), pp. 48–55.

———. *Folktales and Society: Storytelling in a Hungarian Peasant Community*. Bloomington and London: Indiana University Press, 1969.

———. *People in the Tobacco Belt: Four Lives*. National Museum of Man Mercury Series, Canadian Center for Folk Culture Studies, Paper No. 13 (Ottawa, 1975).

———. "Prepared Comments by Linda Degh to Richard M. Dorson's 'Is There a Folk in the City.' " *The Urban Experience and Folk Tradition*, edited by Américo Paredes and Ellen J. Stekert, pp. 54–55. Austin: University of Texas Press, 1971.

———. "Survival and Revival of European Folk Culture in America." *Ethnologia Europea* 2–3 (1968–1969), pp. 97–108.

Dekel, Ephraim. *B'riha: Flight to the Homeland*. Translated by Dina Ettinger. New York: Herzl Press, n. d.

Deshen, Shlomo. " 'The Business of Ethnicity is Finished!'? The Ethnic Factor in a Local Election Campaign." In *The Elections in Israel, 1969*, edited by Alan Arian, pp. 278–302. Jerusalem: Academic Press, 1972.

———. *A Case of Breakdown of Modernization in an Israeli Immigrant Community: An Essay in Applied Sociology*. Kiryat Gat, Israel: Lachish Regional Administration of the Jewish Agency Land Settlement Department, 1964. (Rpt., *Jewish Journal of Sociology* 7 (1965), pp. 63–91; and in *Integration and Development in Israel*, edited by Shmuel Noah Eisenstadt, Rivka Bar Yosef, and Chaim Adler, London: Praeger, 1970.)

———. "Conflict and Social Change: The Case of an Israeli Village." *Sociologia Ruralis* 6 (1966), pp. 31–35.

———. "Ethnic Boundaries and Cultural Paradigms: The Case of Southern Tunisian Immigrants in Israel." *Working Papers in Sephardic and Oriental Jewish Studies*, vol. 2. New York: American Sephardi Federation, 1976 (Rpt., *Ethnos* 4 (1976), pp. 271–294).

———. "Ethnicity and Citizenship in the Ritual of an Israeli Synagogue." *Southwestern Journal of Anthropology* 28 (1972), pp. 69–82.

———. *Immigrant Voters in Israel: Parties and Congregations in a Local Election Campaign*. Manchester: Manchester University Press, 1970.

———. *The Mellah Society: Jewish Community Life in Sherifiyan Morocco*. Chicago: University of Chicago Press, 1989.

———. "Non-Conformists in an Israeli Immigrant Community." *Mankind Quarterly* 9 (1969), pp. 166–177.

———. "Political Ethnicity and Cultural Ethnicity in Israel during the 1960s." In *Urban Ethnicity*, edited by Abner Cohen, pp. 281–309. London: Tavistock, 1974.

———. "Religion among Middle Eastern Immigrants in Israel." In *Israel: A Developing Society*, edited by Asher Arian, pp. 235–246. Assen: Van Gorcum, 1980.

———. "Ritualization of Literacy: The Works of Tunisian Scholars in Israel." *American Ethnologist* 2 (1975), pp. 251–260.

———. "Social Organization and Politics in Israeli Urban Quarters." *The Jerusalem Quarterly* 22 (1982), pp. 21–37.

———. "The Varieties of Abandonment of Religious Symbols." *Journal for the Scientific Study of Religion* 11 (1972), pp. 33–41.

———, ed. *Mahazit Ha-'Umah: Iyunim Be-Tarbut U-Ve-Ma'amad shel Yozei Ha-Mizrah Be-Yisra'el* [Half the nation: Studies in the culture and status of Middle Eastern Jews in Israel]. Ramat Gan: The Kotlar Institute for Judaism and Contemporary Thought, Bar Ilan University, 1986.

Deshen, Shlomo, and Moshe Shokeid. *The Predicament of Homecoming: Cultural and Social Life of North African Immigrants in Israel*. Ithaca and London: Cornell University Press, 1974.

————. "Recent Trends in the Study of North African Jews in Israel." *Jewish Folklore and Ethnology Review* 11 (1989), pp. 26–27.

Deshen, Shlomo, and Walter P. Zenner. *Jewish Societies in the Middle East.* Washington: University Press of America, 1982.

Dorson, Richard M. "Concepts of Folklore and Folklife Studies." *Folklore and Folklife*, edited by Richard M. Dorson, pp. 1–49. Chicago: University of Chicago Press, 1972.

Douglass, William A., and Stanford Lyman. "Ethnicity: Strategies of Collective and Individual Impression Management." *Social Research* 40 (1973), pp. 344–365

Druyan, Nitza. "Yemenite Jews in Israel: Studies of a Community in Transition." *Jewish Folklore and Ethnology Review* 11 (1989), pp. 32–35.

"Du'ah Mehkar shel ha-Merkaz le-Heker ha-Folklor li-Shnat 1981" [Report on research of the Folklore Research Center for 1981]. *Mehkarei Yerushalayim be-Folklor Yehudi* 2 (1982), pp. 176–179.

Eisenstadt, Shmuel Noah. *The Absorption of Immigrants: A Comparative Study Based on the Jewish Community in Palestine and the State of Israel.* London: Routledge and Kegan Paul, 1953. (Rpt. Glencoe, Illinois: Free Press, 1955.)

————. "Evaluation of the Adjustment of Immigrants." *Megamot* 1 (1950), pp. 335–346.

————. *Israeli Society.* London: Weidenfeld and Nicolson, 1967.

————. "Institutionalization of Immigrant Behavior." *Human Relations* 5 (1952), pp. 373–395.

————. "Inter-generation Tensions in Israel." *International Social Sciences Bulletin* 8 (1956), pp. 54–74.

————. *Mavo le-Heker ha-Mivneh ha-Soziyologi shel Edot ha-Mizrah* [An introduction to the sociological structure of Oriental Jewry]. Jerusalem: The Szold Foundation, 1948. (Appeared in English as "The Oriental Jews in Israel." *Jewish Social Studies* 2 (1950), pp. 109–122. Rpt. in *Olim be-Yisra'el* [Immigrants in Israel], edited by Moshe Lissak, et al., pp. 123–147. Jerusalem: Akadmon, 1969.)

————. "The Oriental Jews of Israel." *Jewish Social Studies* 12 (1950), pp. 199–222.

————. "Patterns of Leadership and Social Homogeneity in Israel." *International Social Sciences Bulletin* 8 (1956), pp. 36–53.

————. "Problems of Leadership Training among New Immigrants." *Megamot* 4 (1953), pp. 182–191.

————. "The Process of Absorption of New Immigrants in Israel." *Human Relations* 5 (1952), pp. 223–246. (Rpt. in *Between Past and Future*, edited by Carl Frankenstein, pp. 53–81. Jerusalem: The Szold Foundation, 1953.)

————. "The Social Development of Israel." *Middle Eastern Affairs* 2 (1951), pp. 161–166.

————. "The Social Significance of Education in the Absorption of Immigrants." *Megamot* 3 (1952), pp. 330–341.

————. "Sociological Aspects of the Economic Adaptation of Oriental Immigrants in Israel: A Case Study of Modernization." *Economic Development and Cultural Change* 4 (1956), pp. 269–278.

————. "Sociological Structure of the Jewish Community in Palestine." *Jewish Social Studies* 10 (1948).

————. "Some Comments on the 'Ethnic' Problem in Israel." *Israel Social Science Research* 1 (1983), pp. 20–29.

————. "Youth Culture and Social Structure in Israel." *British Journal of Sociology* 3 (1951), pp. 105–114.

Eisenstadt, Shmuel Noah, Haim Adler, Rivka Bar Yosef, and R. Kahana, eds. *Ha-Mivneh Ha-Hevrati shel Yisra'el* [The Social Structure of Israel]. Jerusalem: Publishing House of the Hebrew University Student Organization, 1966.

Eisenstadt, Shmuel Noah, Rivka Bar Yosef, and Haim Adler, eds. *Integration and Development in Israel.* London: Praeger, 1970.

Eisenstadt, Shmuel Noah, and Avraham Zloczower, eds. *Mizug Galuyot: Yemei Iyun ba-Universitah ha-Ivrit ba-Yerushalayim* [The merging of the exiles: Conference held at the Hebrew University of Jerusalem]. Jerusalem: Magnes Press, 1969.

Frankenstein, Carl, "The Problems of Ethnic Differences in the Absorption of Immigrants." In *Between Past and Future*, pp. 13–32.
————, ed. *Between Past and Future: Essays and Studies on Aspects of Immigrants' Absorption in Israel*. Jerusalem: Szold Foundation, 1953.
Georges, Robert A. "Greek-American Folk Beliefs and Narratives: Survivals and Living Traditions." Diss., Indiana University, 1964.
Georges, Robert A., and Stephen Stern. *American and Canadian Immigrant and Ethnic Folklore: An Annotated Bibliography*. New York and London: Garland Publishing, 1982.
Gerson-Kiwi, Edith. "Synthesis and Symbiosis of Styles in Jewish Oriental Music." In *Studies in Biblical and Jewish Folklore*, edited by Raphael Patai, Francis Lee Utley, and Dov Noy. Bloomington: Indiana University Press, 1960.
Gilad, Lisa. *Ginger and Salt: Yemenite Jewish Women in an Israeli Town*. Boulder, Colorado: Westview Press, 1989.
Gluckman, Max. Foreword. *Immigrant Voters in Israel: Parties and Congregations in a Local Election Campaign*, by Shlomo Deshen, pp. xiii–xxviii. Manchester: Manchester University Press, 1970.
Goitein, S. D. F. *Jemenica: Sprichwörter und Redensarten aus zentral Jemen mit zahlreichen Sach und Worterläuterungen*. Leipzig: Kommisionsverlag von O. Harrassowitz, 1934.
————. "Jewish Education in Yemen as an Archetype of Traditional Jewish Education." In *Between Past and Future*, edited by Carl Frankenstein, pp. 109–146. Jerusalem: The Szold Foundation, 1953.
Goldberg, Harvey. "Acculturation, Continuity and Youth in an Israeli Immigrant Village." Diss., Harvard University, 1966.
————. "Anthropology in Israel." *Current Anthropology* 17 (1976), pp. 119–121.
————. *Cave Dwellers and Citrus Growers: A Jewish Community in Libya and Israel*. Cambridge: Cambridge University Press, 1972.
————. "The Changing Meaning of Ethnic Affiliation." *The Jerusalem Quarterly* 29 (1987), pp. 39–50.
————. "Culture Change in an Israeli Village: The Twist Came to Even Yosef." *Middle Eastern Studies* 9 (1973), pp. 73–80.
————. "Domestic Organization and Wealth in an Israeli Immigrant Village." *Human Organization* 28 (1969), pp. 58–63.
————. "Egalitarianism in an Autocratic Village in Israel." *Ethnology* 8 (1969), pp. 54–75.
————. "FBD Marriage and Demography among Tripolitanian Jews in Israel." *Southwestern Journal of Anthropology* 23 (1967), pp. 176–191.
————. "From Shaikh to Mazkir: Structural Continuity in the Leadership of a Tripolitanian Jewish Community." In *Folklore Research Center Studies*, vol. 1, edited by Dov Noy and Issachar Ben-Ami, pp. 29–41. Jerusalem: The Magnes Press, 1970.
————. *Greentown's Youth: Disadvantaged Youth in an Israeli Development Town*. Assen: Van Gorcum, 1984.
————. "Historical and Cultural Dimensions of Ethnic Phenomena in Israel." In *Studies in Israeli Ethnicity: After the Ingathering*, edited by Alex Weingrod, pp. 179–200. New York: Gordon and Breach, 1985.
————. Introduction. "Culture and Ethnicity in the Study of Israeli Society." *Ethnic Groups* 1 (1977), pp. 163–186.
————. *Jewish Life in Muslim Libya*. Chicago: University of Chicago Press, 1990.
————. "The Mimouna and the Minority Status of the Moroccan Jews." *Ethnology* 17 (1978), pp. 75–88.
————. "The Social Context of North African Jewish Patronyms." In *Folklore Research Center Studies*, vol. 3, edited by Dov Noy and Issachar Ben-Ami. Jerusalem: The Magnes Press, 1972.
————. "Tripolitanian Jewish Communities: Cultural Boundaries and Hypothesis Testing." *American Ethnologist* 1 (1974), pp. 619–634.
————, ed. and trans. *The Book of Mordechai: A Study of the Jews of Libya: Selections from the Highid Mordekhai of Mordechai Hakohen*. Philadelphia: ISHI Press, 1980.

Goodenough, Ward H. *Culture, Language, and Society*. Addison-Wesley Modular Publications, module no. 7, 1971.

Goren, J. *The Villages of New Immigrants in Israel*. Tel Aviv: Ministry of Agriculture, 1960.

Guttman, Louis. Introduction. *Immigrants on the Threshold*, by Judith T. Shuval, pp. vii–xiii. New York: Atherton Press, 1963.

Halper, Jeff. "The Absorption of Ethiopian Immigrants: A Return to the Fifties." *Israel Social Science Research* 3 (1985), pp. 112–136. (Rpt. in *Ethiopian Jews and Israel*, Michael Ashkenazi and Alex Weingrod, eds., pp. 112–139. New Brunswick, New Jersey: Transaction Books, 1987.)

———. "The Persian Jews of Nevei Shalom: A Study in Mobility." *Ariel* 53 (1983), pp. 34–50.

Handelman, Don. "Gossip in Encounters: The Transmission of Information in a Bounded Setting." *Man* 8 (1973), pp. 210–227.

———. "The Organization of Ethnicity." *Ethnic Groups* 1 (1977), pp. 187–200.

———. *Work and Play among the Aged: Interaction, Replication and Emergence in a Jerusalem Setting*. Assen: Van Gorcum, 1977.

Handelman, Don, and Shlomo Deshen. *The Social Anthropology of Israel: A Bibliographical Essay with Primary Reference to Loci of Social Stress*. Tel Aviv: Tel Aviv University Institute for Social Research, 1975.

Handelman, Don, and Bruce Kapferer. "Forms of Joking Activity: A Comparative Approach." *American Anthropologist* 74 (1972), pp. 484–517.

Harman, Zena. "The Assimilation of Immigrants into Israel." *The Middle East Journal* 5 (1951), pp. 303–315.

Hasan-Rokem, Galit, and Eli Yassif. "The Study of Jewish Folklore in Israel." *Jewish Folklore and Ethnology Review* 11 (1989), pp. 2–11.

Hymes, Dell. *Foundations of Sociolinguistics: An Ethnographic Approach*. Philadelphia: University of Pennsylvania Press, 1974.

Ichilov, Orit, and Yehudith Stern. "Patterns of Ethnic Separatism among the Karaites in Israel." *Ethnic Groups* 2 (1978), pp. 17–34.

Inbar, Michael, and Chaim Adler. *Ethnic Integration in Israel: A Comparative Case Study of Moroccan Brothers Who Settled in France and Israel*. New Brunswick, New Jersey: Transaction Books, 1977.

Isaacs, Y. "Israel—A New Melting Pot." In *The Cultural Integration of Immigrants*, edited by W. D. Borrie, pp. 234–265. Paris: UNESCO, 1956.

Jason, Heda. "Types of the Jewish Oriental Tales." *Fabula* 7 (1964–1965), pp. 115–224.

Jewish Folklore and Ethnology Review, special issue on Jewish Folk Literature, edited by Haya Bar-Itzhak, Vol. 14, nos. 1–2 (1992).

Katriel, Tamar. "Israeli Speechways: An Overview of Discourse Related Studies." *Jewish Folklore and Ethnology Review* 11 (1989), pp. 12–18.

———. *Talking Straight: Dugri Speech in Israeli Sabra Culture*. Cambridge: Cambridge University Press, 1986.

Katz, Elihu and Shmuel Noah Eisenstadt. "Some Sociological Observations on the Response of Israeli Organizations to New Immigrants." *Administration Science Quarterly* 1 (1966), pp. 113–133. (Rpt. in *Olim be-Yisra'el* [Immigrants in Israel], edited by Moshe Lissak, Beverly Mizrahi, and 'Ofra Ben-David, pp. 395–417. Jerusalem: Akadmon, 1969).

Katz, Elihu, and Avraham Zloczower. "Ethnic Continuity in an Israeli Town." *Human Relations* 14 (1961), pp. 293–327.

Klaff, Vivian. "Ethnic Segregation in Urban Israel." *Demography* 10 (1973), pp. 161–184.

Klymasz, Robert. "Ukrainian Folklore in Canada: An Immigrant Complex in Transition." Diss. Indiana University, 1970.

Köngäs-Miranda, Elli. "Finnish-American Folklore: Quantitative and Qualitative Analysis." Diss., Indiana University, 1963.

Krausz, Ernest, ed. *Migration, Ethnicity and Community*. Studies in Israeli Society, vol. 1. New Brunswick, New Jersey: Transaction Books, 1980.

Leket Mekorot la-Nose "Me-Edot le-Am" [A Collection of Sources on the Topic "From Ethnic

Groups to a People."]. N.p. Education Department of Ha-Kibbutz Ha-'Arzi Ha-Shomer Ha-Za'ir, 1964.

Lewis, Herbert. *After the Eagles Landed: The Yemenites of Israel*. Boulder, Colorado: West-view Press, 1989.

Lissak, Moshe, Beverly Mizrahi, and 'Ofrah Ben-David, eds. *Olim be-Yisra'el* [Immi-grants in Israel]. Jerusalem: Akadmon, 1969.

Marx, Emmanuel. "Anthropological Studies in a Centralized State: Max Gluckman and the Bernstein Israel Research Project." *Jewish Journal of Sociology* 17 (1975), pp. 131–150.

———. *A Composite Portrait of Israel*. London: Academic Press, 1980.

———. *The Social Context of Violent Behavior: A Social Anthropological Study in an Israeli Town*. London: Routledge and Kegan Paul, 1976.

Matras, Judah. *Social Change in Israel*. Chicago: Aldine Publishing Company, 1965.

Mehkarei Yerushalayim Be-Folklor Yehudi [Jerusalem studies in Jewish folklore]. 1981–

Noy, Dov. "Archiving and Presenting Folk Literature in an Ethnological Museum." *Journal of American Folklore* 75 (1962), pp. 23–28.

———. "Eighty Years of Jewish Folkloristics: Achievements and Tasks." In *Studies in Jewish Folklore: Proceedings of a Regional Conference of the Association for Jewish Studies Held at the Spertus College of Judaica, Chicago, May 1–3, 1977*, edited by Frank Talmage, pp. 1–12. Cambridge, Massachusetts: Association for Jewish Studies, 1980.

———. "The First Thousand Folktales in the Israel Folktale Archives." *Fabula* 4 (1961), pp. 99–110.

———. "Folklore in Israel: Collecting, Application, Research." In *Cultural Absorption of the New Immigration: A Survey of the Activities and Conclusions*, edited by Zvi Rotem. Jerusalem, n.p., 1962.

———. *Jefet Schwili erzählt: hundertneunundsechzig jemenitische Volkserzählungen aufge-zeichnet in Israel 1957–1960*. Berlin: Walter De Gruyter and Company, 1963.

———, ed. *Moroccan Jewish Folktales*. New York: Herzl Press, 1966.

Noy, Dov, and Issachar Ben-Ami, eds. *Folklore Research Center Studies*, vols. 1–5. Jerusa-lem: Magnes Press, 1970–1975.

Noy, Dov, with the assistance of Dan Ben-Amos, trans. Gene Baharav. *Folktales of Israel*. Chicago: University of Chicago Press, 1963.

Oring, Elliot. *Israeli Humor: The Content and Structure of the Chizbat of the Palmah*. Albany: State University of New York Press, 1981.

Palgi, Phyllis. "Cultural Components of Immigrants' Adjustment." In *Migration, Mental Health and Community Services*, edited by H. P. David, pp. 71–82. Geneva: American Joint Distribution Committee, 1966.

———. "Immigrants, Psychiatrists and Culture." *The Israel Annals of Psychiatry and Re-lated Disciplines* 1 (1963), pp. 43–48. (Rpt. in *Olim be-Yisra'el* [Immigrants in Israel], edited by Moshe Lissak, Beverly Mizrahi, and 'Ofrah Ben-David, pp. 723–743. Jerusalem: Akadmon, 1969.)

———. "Mental Health, Traditional Beliefs, and the Moral Order among Yemenite Jews in Israel." In *The Anthropology of Medicine: From Culture to Method*, edited by L. Romanucci-Ross, D. E. Moerman, and L. Tancredi, pp. 319–335. New York: Praeger, 1982.

Paredes, Américo, and Richard Bauman, eds. *Toward New Perspectives in Folklore*. Austin and London: University of Texas Press, 1972.

Patai, Raphael. "Anthropology during the War VI: Palestine." *American Anthropologist* 48 (1946), pp. 477–482.

———. "Ha-Folklor ve-ha-Etnologiyah shel Am Yisra'el: Be'ayot ve-Tafkidim" [Jewish Folklore and Ethnology: Problems and Tasks]. *Edoth* 1 (1945), pp. 1–12. (Ap-peared in English as "Problems and Tasks of Jewish Folklore and Ethnology." *Journal of American Folklore* 59 (1946), pp. 25–39. Rpt. in his *On Jewish Folklore*, pp. 17–34. Detroit: Wayne State University Press, 1983.)

———. *Israel between East and West*. Philadelphia: Jewish Publication Society of America, 1953.

———. "Jewish Folklore and Jewish Tradition." In *Studies in Biblical and Jewish Folklore*, edited by Raphael Patai, Francis Lee Utley, and Dov Noy, pp. 11–24. Bloomington: Indiana University Press, 1960.

———. "On Culture Contact and Its Working in Modern Palestine." *American Anthropologist* 49 (1947), pp. 5–48.

———. *On Jewish Folklore.* Detroit: Wayne State University Press, 1983.

———, ed. *Edoth*, vols. 1–5. Jerusalem: Palestine Institute for Folklore and Ethnology, 1945–1947.

———, ed. *Encyclopedia of Zionism and Israel.* 2 Vols. New York: Herzl Press/McGraw Hill, 1972.

Patai, Raphael, Francis Lee Utley, and Dov Noy, eds. *Studies in Biblical and Jewish Folklore.* Indiana University Folklore Series, Vol. 13. American Folklore Society Memoir Series, no. 51. Bloomington, Indiana: Indiana University Press, 1960.

Paulsen, Frank. "Danish American Folk Traditions: A Study of Fading Survivals." Diss., Indiana University, 1967.

Peretz, Don. *The Government and Politics of Israel.* Boulder, Colorado: Westview Press, 1983.

Poll, Solomon, and Ernest Krausz, eds. *On Ethnic and Religious Diversity in Israel.* Ramat Gan, Israel: Institute for the Study of Ethnic Relations and Religious Groups, 1975.

Reiger, Hagith. "Some Aspects of the Acculturation of Yemenite Youth Immigrants." In *Between Past and Future,* edited by Carl Frankenstein, pp. 82–108. Jerusalem: The Szold Foundation, 1953.

Rivlin, Yosef Yo'el. *Shirat Yehudei Ha-Targum: Pirkei 'Alilah u-Gvurah Be-Fi Yehudei Kurdistan* [The songs of the Jews of the Targum: Chapters, deeds and heroism of the Jews of Kurdistan]. Jerusalem: The Bialik Institute, 1959.

Rosen, Sherry. "Intermarriage and the 'Blending of the Exiles' in Israel." *Research in Race and Ethnic Relations* 3 (1982), pp. 79–101.

Rubin, Morton. *The Walls of Acre: Intergroup Relations and Urban Development in Israel.* New York: Holt, Rinehart and Winston, 1974.

Rubin, Ruth. "First World Conference on Jewish Folklore Research." *Journal of American Folklore Supplement* (April 1960), pp. 18–20.

Sabar, Yona. "First Names, Nicknames and Family Names among the Jews of Kurdistan." *Jewish Quarterly Review* 65 (1974–1975), pp. 43–51.

———. "Studies of the Folklore, Ethnography and Literature of the Kurdistani Jews: An Annotated Bibliography." *Jewish Folklore and Ethnology Review* 11 (1989), pp. 35–38.

Schoenfeld, Elisheva. "Jüdische-orientalische Märchenerzähler in Israel." In *Internationaler Kongress der Volkserzählungsforscher in Kiel und Kopenhagen,* pp. 385–390. Berlin, 1961.

Schwarz, Leslie Perelman. "Something Old, Something New: The Domestic Side of Moroccan-Jewish Ethnicity." Diss., University of Wisconsin-Madison, 1983.

Schwarzbaum, Haim. "The Seventh Annual Hebrew Folk-Narrative Conference." *Fabula* 6 (1963), pp. 180–181.

———. "Some Recent Works on the Ethnology and Folklore of Various Jewish Communities." *Jewish Book Annual* 19 (1961–1962), pp. 23–33.

———. *Studies in Jewish and World Folklore.* Berlin: Walter De Gruyter, 1968.

Shai, Donna. *Yahasei Shhenut Be-Uchlosiyat Olim: Mehkar Antropologi-Khevrati* [Neighborly relations among an immigrant population: A social-anthropological study]. Research Report no. 149. Publication no. 449. Jerusalem: Henrietta Szold Foundation and National Foundation for Behavioral Sciences Research, 1970.

Sharot, Stephen. ". . . Lo Nekhshalim ela Menukhshalim." Review of *Orientals and Ashkenazim in Israel: The Ethnic Division of Labor,* by Shlomo Swirski. *Israel Social Science Research* 1 (1983), pp. 79–85.

Shiloah, Amnon, and Erik Cohen. "The Dynamics of Change in Jewish Oriental Music in Israel." In *Studies in Israeli Ethnicity: After the Ingathering,* edited by Alex Weingrod, pp. 317–340. New York: Gordon and Breach, 1985.

Shokeid, Moshe. *Children of Circumstances: Israeli Emigrants in New York.* Ithaca, New York: Cornell University Press, 1988.

————. "Cultural Ethnicity in Israel: The Case of Middle Eastern Jews' Religiosity." *Association for Jewish Studies Review* 9 (1985), pp. 247–271.

————. *The Dual Heritage: Immigrants from the Atlas Mountains in an Israeli Village*. Manchester: Manchester University Press, 1971.

————. "From Personal Endowment to Bureaucratic Appointment: The Transition in Israel of the Communal Religious Leaders of Moroccan Jews." *Journal for the Scientific Study of Religion* 19 (1980), pp. 105–113.

————. "Immigration and Factionalism: An Analysis of Functions in Rural Israeli Communities of Immigrants." *British Journal of Sociology* 19 (1968), pp. 385–406.

————. "The Manchester School in Africa and Israel Revisited: Reflections on the Sources and Method of an Anthropological Discourse." *Israel Social Science Research* 6 (1988/1989), pp. 9–23.

————. "Old Conflicts in a New Environment: A Study of a Moroccan Atlas Mountains Community Transplanted to Israel." *Jewish Journal of Sociology* 9 (1967), pp. 191–208.

————. "Reconciling with Bureaucracy: Middle Eastern Immigrants' Moshav in Transition." *Economic Development and Social Change* 29 (1980), pp. 185–205.

————. "The Regulation of Aggression in Daily Life: Aggressive Relationships among Moroccan Immigrants in Israel." *Ethnology* 21 (1982), pp. 271–281.

Shumsky, Abraham. *The Clash of Cultures in Israel*. New York: Columbia University Press, 1955.

Shuval, Judith T. "Class and Ethnic Correlates of Casual Neighboring." *American Sociological Review* 21 (1956), pp. 453–458.

————. "Class and Ethnicity: A Study in Community Structure and Interpersonal Relations." Diss., Radcliffe College, 1955.

————. "Emerging Patterns of Social Strain in Israel." *Social Forces* 40 (1962), pp. 323–330.

————. *Immigrants on the Threshold*. London: Prentice-Hall International, 1963.

————. "The Micro Neighborhood: An Approach to Ecological Patterns of Ethnic Groups." *Social Problems* 9 (1961), pp. 272–280.

————. "Patterns of Intergroup Tensions and Affinity." *International Social Sciences Bulletin* 8 (1956), pp. 75–103.

————. "The Role of Class in Structuring Inter-Group Hostility." *Human Relations* 10 (1957), pp. 61–75.

————. "The Role of Ideology as a Predisposing Frame of Reference for Immigrants." *Human Relations* 12 (1959), pp. 51–63. *Human Relations* 10 (1957), pp. 61–75.

————. "Self-Rejection among North African Immigrants to Israel." *Israel Annals of Psychiatry and Related Disciplines* 4 (1966), pp. 101–110.

————. "Some Persistant Effects of Trauma: Five Years After the Nazi Concentration Camps." *Social Problems* 5 (1957–1958).

————. "Value Orientations of Immigrants in Israel." *Sociometry* 26 (1963), pp. 247–259.

Sicron, Moshe. *Immigrants to Israel 1948–1953*. Jerusalem: Falk Institute, 1957. (Rpt. in *Olim be-Yisra'el* [Immigrants to Israel], edited by Moshe Lissak, Beverly Mizrahi, and 'Ofrah Ben-David, pp. 105–121. Jerusalem: Akadmon, 1969.)

Simon, Rita James. *Continuity and Change: A Study of Two Ethnic Communities in Israel*. Cambridge: Cambridge University Press, 1978.

Sklute, Babro. "Legends and Folk Beliefs in a Scandinavian American Community: A Study in Folklore and Acculturation." Diss., Indiana University, 1970.

Smooha, Sammy. *Israel: Pluralism and Conflict*. London: Routledge and Kegan Paul, 1978.

————. *Social Research of Jewish Ethnicity in Israel 1948–1986: Review and Selected Bibliography with Abstracts*. Haifa: Haifa University Press, 1987.

————. "Three Approaches to the Sociology of Ethnic Relations in Israel." *Jerusalem Quarterly* 40 (1986), pp. 31–61.

Spiro, Melford. *Children of the Kibbutz: A Study in Child Training and Personality*. Revised Edition. Cambridge, Massachusetts: Harvard University Press, 1975.

————. *Gender and Culture: Kibbutz Women Revisited*. New York: Schocken Books, 1979.

Stahl, Avraham. "Hishtanuto shel ha-Sipur ha-'Amami shel Yehudei ha-Mizrah le-ahar 'Aliyatam 'Artsah." [The change in the folk tales of Oriental Jewry following their immigration to Israel]. In *Folklore Research Center Studies*, vol. 1, edited by Dov Noy and Issachar Ben-Ami, pp. 344–349. Jerusalem: Magnes Press, 1970.

Stern, Stephen. "Ethnic Folklore and the Folklore of Ethnicity." In *Folklore and Ethnicity*, edited by Larry Danielson, pp. 7–32. Los Angeles: California Folklore Society, 1977.

Swirsky, Shlomo. "The Oriental Jews in Israel: Why Many Tilted Toward Begin." *Dissent* (winter 1984), pp. 71–91.

Talmage, Frank, ed. *Studies in Jewish Folklore: Proceedings of a Regional Conference of the Association for Jewish Studies Held at the Spertus College of Judaica, Chicago, May 1–3, 1977.* Cambridge, Massachusetts: Association for Jewish Studies, 1980.

Talmon-Garber, Yonina. "Social Differentiation in Cooperative Communities." *British Journal of Sociology* 3 (1952), pp. 339–357.

Thigpen, Kenneth A. "Folklore and the Ethnicity Factor in the Lives of Romanian Americans." Diss., Indiana University, 1973.

Thompson, Stith. *The Folktale.* New York: Holt, Rinehart and Winston, 1946. (Rpt. Berkeley: University of California Press, 1977.)

Van Teeffelen, Toine. *Anthropologists on Israel: A Case Study in the Sociology of Knowledge.* Papers on European and Mediterranean Societies no. 9. Amsterdam: Universiteit Van Amsterdam: 1977.

Weiker, Walter F. "Stratification in Israeli Society: Is there a Middle Category?" *Israeli Social Science Research* 1 (1983), pp. 30–56.

———. *The Unseen Israelis: The Jews from Turkey in Israel.* Lanham, Maryland: University Press of America, 1988.

Weil, Shalva. "Ethiopian Jews in Israel: A Survey of Research and Documentation." *Jewish Folklore and Ethnology Review* 11 (1989), pp. 28–32.

———. "Names and Identity among the Bene Israel." *Ethnic Groups* 1 (1977), pp. 187–219.

Weinberg, Abraham A. *Migration and Belonging: A Study of Mental Health and Personal Adjustment in Israel.* The Hague: Martinus Nijhoff, 1961.

Weingrod, Alex. "Administered Communities: Some Characteristics of New Immigrant Villages in Israel." *Economic Development and Social Change* 2 (1962).

———. "Israel: An Annotated Bibliography." In *The Central Middle East*, edited by Louise Sweet, pp. 357–420. New Haven: HRAFlex Books, 1968.

———. *Israel: Group Relations in a New Society.* Westport, Connecticut: Greenwood Press, 1965.

———. "Recent Trends in Israeli Ethnicity." *Ethnic and Racial Studies* 2 (1979), pp. 55–65.

———. *Reluctant Pioneers: Village Development in Israel.* Ithaca, New York: Cornell University Press, 1966.

———. "Reciprocal Change: A Case Study of a Moroccan Immigrant Village in Israel." *American Anthropologist* 64 (1962), pp. 115–131.

———. *The Saint of Beersheba.* Albany: State University of New York Press, 1990.

———, ed. *Studies in Israeli Ethnicity: After the Ingathering.* New York: Gordon and Breach, 1985.

Weintraub, Dov. "Patterns of Social Change in New Immigrants' Smallholders' Cooperative Settlements." Diss., Hebrew University, 1962.

Weintraub, Dov, and Moshe Lissak. "The Absorption of North African Immigrants in Agricultural Settlements in Israel." *Jewish Journal of Sociology* 3 (1961), pp. 29–54.

Weintraub, Dov, Moshe Lissak, and Yaakov Azmon, eds. *Moshava, Kibbutz, and Moshav: Patterns of Jewish Rural Settlement Development in Palestine.* Ithaca and London: Cornell University Press, 1969.

Weintraub, Dov, et al., *Immigration and Social Change: Agricultural Settlements of New Immigrants in Israel.* New York: Humanities Press, 1971.

Weitz, Raanan. "The Sociologists and the Policy Makers: A Case Study of Agricultural Settlements in Israel." *Transactions of the Fifth World Congress of Sociology* 1 (1962), pp. 59–75.

Weller, Leonard. *Sociology in Israel.* Westport, Connecticut: Greenwood Press, 1974.

Willner, Dorothy. *Nation-Building and Community in Israel*. Princeton: Princeton University Press, 1969.
Yassif, Eli. *Jewish Folklore: An Annotated Bibliography*. New York: Garland Publishing, 1986.
――――. "Storytelling of the 'Repentence Movement': Rhetoric, Folklore and Cultural Debate in Contemporary Israel." *Jewish Folklore and Ethnology Review* 14 (1992), pp. 26–31.
Zenner, Walter P. "Ambivalence and Self-Image among Oriental Jews in Israel." *Jewish Journal of Sociology* 5 (1963), pp. 214–223.
――――. "The Israeli Sephardim and Religion." *Alliance Review* 39 (1965), pp. 26–27.
――――. "Joking and Ethnic Stereotyping." *Anthropological Quarterly* 43 (1970), pp. 93–113.
――――. "Sephardic Communal Organizations in Israel." *Middle East Journal* 21 (1967), pp. 173–186.
――――. "Syrian Jewish Identification in Israel." Diss., Columbia University, 1965.
――――. "Syrian Jews in Three Social Settings." *Jewish Journal of Sociology* 10 (1968), pp. 101–120.
Zerubavel, Ya'el. "The Last Stand: On the Transformation of Symbols in Modern Israeli Culture." Diss., University of Pennsylvania, 1980.

Bulgarian Jewry

Ainsztein, Reuben. *Jewish Resistance in Nazi-Occupied Eastern Europe*. New York: Barnes and Noble, 1974.
Alcalay, Ora. "Bulgaria." *European Judaism* 3 no. 2 (winter 1968–1969), pp. 26–33.
Almanakh na Bulgarskata aliya: 25 godini Izrael [Almanac of the Bulgarian aliyah: 25 years in Israel]. N.p. 1973.
Annual of the Social, Cultural and Educational Association of the Jews in the Peoples Republic of Bulgaria 24 (1989).
Arditi, Binyamin. *Ha-Sifrut Ha-Antishemit Be-Bulgariyah: Reshimah Bibliografit* [Antisemitic literature in Bulgaria: A bibliography]. Holon, Israel: the author, 1972.
――――. "Purvite Evrei v Bulgariya" [The first Jews in Bulgaria]. *Evreite v istoriyata, literaturata i politikata―-Sbornik na Evreiskiya Naroden Universitet* [Jews in History, Literature and Politics: Journal of the Jewish People's University] (1933), pp. 5–22.
――――. *Rolyata na Tsar Boris III pri izselvaneto na Evreite ot Bulgariya* [The role of King Boris III in the deportation of the Jews from Bulgaria]. Tel Aviv: n.p., 1952.
――――. *Vidni Evrei v Bulgariya: galeriya na zabravenite* [Prominent Jews in Bulgaria: Gallery of the forgotten], vol. 3. Tel Aviv: the author, 1971.
――――. *Yehudei Bulgariyah Bi-Shnot Ha-Mishtar Ha-Nazi: 1940–1944* [The Jews of Bulgaria during the years of the Nazi regime: 1940–1944]. Tel Aviv: Israel Press, 1962.
――――. *Yehudei Bulgariyah: Kehilat Shumlah* [The Jews of Bulgaria: The community of Shumlah]. Holon, Israel: the author, 1968.
Bahar, Avraham. *Zihronot Har-Tuv* [Memories of Har-Tuv] Jerusalem: Published by the family, 1970, (repr. 1990).
Baruh, Eli. *Iz istoriyata na Bulgarskoto Evreistvo: nashite stradaniya v evreiskite trudovi lageri prez fashistkiya rezhim v Bulgaria: 1941–1944* [From the history of Bulgarian Jewry: Our suffering in the Jewish labor camps during the Fascist regime in Bulgaria: 1941–1944]. Tel Aviv: Yafor Printing House, 1960.
Barukh, Nir. *Ha-Kofer: Bulgariyah Ve-Yehudeyha Be-Mesheh Ha-Dorot* [The ransom: Bulgaria and her Jews across the ages] Tel Aviv: Shvilim Publishing House, 1990.
Barouh, Victor. *Beyond the Law*. Sofia: Foreign Languages Press, 1965.
Ben, Yosef. *Mishpat Eichmann Ve-Yahadut Bulgariyah* [The Eichmann trial and Bulgarian Jewry]. Tel Aviv: A. Pardo Holocaust Research Institute, 1962.
Benardete, Maír Jose. *Hispanic Culture and the Character of the Sephardi Jews*. New York: Hispanic Institute in the United States, 1952.

Benaroyo, Reuven (Doti). *Nedovursheniyat put na Negovo Velichestvo: iz spomenite na edin ot mnogoto evreiskite trudovi lageri* [His majesty's unfinished road: Recollections of one of many Jewish labor camps]. Tel Aviv: n.p., 1975.

Beni, Albert. *Feiletoni* [Feuilletons]. Jaffa: the author, 1978.

———. *Sto intervyuta* [One hundred interviews]. Tel Aviv: n.p., 1971.

———. *Yehudei Bulgariyah Ba-Ma'avak Neged Ha-Nazim* [The Jews of Bulgaria in the struggle against the Nazis]. Tel Aviv: The World Zionist Organization, Department of Zionist and Social Activity among Sephardic Communities and Immigrants from Oriental Countries, 1980.

Black, Cyril E. *The Establishment of Constitutional Government in Bulgaria*. Princeton: Princeton University Press, 1944.

Black, Floyd H. *The American College in Sofia: A Chapter in American-Bulgarian Relations*. Boston: The Trustees of the Sofia American Schools, 1958.

Blaine, Harden. "Bulgaria and its Jews." *The Washington Post* (December 31, 1990), p. 10.

Brown, J. F. *Bulgaria under Communist Rule*. New York: Praeger, 1970.

Bunis, David M. *Sephardic Studies: A Research Bibliography Incorporating Judezmo Languages Literature, Folklore and Historical Background*. New York and London: Garland Publishing Inc., 1981.

Butler, Thomas. Introduction. In his *Bulgaria: Past and Present*, pp. xi–xiv. Columbus, Ohio: American Association for the Advancement of Slavic Studies, 1973.

Chary, Frederick B. "Bulgaria and the Jews: 'The Final Solution,' 1940–1944." Diss., University of Pittsburgh, 1968.

———. *The Bulgarian Jews and the Final Solution, 1940–1944*. Pittsburgh: University of Pittburgh Press, 1972.

Cohen, Israel. "Dissolving Jewries: The Jews of Bulgaria." *Congress Bi-Weekly* 18, no. 10 (March 12, 1951), pp. 9–11.

Cornescu, A. "Sepharad and Ashkenaz Jews in the Balkans." *Astes du Premier Congres International des Etudes Balkaniques et Sud-est Europeenes* 3 (1969), pp. 781–783.

Crampton, R. J. "Bulgarian Society in the Early 19th Century." In *Balkan Society in the Age of Greek Independence*, edited by Richard Cligg, pp. 157–204. Totowa, New Jersey: Barnes and Noble Books, 1981.

Daniel, Jean. "Kavim Le-Toldot Po'alei Ziyon" [Approaches to the history of Po'alei Ziyon]. In *Aharon Ben-Yosef: Ha-Ish U-Fa'alo* [Aharon Ben-Yosef: The man and his work], edited by Yosef Shapira, pp. 187–202. Tel Aviv: The Aharon Ben-Yosef Committee, 1953–1954.

Dellin, L. A. D., ed. *Bulgaria*. New York: Free Europe Committee, 1957.

Dvadeset i pet godini ot osnovaveneto na "Po'alei Tsiyon" v Bulgaria [Twenty-five years of Po'alei Tsiyon in Bugaria]. Tel Aviv: n.p., 1955.

Einfeld, Zevi. "Batei Sefer Ha-'Ivriyim Be-Sofia" [The Hebrew schools in Sofia]. *Ha-'Olam* (London) 17, no. 4 (January 1929), pp. 73–75.

Encyclopedia Judaica. Jerusalem: Keter, 1972.

Evans, Stanley George. *A Short History of Bulgaria*. London: Lawrence and Wishart, 1960.

Evrei zaginali v anti-fashistkata borba [Jews killed in the anti-Fascist battle]. Sofia: Natsionalen Komitet na Otechestven Front, 1958.

Gelber, N. M. "Jewish Life in Bulgaria." *Jewish Social Studies* 8 (1946), pp. 103–126.

Georgieff, Peter, and Basil Spiru. *Bulgariens Volk im Wiederstand: 1941–1944*. East Berlin: n.p., 1962.

Godishnik na Bulgarskata Aliya [Yearbook of the Bulgarian aliya]. N.p, 1974–1975; 1975–1976; 1978–1979.

Grinberg, Natan. *Hitleristkiyat natisk za unishtozhavene na Evreite ot Bulgariya* [The Hitlerist pressure for destroying the Jews of Bulgaria]. Tel Aviv: 'Amal, 1961.

Groueff, Stephane. *Crown of Thorns*. Lanham, Massachusetts: Madison Books, 1987.

Hananel, Asher. "Jewish Life in Bulgaria." *Jewish Chronicle* (London), (July 18, 1952), p. 12.

Harris, Tracy K. "Editor's Note: The Name of the Language of the Eastern Sephardim." *International Journal of the Sociology of Language* 37 (1982), p. 5.

———. "Reasons for the Decline of Judeo-Spanish." *International Journal of the Sociology of Language* 37 (1982), pp. 71–97.

Haskell, Guy H. "Bulgarian Folklore and Ethnography: A Bibliographical Essay." *East European and Slavic Folklore Newsletter* 1 (1980), pp. 1–10.
———. "The Jews of Bulgaria." *Jewish Folklore and Ethnology Newsletter* 5 (1982), pp. 10–11.
Hazzan, Baruch. "The Jewish Community of Bulgaria." In *The Balkan Jewish Communities: Yugoslavia, Bulgaria, Greece and Turkey*, edited by Daniel J. Elazar, pp. 59–101. Lanham, Maryland: University Press of America, 1984.
Heiber, Helmut. "Der Tod des Zaren Boris." *Vierteljahrshefte für Zeitgeschichte* 9 (1961), pp. 384–416.
Hilberg, Raul. *The Destruction of the European Jews*. Chicago: Quadrangle, 1961.
Isakov, Simcho. *Alfred Sason*. Tel Aviv: Albert Beni, 1980.
———. *'Andarta: Mehaber Shirim* [Memorial to a poet]. Trans. Rafa'el Eli'az. Tel Aviv: Committee for Publishing the Works of Simcho Isakov of the Union of Bulgarian Immigrants, 1973.
The Jewish Communities of Nazi Occupied Europe. N.p.: The Research Institute on Peace and Post War Problems of the American Jewish Committee, 1944. (Rpt. New York: Howard Fertig,)1982.
Kalev, Albert. "Ha-Histadrut Le-Safah Ve-Le-Tarbut Ha-'Ivrit" [The Hebrew language and culture federation]. In *Aharon Ben-Yosef: Ha-Ish U-Fa'alo* [Aharon Ben-Yosef: The man and his work], edited by Yosef Shapira, pp. 175–178. Tel Aviv: The Aharon Ben-Yosef Committee, 1953–1954.
Kalev, Marcel. "Yahadut Bulgariyah Ve-Tnu'atah Ha-Ziyonit" [Bulgarian Jewry and its Zionist movement]. In *Aharon Ben-Yosef: Ha-Ish U-Fa'alo* [Aharon Ben-Yosef: The man and his work], edited by Yosef Shapira, pp. 135–158. Tel Aviv: The Aharon Ben-Yosef Committee, 1953–1954.
Kashani, Re'uven. *Skirat Sfarim al Ha-Yahadut Be-Bulgariyah* [A study of books on Jewry in Bulgaria]. Jerusalem, n.p., 1962.
Kazasov, Dimo. *Burni Godini* [Stormy years]. Sofia: n.p., 1949.
Keshales, Haim. "Dorot Ha-Rishonim" [The first generations]. In *Yahadut Bulgaria* [Bulgarian Jewry] Enziklopediyah shel Galuyot: Sifrei Zikaron Le-Arzot Ha-Golah Ve-'Edoteyha [The encyclopedia of the Jewish diaspora: Memorial volumes to the lands of the diaspora and their communities], vol. 10., edited by Albert Romano, et al., pp. 319–356. Jerusalem-Tel Aviv: Encyclopedia of the Diaspora, 1967.
———. *Korot Yehudei Bulgariyah* [History of the Jews of Bulgaria]. Tel Aviv: Davar, vol. 1, 1971; vol. 2, 1972; vol. 3, 1969; vol. 4, 1969; vol. 5, 1973.
Koen, Albert. *Le Sauvetage des Juifs en Bulgarie: 1941–1944*. Sofia: Septemvri, 1977.
Kohen, Nisim. "Ha-Shomer Ha-Za'ir." In *Aharon Ben-Yosef: Ha-Ish U-Fa'alo* [Aharon Ben-Yosef: The man and his work], edited by Yosef Shapira, pp. 179–186. Tel Aviv: The Aharon Ben-Yosef Committee, 1953–1954.
Konfino, Baruh. *Aliyah Bet Mi-Hofei Bulgariyah, 1938–1940, 1947–1948: Hisul Galut Bulgariyah, 1948–1949* [Illegal Immigration from the Shores of Bulgaria, 1938–1940, 1947–1948: Dissolution of the Bulgarian community, 1948–1949]. Sason Levi, trans. Jerusalem-Tel Aviv: Ahiyasaf Publishing House, 1965.
Krispin, Haim. "Hilkah shel Yahadut Bulgariyah be-Hityashvut." In *Aharon Ben-Yosef: Ha-Ish U-Fa'alo* [Aharon Ben-Yosef: The man and his work], edited by Yosef Shapira, pp. 224–227. Tel Aviv: The Aharon Ben-Yosef Committee, 1953–1954.
Lang, David Marshall. *The Bulgarians: From Pagan Times to the Ottoman Conquest*. London: Thames and Hudson, 1976.
Leviev, Misho, ed. *Nashata blagadarnost* [Our thanks]. Sofia: Sbornik "Kadima," 1946.
Malinowski, Arlene. "A Report on the Status of Judeo-Spanish in Turkey." *International Journal of the Sociology of Language* 37 (1982), pp. 7–23.
Marcus, Simon. "'Al Ashkenazim Sfaradim ve'al Ashkenazim Stam Be-Bulgariyah." *Sinai Yerushalayim* 26 (1950), pp. 236–246.
———. *Ha-Safah Ha-Sfaradit-Yehudit* [The Judeo-Spanish Language]. Jerusalem: Kiryat Sefer, 1965.
———. "Romaniots." *Encyclopedia Judaica*, vol. 14, p. 231. Jerusalem: Keter, 1972.
Margalit, Emanu'el. "Ha-Ma'avak Ha-Ziyoni shel Yehudei Bulgariayah 'im Hishtaltut Ha-Komunistim" [The Zionist struggle of the Jews of Bulgaria with the Communist regime]. *Gesher* 3 (1957), pp. 92–105.

Mashiah, Avidan. "Bulgarian Jews in Israel." *Encyclopedia of Zionism and Israel*, edited by Raphael Patai, pp. 169–170. New York: Herzl Press/McGraw Hill, 1971.

Matkowski, Alexander. "The Destruction of Macedonian Jewry in 1943." *Yad Vashem Studies* 3 (1959), pp. 203–259.

———. *A History of the Jews in Macedonia*. Skopje: Macedonian Review Editions, 1982.

———. *Tragedijata na Evreite ot Makedonija* [The tragedy of the Jews of Macedonia]. Skopje: Kultura, 1962.

Meyer, Peter. "Bulgaria." In *The Jews of the Soviet Satellites*, edited by Peter Meyer, pp. 559–569. Syracuse, New York: Syracuse University Press, 1953.

Mezan, Saul. *Les juifs espagnols en Bulgarie*. Sofia: Editions d'Essai, 1925.

Miller, Marshall Lee. *Bulgaria during the Second World War*. Stanford, California: Stanford University Press, 1975.

Nitsani, Ya'akov. "Kehilat Plovdiv: 'Em Ha-Ziyonut Be-Bulgariyah" [The Jewish community of Plovdiv: Mother city of Zionism in Bulgaria]. *Rushumot*, n.s. 5 (1953), pp. 25–50.

Oliver, Haim. *We Were Saved: How the Jews of Bulgaria Were Kept from the Death Camps*. V. Izmirliev, trans. Sofia: Sofia Press, 1978.

Omarchevsky, Stoyan. "The Jews in Bulgaria." *Reflex* 4 (1929), pp. 48–51.

Oren, Nissan. "Bulgaria." *Enclyclopedia Judaica*, vol. 2, pp. 1480–1494.

———. *Bulgarian Communism, 1934–1944*. New York and London: Columbia University Press, 1971.

———. "The Bulgarian Communist Party, 1934–1944." Diss., Columbia University, 1960.

———. "The Bulgarian Exception: A Reassessment of the Salvation of the Jewish Community." *Yad Vashem Studies* 7 (1968), pp. 83–106.

———. *Revolution Administered: Agrarianism and Communism in Bulgaria*. Baltimore and London: Johns Hopkins University Press, 1973.

Petdeset avtori pod edin pokriv. [Fifteen authors under one roof]. Tel Aviv-Jaffa: n.p., 1978.

Petdeset avtori vi razkazvat: literaturen sbornik [Fifteen authors narrate: A literary journal]. Tel Aviv: n.p., 1970.

Piti, Buko. *Bulgarskata obshtestvenost za rasizma i antisemitizma* [Bulgarian public opinion on rascism and antisemitism]. Sofia: n.p., 1937.

———. *Te, spasitelite* [They, the rescuers.] Tel Aviv: n.p., 1969.

Prouchvaniya za istoriyata na evreiskoto naselenie v-bulgarsite zemi xv–xx vek [Studies in the history of the Jewish population of Bulgarian lands: XV–XX Centuries]. Sofia: Bulgarian Academy of Sciences, 1980.

Pundeff, Martin V. "Bulgaria's Place in Axis Policy." Diss., University of Southern California, 1958.

Rodrigue, Aaron. *French Jews, Turkish Jews: The Alliance Israélite Universelle and the Politics of Jewish Schooling in Turkey, 1860–1925*. Bloomington: Indiana Unviersity Press, 1990.

Romano, Albert. " 'Agudot 'Maccabi' Be-Bulgariyah" [The Maccabi organizations in Bulgaria]. In *Yahadut Bulgaria* [Bulgarian Jewry] Enziklopediyah shel Galuyot: Sifrei Zikaron Le-Arzot Ha-Golah Ve-'Edoteyha [The encyclopedia of the Jewish diaspora: Memorial volumes to the lands of the diaspora and their communities], vol. 10., edited by Albert Romano, et al., pp. 319–356. Jerusalem-Tel Aviv: Encyclopedia of the Diaspora, 1967.

———. "Ha-Yahadut Ve-Ha-Tnu'ah Ha-Ziyonit Be-Bulgariyah" [Bulgarian Jewry and the Zionist movement]. In *Yahadut Bulgaria* [Bulgarian Jewry]. Enziklopediyah shel Galuyot: Sifrei Zikaron Le-Arzot Ha-Golah Ve-'Edoteyha [The encyclopedia of the Jewish diaspora: Memorial volumes to the lands of the diaspora and their communities], vol. 10, edited by Albert Romano, et al., pp. 164–606. Jerusalem-Tel Aviv: Encyclopedia of the Diaspora, 1967.

———, et al., eds, *Yahadut Bulgaria* [Bulgarian Jewry]. Enziklopediyah shel Galuyot: Sifrei Zikaron Le-Arzot Ha-Golah Ve-'Edoteyha [The encyclopedia of the Jewish diaspora: Memorial volumes to the lands of the diaspora and their communities], vol. 10. Jerusalem-Tel Aviv: Encyclopedia of the Diaspora, 1967.

Rosanes, Solomon. *Divrei Yemei Yisra'el Be-Togarmah* [History of the Jews in Turkey]. (Reprinted as *Korot Ha-Yehudim Be-Turkiyah Ve-'Arzot Ha-Kedem* [History of the Jews in Turkey and ancient lands].) Tel Aviv: Dvir, 1930, vol 1; Sofia: 1934–1938, vols. 2–5; Jerusalem, 1948, vol. 6.

Rothschild, Joseph. *The Communist Party of Bulgaria: 1883–1936*. New York: Columbia University Press, 1959.

Russel, William F. *Schools in Bulgaria*. New York: Teacher's College, Columbia University, 1924.

Sciaky, Leon. *Farewell Solonika*. New York: Current Books, 1946.

Sevilya, Metin B. "The Psychological Aspects of Sephardic Identity." *The Sephardic Scholar* 3 (1977–1978), pp. 75–82.

Shalti'el, Shlomo. *Iyunim Be-Toldot Yahadut Bulgariyah 'ad Sof Ha-Me'ah Ha-19* [Studies in Bulgarian Jewry until the end of the 19th century]. Tel Aviv: n.p. 1970.

Shapira, Yosef, ed. *Aharon Ben-Yosef: Ha-Ish u-Fa'alo* [Aharon Ben-Yosef: The man and his work]. Tel Aviv: The Aharon Ben-Yosef Committee, 1953–1954.

Sharf, Andrew. *Byzantine Jewry: From Justinian to the Fourth Crusade*. New York: Schocken Books, 1971.

Starr, Joshua. *The Jews in the Byzantine Empire, 641–1204*. New York: B. Franklin, 1939.

———. "The Socialist Federation of Soloniki." *Jewish Social Studies* 7 (1945), pp. 323–336.

Tabakov, George. "King Boris III and His People Saved the Bulgarian Jews—In Its Time—A Unique Triumph." *Macedonian Tribune* (September 29, 1983).

Tamir, Vicki. *Bulgaria and Her Jews: The History of a Dubious Symbiosis*. New York: Sepher Hermon Press for Yeshiva University Press, 1979.

Todorov, Nikolai. "The City in the Bulgarian Lands from the Fifteenth to the Nineteenth Century." In *Bulgaria: Past and Present*, edited by Thomas Butler, pp. 15–30. Columbus, Ohio: American Association for the Advancement of Slavic Studies, 1973.

———. "Evreiskoto naselenie v balkanskite rovintsii na Osmanskata Imperiya prez xv–xix vek" [The Jewish population of the Balkan provinces of the Ottoman Empire from the xv–xix centuries]. In *Prouchvaniya za istoriyata na evreiskoto naselenie v-bulgarskite zemi xv–xx vek* [Studies in the history of the Jewish population of Bulgarian lands: XV–XX Centuries], pp. 7–21. Sofia: Bulgarian Academy of Sciences, 1980.

Topalov, Vladislav. "L'opinion publique bulgare contre les persecutions des juifs (octobre 1940–9 septembre 1944)." *Etudes Historiques a l'occasion du XXIIe Congres Internationale des Sciences Historiques-Vienne, aout-septembre, 1965*, vol. 2. Sofia: BAN, 1965.

Totev, Anastas Iv. "Characteristic Demographic Features of Bulgaria, 1880–1980." In *Bulgaria: Past and Present*, edited by Thomas Butler, pp. 132–141. Columbus, Ohio: American Association for the Advancement of Slavic Studies, 1973.

Vasileva, Nadejda Slavi. "On the Catastrophe of the Thracian Jews: Recollection." *Yad Vashem Studies* 3 (1959), pp. 295–302.

Versano, Albert. "Hit'ahdut Makabi [The Maccabi union]. In *Aharon Ben-Yosef: Ha-Ish U-Fa'alo* [Aharon Ben-Yosef: The man and his work], edited by Yosef Shapira, pp. 170–175. Tel Aviv: The Aharon Ben-Yosef Committee, 1953–1954.

———. *Maccabi Bulgariyah*. Tel Aviv: Albert Kiyoso Circle, 1976.

Vital, Haim. "The Jews of Bulgaria." *Congress Bi-Weekly* 8, no. 37 (November 14, 1941), pp. 12–13.

Weich-Shahak, Susan. "The Wedding Songs of the Bulgarian-Sephardi Jews: A Preliminary Study." *Orbis Musicae* 7 (1978–1980).

Yulzari, Matei. "The Bulgarian Jews in the Resistance Movement." In *They Fought Back: The Story of the Jewish Resistance in Nazi Europe*, edited and translated by Yuri Suhl, pp. 275–281. New York: Crown Publishers, 1967.

Zion, Dan. *Pet godini pod fashistki gnet* [Five years under fascist oppression]. Sofia: n.p., 1945.

Zwergbaum, Aharon. "Zionism." *Encyclopedia Judaica*, vol. 16, pp. 1108–1109. Jerusalem: Keter, 1972.

Index

Books in the Jewish Folklore and Anthropology Series